# The Interpreter's Resource

**TOPICS IN TRANSLATION**
**Series Editors: Susan Bassnett,** *University of Warwick* and Edwin Gentzler, *University of Massachusetts, Amherst*
**Editor for Translation in the Commercial Environment:** Geoffrey Samuelsson-Brown, *University of Surrey*

**Other Books in the Series**
Annotated Texts for Translation: French–English
  *Beverly Adab*
Annotated Texts for Translation: English–French
  *Beverly Adab*
Constructing Cultures: Essays on Literary Translation
  *Susan Bassnett and André Lefevere*
Culture Bumps: An Empirical Approach to the Translation of Allusions
  *Ritva Leppihalme*
Linguistic Auditing
  *Nigel Reeves and Colin Wright*
Paragraphs on Translation
  *Peter Newmark*
Practical Guide for Translators
  *Geoffrey Samuelsson-Brown*
The Coming Industry of Teletranslation
  *Minako O'Hagan*
The Pragmatics of Translation
  *Leo Hickey (ed.)*
Translation, Power, Subversion
  *Román Alvarez and M. Carmen-Africa Vidal (eds)*
Translation and Nation: A Cultural Politics of Englishness
  *Roger Ellis and Liz Oakley-Brown (eds)*
Time Sharing on Stage: Drama Translation in Theatre and Society
  *Sirkku Aaltonen*
Words, Words, Words. The Translator and the Language Learner
  *Gunilla Anderman and Margaret Rogers*

**Other Books of Interest**
About Translation
  *Peter Newmark*
Cultural Functions of Translation
  *C. Schäffner and H. Kelly-Holmes (eds)*
Discourse and Ideologies
  *C. Schäffner and H. Kelly-Holmes (eds)*
More Paragraphs on Translation
  *Peter Newmark*
Translation and Quality
  *Christina Schäffner (ed.)*
Translation and Norms
  *Christina Schäffner (ed.)*
Word, Text, Translation: Liber Amicorum for Peter Newmark
  *Gunilla Anderman and Margaret Rogers (eds)*

**Please contact us for the latest book information:**
**Multilingual Matters, Frankfurt Lodge, Clevedon Hall,**
**Victoria Road, Clevedon, BS21 7HH England**
http://www.multilingual-matters.com

TOPICS IN TRANSLATION 19

# The Interpreter's Resource

Mary Phelan

**MULTILINGUAL MATTERS LTD**
Clevedon • Buffalo • Toronto • Sydney

**Library of Congress Cataloging in Publication Data**
Phelan, Mary
The Interpreter's Resource/Mary Phelan
Topics in Translation: 19
Includes bibliographical references.
1. Translating and interpreting. I. Title. II. Series.
P306.2.P486 2001
418'.02–dc21                    00-050114

**British Library Cataloguing in Publication Data**
A catalogue entry for this book is available from the British Library.

ISBN 1-85359-516-0 (hbk)
ISBN 1-85359-515-2 (pbk)

**Multilingual Matters Ltd**
*UK*: Frankfurt Lodge, Clevedon Hall, Victoria Road, Clevedon BS21 7HH.
*USA*: UTP, 2250 Military Road, Tonawanda, NY 14150, USA.
*Canada*: UTP, 5201 Dufferin Street, North York, Ontario M3H 5T8, Canada.
*Australia*: Footprint Books, Unit 4/92a Mona Vale Road, Mona Vale, NSW 2103, Australia.

Typeset by Wyvern 21 Ltd.
Printed and bound in Great Britain by the Cromwell Press Ltd.

# Contents

## 9. Other International Organizations                              138

## 10. Interpreters' Associations                                    160

# Acknowledgements

I would like to thank the following individuals and organizations that kindly took the time to provide information and answer my questions:

African Development Bank; Association of South East Asian Nations; Niels Agger-Gupta of the Fielding Institute; Arte TV, Janice Barahona, Pan American Health Organization; Susan Bartolo, United Nations Economic Commission for Europe; C.Baviera-Betson, Court of Justice of the European Communities; Laurence Blairon, information officer at the International Court of Justice; Rita Boren-Gomez, Inter-American Development Bank; D. Brassens of the Council of Europe; Claude Briand, International Telecommunications Union; Bruce Cadbury, Language Line; Alfred Cahen, Atlantic Treaty Association; Jan Cambridge; Helen Campbell, SCIC; Terry Chesher, FIT Community based Interpreting Committee; Ruth Coles, Director of Diversity at Providence Health Care, British Columbia, Canada; Jean Louis Cougnon, European Parliament; Janice Driscoll, World Intellectual Property Organization; Susana Eri, International Monetary Fund; The European Commission; Rita Ezrati, International Civil Aviation Organization; Christina M Goodman, European Central Bank; Carola E. Green, Vice President of California Healthcare Interpreters Association; Beverley Harrison, European Bank for Reconstruction and Development; Ayla Kayalar, UNIDO; Romy Kluge, Committee of the Regions; Liese Katschinka, FIT committee on court interpreting; Peter Mertvago, United Nations, New York; F. Moore, Western European Union; Shuja Nawaz, International Atomic Energy Association; North Atlantic Treaty Organization; Luigi Lehmann, Nestec Ltd.; Britt Mathez, Universal Postal Union; Brian Mc Ginley, European Patent Office; Farouk U. Muhammed, Organization of the Petroleum Exporting Countries; Office of the High Commissioner for Human Rights; Organization of American States; Julia Puebla Fortier, Director of Resources for Cross Cultural Health Care; Bruno René-Bazin, ISM Interprétariat and President of Babelea; Greg Richards, Tilburg University, The Netherlands; M. Samsonetti-Ferrante, International Fund for Agricultural Development; Alec Singh, ACP; Arlette-Josiane Skinner, International Electrotechnical Commission; Agneta Speed, European Court of Auditors; Nagy Tawfik, United Nations, Geneva; Valérie Thill, European Investment Bank; United Nations Economic and Social Commission for Asia and the Pacific; Jean-Marie Vacchiani, South Pacific

Commission; Yolande Van Coppenolle, Council of the European Union; Sergio Viaggi, United Nations, Vienna; Bill Weber, International Olympic Committee; Elisabeth Wolff, Economic and Social Committee of the European Union; World Customs Organization; Qifeng Zhang, Asian Development Bank.

The First Babelea Conference on Community Interpreting held in Vienna, Austria, in November 1999 was particularly informative and is the source of the information in this volume on Community Interpreting in France, Italy, the Netherlands and the United Kingdom.

I attended the Agnese Haury Institute for Court Interpreting at the University of Arizona in July 2000. The course helped to clarify my ideas on court interpreting and I am particularly grateful to Joyce García for her lecture on wiretapping and tape transcription. The section on this topic in the present volume is based on that lecture.

My thanks to my colleagues Michael Cronin, Niobe Hernández, Sylvie Kleinmann-Batt, Helga Leifer-Zink, Christelle Petite and Jenny Williams at Dublin City University.

Wilhelm K. Weber's 1990 booklet on *Interpretation in the United States* provided practical information on the situation pertaining in America.

I would like to thank the members of the US National Council for Interpretation in Health Care Mail List (NCIHC-list@diversityRx.org) for drawing my attention to the Massachusetts Emergency Room Interpreter Bill and to Edward Wong's article on medical interpreting in *The New York Times*.

The population figures given in this volume are based on censuses mentioned in Encarta 98 Encyclopedia on CD-ROM.

I am grateful to the following for permission to reproduce material:

▤  The American Association of Language Specialists for permission to quote the TAALS Standards of Professional Practice for Conference Interpreters.

▤  Ruth Coles of Providence Health Care for permission to quote the Vancouver Health Care Interpreter Standards of Practice.

▤  The AIIC Secretariat for permission to cite the AIIC Code of Conduct.

▤  The Institute of Linguists for permission to quote the NRPSI Code of Conduct for Public Service Interpreters.

▤  The Registry of Interpreters for the Deaf in the United States for permission to include their Code of Ethics.

▤  National Geographic for permission to reproduce the Xpeditions maps in the Appendix.

# Preface

Interpreting is a relatively new area of research that is all too often subsumed under the heading of translation. For example, many Translators' Associations include Interpreters. Many books on translation will include a section on Interpreting. Of course there is an overlap between the two areas that are so alike and yet so different – many translators do some interpreting work and vice versa. All of this has led to a confusing situation where interpreting is still in the process of establishing itself as a discipline in its own right. The general public is confused about what exactly interpreting is. The very word interpreting is most unsatisfactory. If you do a search in an OPAC library catalogue on Interpreting you could find anything from interpreting statistics to interpreting Bach at the Keyboard. Similarly, an Internet search can turn up all kinds of results, from interpreting ancient manuscripts to interpreting the Irish Famine.

My aim in this volume is to provide an overview of interpreting in the year 2000 to anyone interested in interpreting in general or indeed in becoming an interpreter. A number of specialist books have been published in recent years, all on specific areas of interpreting. I would like to provide a fuller picture. To this end I set about collecting information about international and regional Organizations in particular. My starting point was a booklet published by AIIC, the International Association of Conference Interpreters in 1997. The booklet, *Conseils aux étudiants souhaitant devenir interprète de conférence,* contains a list of international organizations around the world that employ interpreters. However, it does not contain any information on the numbers of interpreters employed or on the organizations themselves. I wanted to collect information on the numbers of interpreters employed around the world. Conference interpreting is the most prestigious type of interpreting and the best paid. I was quite surprised by some of the results of the questionnaire that many of the organizations kindly completed for me. Firstly, with the exceptions of the European Union and the United Nations, the actual numbers of interpreters employed by many organizations is quite small. Secondly, I have not found any support for the notion that interpreters suffer from burnout, that they work solidly for five years or so, earning quite a lot of money, and then disappear into the sunset. On the contrary, they continue to work as interpreters until retirement age and in some cases beyond it. Thirdly, English is the international language of business and is used in boardrooms and business meetings throughout the world. English is also the international language of science. In the 1960s and 1970s when foreign languages were not widely taught, international meetings of doctors or scientists needed interpreters. Nowadays most educated people learn foreign languages and as a result the need for interpreters at this type of meeting has diminished.

However, the need for Community and Court interpreters has increased dramatically. There is far greater movement of people now than ever before. These include tourists, people living and working in foreign countries, illegal immigrants, refugees and asylum seekers. The training and testing of Community and Court interpreters varies from none at all in some countries to well thought out programmes in others.

The Internet has been a wonderful source of information. Of course, it must be said that many Web sites are poorly organized, out of date or just do not have the information one is looking for. All are unrelentingly positive regarding their achievements and rarely mention negative aspects. I have included Web site addresses for those readers who wish to update the information or to check out on employment possibilities – quite a lot of Web sites include a vacancies section. When writing about the international organizations I have drawn heavily on such resources as information booklets and the Internet – in many cases these are the exact same. My aim has been to summarise the objectives and explain the management structure of each organization. I have also included information about interpreting staff and working languages gleaned from my questionnaire. This information is not given for a number of organizations that did not respond to my request for information. Obviously, a great deal more could be written about many of the organizations but my aim here has been to provide essential information only.

Any errors that appear in this volume are my own. A word of warning: it is the nature of this type of information to date quite quickly. For example, the next EU Treaty will bring substantial changes to the organization of the European Union. If enlargement goes ahead there will be changes in the numbers of members of the European Parliament from each member state. There will also be changes in the European Commission. The system of qualified majority voting in the Council of the European Union will have to be refined. On the other hand, I would expect the United Nations to continue without any major changes.

*Mary Phelan*
*September 2000*

# 1 A Brief History of Interpreting

Comparatively little research has been done on Interpreting throughout history. In part, this is because often there is no written record of the spoken word. There may be very little evidence of the interpreter's work. It may be clear from the context that an interpreter was present but all too often the interpreter is not specifically named or mentioned in historical documents. The interpreter may have been a linguist or a diplomat who was asked or offered to interpret.

Interpreting has existed for a long time. Whenever people met who had no common language they had to make do with sign language or find someone who could speak both languages. Some people grew up in a bilingual environment, because they lived in a border area or because their parents spoke different languages. Others moved from one country to another and acquired a second language.

At times in history groups of educated people have shared a common language across borders. A prime example is Latin, which was the language of the Catholic Church and was also used by scientists, writers and diplomats.

When Europeans began to move outside their own countries they had no knowledge of the languages of the peoples of America, Africa or Asia. In the process of colonisation of new continents language was important. The indigenous peoples outnumbered the colonisers and communication was the key to power and control. In their chapter titled *Interpreters and the Making of History* which appeared in *Translators Through History* (1995), Margareta Bowen, David Bowen, Francine Kaufmann and Ingrid Kurz provide a fascinating and detailed account of interpreters down through the ages. Their examples include the following: Christopher Columbus took six native Indians back to Spain with him so that they could learn to speak Spanish and then be used as interpreters once they returned to Central America. Other colonisers such as the French in Canada repeated this pattern. Subsequently the colonisers imposed their own language on the native people, thus reducing the need for interpreters. Some Europeans became proficient in the native Indian languages after being shipwrecked or captured. Missionary priests intent on spreading the Catholic faith drew up glossaries and dictionaries of the native languages.

French was the international language of diplomacy until the peace

1

talks that took place in 1919 after the First World War. These were a turning point because for the first time English was used as a working language. According to historian David Thomson, most of the great powers were represented by their Prime Ministers and Foreign Ministers rather than by kings and queens. President Woodrow Wilson of the United States and Prime Minister Lloyd George of the United Kingdom did not speak French. This was the beginning of conference interpreting. Consecutive interpreting was the order of the day with some interpreters exhibiting an amazing ability to recall speeches lasting up to fifty minutes.

Margareta Bowen *et al.* relate how in the 1920s another milestone was reached with the invention of equipment for simultaneous interpreting by Edward Filene, a businessman, Gordon Finlay, an electrical engineer and Thomas Watson, the president of IBM. Simultaneous interpreting was first used at the International Labour Organization Conference in Geneva in 1927. However, technical difficulties meant that almost twenty years would elapse before simultaneous interpreting was provided in English, French, German and Russian at the Nuremberg Trials, which lasted from November 1945 to October 1946. Some of the interpreters at the Trials went on to work as conference interpreters at the United Nations. In his article, *How Conference Interpretation Grew*, Jean Herbert related how, gradually, simultaneous interpreting began to be used in the United Nations in particular, first in French and English and later in the other official UN languages, Arabic, Chinese, Russian and Spanish. The development of simultaneous interpreting was to facilitate the growth of international organizations after the Second World War. The interpreter's role also changed as the interpreter moved from a very visible, high profile position as consecutive interpreter to being a voice from a booth at the back of a venue.

Some of the first conference interpreters, such as Jean Herbert, wrote about their experiences. Many of those who worked as consecutive interpreters were really in the thick of things. However, although fascinating, these were personal memoirs and more historical documents than research into what exactly is going on when an interpreter is at work.

The first conference interpreters became interpreters by accident. They had one or more foreign languages and found themselves in the right place at the right time. As interpreting developed, universities began offering courses in the subject. This helped interpreters attain professional status. The University of Geneva School of Interpreting was founded in 1940 and the Vienna School of Interpreting in 1943. Georgetown University Division of Interpreting and Translation was founded in the United States in 1949. In 1952, Jean Herbert, a practising interpreter, wrote a book called *Manuel de l'Interprète* which was followed in 1956 by Jean-François Rozan's book *La prise de notes en Consécutive*. Both books were published by University of Geneva Press. AIIC, the International Association of Conference Interpreters, was set up in 1953 and became a proponent of better conditions for its members. Over the decades interpreting became a growth area. In 1957 two schools of Interpreting were established in Paris, the Institut Supérieur d'Interprétation et de Traducteurs (ISIT) and the École Supérieure d'Interprètes et de Traducteurs (ESIT). In 1965 Westminster was established, in 1967 Zurich and in 1968 Monterey Graduate School of Translation and Interpreting. More and more interpreting schools and courses were established around the developed world until interpreter training became the norm.

Once university courses were established, academics began to do research into interpreting. Some early research was not very scientific, being based more on personal judgement than on verifiable results. In the 60s research was done on Ear–Voice Span, i.e. the time lapse between what the speaker says and when the interpreter speaks. In the 70s Danica Seleskovitch of ESIT in Paris wrote about her 'théorie du sens'. Studies were carried out on interpreting errors and their causes. In the 80s and 90s research began on what happens in the brain while a subject is interpreting. Daniel Gile has provided a comprehensive account of conference interpreting research in his book *Regards sur la Recherche en Interprétation de Conférence*. Some researchers unearthed references to interpreters throughout history. Others studied interpretation from the point of view of discourse analysis. Gradually, interest grew in other types of interpreting. A considerable body of work was carried out on court interpreting in the United States. At the end of the 90s some researchers became concerned about community interpreting and used their research to reveal problems associated with this type of interpreting.

All universities which offer courses in interpreting have stringent entrance tests whereby candidates are tested on their knowledge of languages and current affairs and in some cases their ability to cope when being bombarded with information. Despite this rigorous selection procedure many schools find that a considerable number of students drop out or fail interpreting exams. Nowadays a university qualification in interpreting is a prerequisite to a career as an interpreter. Depending on the course, would be interpreters may either study interpreting as part of an undergraduate degree or add an interpreting qualification on to an existing degree. Most courses cover two foreign languages and students usually work into their mother tongue. The primary degree does not have to be in languages. Indeed, in the past the EU preferred to take on people with a background in law or economics or other specialised areas plus knowledge of languages and train them in the skills of interpreting.

Even those who successfully complete an interpreting course may not find employment as interpreters. Finding work can demand a great deal of persistence. It takes time to become an established interpreter. Typically, after qualification as an interpreter, people apply for work to organizations near where they live or move abroad to work. They also apply to agencies for work. Interpreters have to build up experience and often there is a temptation for new interpreters to cut prices in order to be able to work. This is not really a good idea in the long term. Freelance interpreters should always make sure that a contract is drawn up specifying details of their assignment and pay.

A lot depends on where the interpreter lives and the need for interpreting in a particular area. Some organizations prefer to recruit locally rather than cover transport and accommodation costs. There is a great deal of competition for posts in the international organizations. The United Nations has been engaged in cost cutting exercises over a number of years and does not present much hope for would be interpreters. Of course conferences take place all the time on a huge variety of topics and are a useful source of work for freelance interpreters.

Conference interpreting continues to play an important role around the world today both at an international level and on a regional level. It has facilitated the growth of international organizations around the world. The following chart contains the numbers of interpreters employed at the larger international organizations in 1999:

|  | Staff interpreters | Pool of freelance interpreters |
| --- | --- | --- |
| European Commission (SCIC/JICS) | 530 | 1,700 |
| European Parliament | 180 | 1,000 |
| European Court of Justice | 40 | 150 |
| United Nations Office in New York | 110 | 350 |
| UN Office in Geneva | 84 | 30–40 per week |
| UN Office in Vienna | 13 | 60 at peak times |
| NATO | 42 | 100 |
| Total | 1,000 | 3,400 |

**Table 1** *Numbers of interpreters employed at major international organizations*

The remaining international organizations employ very few or no staff interpreters and take on freelance interpreters as needed.

Conference interpreters will need an excellent knowledge of at least two foreign languages. In the case of the European Parliament, four languages are required and a fifth is desirable. Most mainstream languages such as English, French, German, Italian and Spanish are well covered by existing interpreters. In the future within the EU the need will be for Eastern European languages such as Romanian, Turkish, Czech and so on. Of course, knowledge of languages must be accompanied by knowledge of the culture.

Intellectual curiosity is essential for conference interpreters in particular. As conferences can be on any topic interpreters need to be well informed as regards current affairs. EU interpreters would also benefit from a thorough understanding of how the EU is organized and how it works.

Interpreting is a demanding job in that when an interpreter is working he or she cannot afford to have a bad day. One bad interpreter can ruin a conference. The interpreter needs a good short-term memory to retain what he or she has just heard and a good long-term memory to put the information into context. Ability to concentrate is a factor as is the ability to analyse and process what is heard.

Whether an interpreter is working at a conference or in a court or in a hospital, preparation is the key. The first task is to find out as much information as possible about the context. Then the interpreter will set about organizing a terminology glossary that corresponds to the assignment and reading around the subject area. This is when access to up to date dictionaries is essential.

Other forms of interpreting have also become important. Court interpreting is one. Another is community interpreting. As multiculturalism became a feature of life in Australia, Canada, Europe and the United States, people gradually realised that they could not just expect foreigners to become proficient in the language of the country in which they found themselves. In some countries there is no training for would be interpreters. If they speak two languages and are willing to interpret, they will find work. This is partly because some governments have no policy on community interpreting and partly because the people who need this type of interpreting speak lesser-used languages in the countries where they are resident. Furthermore, language needs constantly change as new groups move from one country to another. This makes it difficult to find interpreters with new languages.

Community interpreting will be the next growth area. There is a widespread need for community interpreting to be recognised, for courses to be set up at university level and for community interpreters to gain recognition.

# 2 The Different Types of Interpreting

Interpreting takes place when one person translates orally what he or she hears into another language. Many people are confused about the difference between translating and interpreting. The difference is quite simple: a translation is written down whereas interpreting is spoken.

The three types of interpreting are bilateral or liaison, consecutive and simultaneous.

Because the interpreter takes the place of the original speaker, interpreters use the first person singular, 'I' when interpreting.

## Conference Interpreting

The term Conference Interpreting refers to the use of consecutive or simultaneous interpreting at a conference or a meeting. Nowadays, simultaneous is far more common and is used almost exclusively in international organizations. Conference interpreting is the most prestigious form of interpreting and the most financially rewarding. Degrees or postgraduate qualifications in conference interpreting are available in many countries.

## Simultaneous Interpreting

In simultaneous interpreting the listener hears the interpretation at the same time as the speech is made. The interpreter sits in a booth wearing headphones with a microphone. There is a booth for each language and two or sometimes three interpreters in each booth. A *chef d'équipe* liaises between the interpreters and the conference organizers and delegates. The interpreter hears the speech through the headphones and simultaneously interprets. In some cases interpretation is recorded but the interpreters' permission is required for this. The booth contains a button for volume control, a mute button and a relay button. If the interpreter needs to cough he or she presses the mute button so that the audience will not hear. Meanwhile the listeners are equipped with headphones that they can switch to the language they require.

The **relay** button is switched on to listen to an interpretation from another booth. For example, in the case of a conference held in London with most speeches in English, if a speaker speaks in another language such as German, the interpreters in the French and Spanish booths will listen to the English version given by the interpreter in the German booth. So, while the German speaker gives the talk in German, the interpreter interprets into English and the other interpreters interpret into French and Spanish. This all happens simultaneously but obviously the quality of the French and Spanish interpretations will be totally dependent on the interpretation from German to English. For this reason over reliance on relay is not recommended.

Because of the high level of concentration required for simultaneous interpreting, interpreters do not usually interpret for more than thirty minutes at a time. There are usually at least two people in any language booth. When the interpreter is not actually interpreting he or she stays in the booth preparing the next speech and remains available to help his or her colleague if necessary. Many of the international organizations contacted in the course of preparing this book emphasised that teamwork is an important aspect of simultaneous interpreting. For example, the Organization of American States representative wrote that the ideal candidate 'would be intellectually curious, have a pleasant voice and smooth delivery when interpreting, and be able to function as a team player.' Willingness to cooperate and flexibility were underlined by the Language Service of the European Patent Office. As the booth is a confined space it is helpful if colleagues are of a pleasant, helpful disposition. Sergio Viaggi, Head Interpreter at the United Nations in Vienna is one of the few commentators to deal with the issue of booth manners. In his keynote presentation to the XIV FIT Congress in Melbourne in 1996 he highlighted the importance of a constant presence in the booth. He said that interpreters should be helpful and have a sociable personality. He also pointed out that interpreters should be careful of distracting noises such as the rustling of papers, background talk or laughter, water being poured, as all these sounds can be picked up by the microphone and transmitted to the audience.

The interpreter has to process incoming information in one language and produce an interpretation in a second language. It is often necessary to wait for more information in order to give a correct interpretation. Sometimes interpreters try to predict the next word or phrase. Interpreters should always keep in mind the fact that they are speaking to an audience. They should not hesitate or leave sentences unfinished. They should be concerned with meaning rather than exact equivalents for individual words. A pleasant voice is a great asset in an interpreter. The interpreter should not sound boring or bored and should not speak at great speed.

As conferences can be on any subject from the environment to computers to electronic engineering, conference interpreters need to have a broad range of interests and to be able to cope with a variety of topics.

Simultaneous interpreters need to have a clear view of the speaker and of any slides, transparencies or videos that may be shown at the conference. A pair of binoculars can be a useful aid in this type of situation.

In some cases the text of the speeches is made available to the interpreters before the conference takes place. This allows the interpreters to find out what the speech is about and to prepare terminology. In many cases, however, the speeches are made available just before the meeting. When a speaker reads from a prepared text he or she tends to speak faster than when speaking off the cuff. Increased speed makes interpreting more intensive, hence the value of actually having a copy of the speech. However, simply having a copy of the speech does not necessarily mean that the interpreter will have no worries. In many cases speakers deviate from their speech to make a point in connection with another speaker's point or because they are keeping to a revised schedule. If the interpreter happens to make a mistake, as can easily occur with figures, he or she may be corrected from the floor in a questions and answers session after the speech. The questions and answers session can also be quite complex because until the person begins to speak the interpreters do not know what language is involved or who is going to have to interpret.

Laptop computers are being used more and more in the booth. They allow the interpreter to access terminology bases very quickly. Organizations such as the European Commission have their own Intranet containing original documents and terminology databases for EU related terms. Many specialised dictionaries can also be accessed online.

Simultaneous without the booth is used for meetings between political leaders for example. If the US President and the German Chancellor are having direct talks, they sit down along with two interpreters at a table. Everyone is equipped with headphones and microphones and simultaneous interpreting can take place. Some Prime Ministers have their own personal interpreters.

Apart from conference settings, simultaneous interpreting is provided in a number of parliaments around the world – in the case of the Nunavut, Canada's third territory, the working language of the legislative assembly is Inuktitut for debate and legislation with simultaneous interpretation into other Inuit dialects, English and French.

Simultaneous interpretation from Welsh into English is provided at the National Assembly for Wales, Web site: www.wales.gov.uk

In Canada, the two official languages are English and French and under the 1988 Official Languages Act 'any oral communication occurring as part of official House of Commons business shall be interpreted into the other official language while, or immediately after, being spoken.' Web site: www.parl.gc.ca

Brian Huebner has designed a very useful Web site for conference interpreters. It consists of links to glossaries, newspapers, radio, interpreter groups, AIIC, search engines, dictionaries, translators' sites and a very entertaining list of 'bloopers' made by conference interpreters. Web site: web.wanadoo.be/brian.huebner/interp.htm

Another useful Internet source is **The Translator's Home Companion**, which has links to dictionaries in many languages. Web site: www.rahul.net/lai/companion.html

## Consecutive Interpreting

In consecutive interpreting the interpreter listens to a speech while taking notes. When the speaker has finished, the interpreter stands up and delivers the speech in his or her native language. The speech could be as long as fifteen minutes nowadays although in the past thirty minutes was not unusual. The interpretation is not a summary; it is a complete rendition of the original speech in another language. Obviously this method is time consuming as the time element is almost doubled. Some practitioners felt that this extra time was useful because it gave people time to think. But if interpretation has to be provided into more than one language the whole process becomes extremely lengthy. However, the widespread use of simultaneous has meant that nowadays consecutive interpreting is confined to situations where simultaneous equipment is not available. Consecutive could be useful for a question and answer session, a press conference or an after dinner speech. Despite the move away from consecutive, it is still taught on all interpreting courses and is part of the selection procedure for entry into most interpreting posts, partly because trainers believe it is an essential part of interpreter training.

In consecutive interpreting, a clear division of the skills involved in interpreting can be seen. Apart from knowledge of the language, memory, concentration and understanding are important factors. The importance of delivery is clear when the interpreter has to stand up in front of the audience and give the speech. Practice at public speaking is useful training.

Notetaking is central to consecutive interpreting. Practising interpreters develop their own techniques for notetaking. Some use a great number of symbols while others hardly use any. One person's notes would probably be totally unintelligible to any other reader. Some interpreters even manage to write down everything they hear although this is not generally recommended because it is so important to be able to analyse the speech and its theme or argument. Most interpreters take notes in the target language rather than the source language as this approach saves time and effort when the time comes to deliver the interpretation. This approach also helps the interpreter to make a conscious effort to move away from the structures and expressions of the source language. One advantage of consecutive interpreting is the fact that there are no booths or equipment between the speaker and the interpreter. If the interpreter is unsure of a point he or she can check with the speaker as to what exactly was meant.

Jean-François Rozan put together some ideas to help interpreters with the task of notetaking in his book *La prise de notes en consécutive*, published by the University of Geneva in 1956. Some of his ideas are still useful today. Rozan established seven basic principles:

Note the idea rather than the exact words used.

Abbreviate long words by noting the first two and the last two letters only. Alternatively, find a short word with the same meaning.

Abbreviations of linking words are important:

| | |
|---|---|
| as, why | to mean because, as, given that, for this reason |
| tho | although, despite |
| but | however, nevertheless |
| if | supposing |
| as to | as regards, regarding, concerning |
| ths | thus, in other words, to conclude, in conclusion |

Negation

| | |
|---|---|
| OK | to approve |
| no OK | to disapprove |

Underlining to stress importance or significance:

| | |
|---|---|
| int | interesting |
| <u>int</u> | very interesting |
| <u>?</u> | an important question |

Work down the page. Group ideas intelligently. Use a line to separate ideas. Number pages to avoid confusion. Cross off each section as you interpret it.

Symbols
*Symbols of expression*

| | |
|---|---|
| : | to express thought or belief |
| " | to express what is said, declared or affirmed |
| ⊙ | symbol of discussion |
| OK | symbol of approbation |

*Symbols of movement*

| | |
|---|---|
| → | A horizontal arrow indicates movement or communication. It can also be used to express leading to or providing with. |
| ↗ | to express increase, development or progress |
| ↘ | to express decrease, reduction or decline |

*Symbols of correspondence*

| | |
|---|---|
| = | to imply equality or correspondence |
| ≠ | unlike, as against |
| + | moreover, in addition |

*Other symbols*

| | |
|---|---|
| ☐ | country, nation, national |
| ☒ | international, foreign |
| W | world, worldwide, global, universal |
| w | work, labour |
| ? | question, problem |
| Ms | members, participants |
| TR | trade, commerce, trade relations |

Some of Rozan's ideas are still useful today and can be combined with other easily recognised symbols include the following:

| | |
|---|---|
| ⓘ | information |
| ⚡ | tension, electricity |
| ⊕ | meeting point |
| Km | kilometre |
| KWh | kilowatt hour |
| O | Oxygen |
| % | percentage |
| ca | circa, roughly |
| ∴ | therefore |
| > | greater than |
| < | less than |
| HR | Human Rights |

Commonly accepted abbreviations used in the postal code and car identification for countries are easy to remember:

| | |
|---|---|
| D | Germany |
| Dk | Denmark |
| F | France |
| 75 | Paris |
| E | Spain |

In some countries the car registration system identifies the province or city where the car is registered:

| | |
|---|---|
| M | Madrid |
| V | Valencia |
| R | Rome |
| To | Turin |

Some interpreters use the following symbols:

| | |
|---|---|
| 0 | -ion ending in many words |
| / | -ly ending for adverbs |

In 1989 Heinz Matyssek published a handbook in two volumes called *Handbuch der Notizentechnik für Dolmetscher* on notetaking techniques. His approach is exhaustive – Volume II is like a dictionary consisting of 280 pages of German words and symbols. Some symbols could be used in any language but others are particular to German. In Volume I Matyssek explains his theory of notetaking and suggests basic symbols which can be developed to express different meanings. For example:

| | |
|---|---|
| Ha | trade (Handel is German for trade) |
| ↙Ha | imports |
| H<u>a</u> | retail trade |
| H̲a | wholesale |
| W | war |
| π | politics |
| P | price |
| ψ | agriculture |
| M | motor |
| Met | metal |
| ♀ | people |
| ♀♀ | family |
| ↑ | market |

Clearly it is impossible to learn symbols for every term and every word one meets when interpreting. They can be useful for terms that occur frequently. They are only worthwhile if the interpreter can recall them speedily and jot them down immediately. If an interpreter has developed any shortcuts in notetaking at lectures for example, those techniques should be incorporated into notetaking for consecutive interpreting. If something works for you, you should use it.

## Whispered Interpreting

Whispered interpreting or *chuchotage* is used when one or two people do not understand the source language. Whispering is not a very accurate description because too much whispering is not very good for the vocal cords. Most interpreters in this situation speak in a low voice rather than whispering. The interpreter listens to the speaker and simultaneously renders the interpretation to the listener or listeners. No equipment is required. This technique could be used at a school meeting for example where one parent does not understand the language being used. Acoustics can be a problem.

## Bilateral or Liaison Interpreting

A number of different types of interpreting have evolved for different situations. The first type of interpreting was bilateral or liaison interpreting (sometimes referred to as *ad hoc* interpreting) where the interpreter uses two languages to interpret for two or more people. This type of interpreting is still used today in informal situations, for business meetings and for community interpreting. Bilateral interpreters may need to be assertive and exert control over how much interlocutors say and when. They may need to ask clients to speak up.

## Sight Translation

Interpreters are often asked to read and translate documents aloud. This could happen in many different situations. For example, an interpreter working at a business meeting could be asked to translate some material. An interpreter in a court setting could be asked to translate a legal document. Interpreters may need time to peruse the document in detail and if this is the case they should request that time.

## Telephone Interpreting

Telephone Interpreting is bilateral interpreting over the phone. It is widely used in a business context, for medical examinations and even in some courts in America. If a factory manager in the United States needs a component that is manufactured in Japan, he contacts a telephone interpreting service and asks for an English-Japanese interpreter. The interpreter interprets everything that is said.

Freelance telephone interpreters are paid a retainer to be available at the end of a phone line. Depending on their conditions of employment, they may be paid by the minute or every five minutes for actual interpreting time.

The advantage of telephone interpreting is that it is available from anywhere, round the clock in a large number of languages. It is obviously ideal for emergency situations and for first contacts. Advances in voice recognition processes mean that machine interpreting may become available over the phone in the future.

Telephone interpreting is highly developed in the United States where it is available from a number of companies. AT&T Language Line Services offer over the phone interpreting in 140 languages. Language Line Services began in 1989 and was originally aimed at businesses and at emergency services such as ambulances, police and the fire brigade. Many hospitals in the United States use Language Line Services. Insurance companies have also found it useful for claims adjustments. In 1990 the service was made available to individual consumers as well. Language Line Services are available through English from any phone in the world and payment can be made by credit card. Connection to an interpreter can be obtained in 25 seconds or less. The cost per minute in 1999 was between US$4.15 and US$7.25 depending on the language required. A complex database has been developed by Language Line Services in order to calculate the number of interpreters and languages required at any given time.

The Language Line Services Internet site contains audio of three 'real–life episodes' of telephone interpreting between a Portuguese asthma sufferer and a hospital, a business transaction between a US company and a Thai company and finally a complaint about some missing items from a mail order purchase.

---

**Language Line Services**
Web site: www.languageline.com

---

NetworkOmni® is another provider of telephone interpreting services in the United States. Founded in 1981 it began with face to face interpreting, then commenced a translation service and in 1992 set up the telephone interpreting section that unfortunately is called Translation Line. Again, it provides a year long round the clock service in 140 languages. NetworkOmni® works with over 2,000 translators and interpreters.

---

**NetworkOmni®**
1329 E Thousand Oaks Blvd, 2nd Floor, Thousand Oaks, CA 91362, USA
Web site: www.networkomni.com

---

In France Alphatrad provides a telephone interpreting service which allows customers to contact others anywhere in the world with the help of an interpreter. This service is aimed mainly at business people.

---

**Alphatrad Head Office**
1, rue du Languedoc, Z.I. de la Moinerie BP no. 48 91223, Bretigny CEDEX, France
Web site: www.alphatrad.com

---

# Sign Language Interpreting

Sign language interpreting is provided for deaf or hearing-impaired people who cannot understand the original speech. It may come as a surprise to some readers to find sign language included in this volume but deaf and hard of hearing people find themselves in the same situation as people who do not speak the language of the country where they are living. Attitudes towards sign language have changed. In the past those working with deaf people were intent on teaching them to speak and sign language was frowned on. Nowadays, sign language is recognised as a language in its own right. Sign language uses gestures of the hands and the rest of the body including the face. A number of sign languages have developed separately in different countries. Within the English speaking world American, British and Irish sign language have all evolved separately. There are dialects within each sign language. Fingerspelling is used to supplement signing. Unlike language interpreters who are often hidden away in their booths at the back of a conference hall, sign language interpreters must be clearly visible to their audience. However, they are generally advised not to wear very bright or distracting colours or designs as this can cause visual fatigue among the deaf or hard of hearing listeners.

Gallaudet University in the United States is a University for deaf and hard of hearing people. Everyone on the campus uses sign language. The Gallaudet Research Institute carries out research in areas of concern to the deaf community such as paediatric cochlea implants, health care services for deaf and hard of hearing patients, hearing loss in adults and in children.

---

**Gallaudet University**
800 Florida Avenue, NE, Washington DC 20002–3695, USA
Web site: www2.gallaudet.edu

**Gallaudet Research Institute**
Web site: gri.gallaudet.edu

---

The Interpreters' Network is 'The Internet Resource for interpreters whose working languages include a signed language'. The Web site includes links to areas of interest to sign language interpreters and to interpreting in general.

---

**The Interpreters' Network**
Suite 230, 1326 Huron Street, London, Ontario, Canada N5V 2E2
Web site: www.terpsnet.com

---

## Television Interpreting

Simultaneous interpreting is provided for television programmes, particularly for interviews with foreign guests. Examples include politicians, musicians and sportsmen and women. This type of concept is not very prevalent in the English speaking world but is quite common in mainland Europe. The Franco-German television station Arte employs a dozen full time interpreters and a large number of freelance interpreters in English, French and German.

AIIC recommends that in the case of programmes recorded live in the studio, the interpreter should sit in a booth where ideally he or she can see the speakers, the set and other interpreters who are working on the programme. All equipment should be checked before recording begins. In particular, satellite connections should be checked to ensure that the interpreter's voice is not sent back.

In the case of interviews recorded outside the studio and some current affairs programmes, the interpreter interprets what he or she hears on a TV monitor. Background noise can be a problem. Ingrid Kurz (1997) has made the point that interpreters are expected to sound as slick and confident as any TV presenter. A convention has developed where male interpreters interpret male voices and female interpreters interpret female voices. All too often we hear interpreters' voices on television programmes and sometimes we actually see them but we rarely see their names. Everyone else involved in making a programme is credited except for the interpreter, without whom the programme could not have been made.

---

**Arte**
2A rue de la Fonderie, F-67080 Strasbourg Cedex, France
Web site: www.arte.fr/

---

# Videoconference Interpreting

Videoconference technology is undergoing rapid development. The Internet offers a great deal of potential for live teleconferencing in the future. In the meantime, a number of different systems are being developed but compatibility and interoperability could well present problems for some time. Technical differences include different network services, different codec equipment and different transmission speeds. According to AT& T Video Center in Atlanta, Georgia, the basic equipment for video conferencing consists of a camera, a codec, a monitor, a microphone, an equipment control pad at each location and Network services to connect the locations. Some multinational companies use video conferencing as part of the recruitment process. Interpreting is an added complication in video conferencing.

---

**AT&T Video Center**
Tips and Techniques – the basics of Video Conferencing
Web site: www.att.com/conferencing/vid_bas.html

---

Video relay interpreting is also used to help deaf people communicate by phone. This could replace text telephone machines where deaf people type in questions or statements. The text is sent to a relay centre where an operator contacts the person the deaf person wants to deal with. Video relay interpreting means that a deaf person who has access to a computer with a video card and a camera can use sign language directly to another deaf person or to an interpreter. This is much faster than the slow procedure of a person typing out what he or she wants to say.

# Wiretapping and Tape Transcription

Many law enforcement agencies in the United States and in the Netherlands use wiretaps to record conversations in private residences and on mobile phone lines in order to gather information about drug-related crime and criminal gangs. According to the Administrative Office of the U.S. Courts, in 1999 there were 1,350 applications for permission to use wiretaps. These applications resulted in 4,372 arrests and 654 convictions. In the United States wiretaps are usually restricted to thirty days although they can be extended to much longer periods.

---

**Administrative Office of the United States Courts (AOUSC)**
Web site: www.uscourts.gov/Press_Releases/press_050100.html

---

(The remainder of this section is based on a lecture given by Joyce García at the July 2000 Agnese Haury Institute for Court Interpretation). If the police find that the recordings include a foreign language they may ask interpreters to transcribe and translate the content of the tapes. This is a very laborious, time consuming process. A great deal depends on the actual quality of the tapes. There may be a lot of background noise although sometimes this can be cleaned up. The interpreter's transcription fee is based on the level of difficulty of the recording.

An office transcriber with a foot pedal to stop and start the tape is a very useful aid in this type of work because it leaves your hands free to use the keyboard.

As the recordings are evidence it is imperative not to work with originals and to take great care to sign off for each item and to return everything once the work is completed. The interpreter may be asked to work from videocassettes, in which case the recording can be transferred to audiotape, but obviously the video will provide clues as to the context and the speakers.

Each call should be treated as a separate document and the transcription should include the source language on the left-hand side of the page and the target language on the right hand side. Each line should be numbered. MV1 will be the first male voice that appears on the tape. FV2 will be the second female voice and so on. All pauses, noise or static should be mentioned. Any inaudible or unintelligible conversation should be labelled as such. A legend can be included at the beginning of the transcript to indicate any of these problems. The translation should be an accurate reflection of the original and should include any poor grammar and inconsistencies that appear on the recording. Any extraneous information provided by the police should be mentioned on the transcript. The interpreter should sign each page to ensure that no changes are made to any section of the transcription. The interpreter must be prepared to justify every single word that appears in the transcript.

In some cases in the United States the work of transcription and translation is done by language specialists at the Federal Bureau of Investigation and then passed on to accredited Federal Court interpreters for certification.

# 3 Hints for Speakers at Conferences

*Before the conference:*

1. If at all possible, speak in your mother tongue. It is silly to insist on speaking a foreign language if interpreting is available from your language.

2. If you have to give a speech in a language other than your mother tongue, ask a native speaker to check through it to ensure that it makes sense and to eliminate any possible grammatical problems or sources of confusion. It could also be a good idea to rehearse your speech with a native speaker or speakers as your audience.

3. Despite increasing globalisation it is a good idea to avoid references to or comparisons with local personalities or events which may mean nothing to people from other countries.

4. Many speakers like to begin their talk with a joke to put their audience at their ease. Very few jokes work when interpreted into other languages. If your joke is based on a pun for example, the chances are that it will be untranslatable.

5. If you plan to work from a prepared speech, send a copy of your speech to the conference organizers well before the date of the conference, ideally a few weeks before. This will allow the interpreters to prepare terminology and will ensure a better standard of interpretation.

6. Consider delivering your speech extemporaneously. For example you could prepare overheads on a computer programme such as PowerPoint. Supply the interpreters with a photocopy showing overhead content. Then talk around the overheads.

*Before you speak:*

7. Sometimes, if the conference is running late for example, the time allocated to you may be reduced. If this happens, do not decide to deliver your speech at top speed in a shorter time. Ask to meet the interpreters and tell them that you intend to delete certain sections of the speech. Specify exactly which parts you will omit. This will mean that the interpreters will not be frantically going through the text trying to locate sections of your paper.

*The speech itself:*

8.  If a microphone is provided, don't forget to use it.
9.  Speak slowly and clearly, particularly if you are reading your speech. Speakers tend to speak faster in this situation than when speaking spontaneously. If you speak quickly you make the interpreter's task more difficult, if not downright impossible. Some speakers speak very quickly due to nervousness but speed is detrimental to understanding by everyone, both audience and interpreters.
10. Take particular care with figures – say them slowly and it may in fact be a good idea to repeat them.
11. Quotations can also be problematic. In the case of well-known literary quotations there may be only one correct, accepted translation. The interpreter may need a few extra seconds to think quickly. Of course, if they have time to go through the speech before the conference, they will be able to find the accepted version.
12. Excessive speed of delivery is particularly counterproductive in the case of very technical material where the interpreter may be struggling to grasp the process being described in order to give an acceptable interpretation. Remember that this is your subject so of course you understand it and it seems simple to you. It may not seem so simple to others.
13. If members of the audience ask questions in your native language, it is a good idea to repeat the questions as this facilitates both the audience and the interpreters.

# 4 Community, Court and Medical Interpreting

## Community Interpreting

Community or public service interpreting is provided face to face and over the phone in the spheres of health, social services, the law and education. There is a certain amount of confusion about what term to use to describe this type of interpreting. Public service interpreting is the term used in the United Kingdom. Most other countries use the term community interpreting. In Australia the preferred term is community based interpreting. Some commentators prefer the term *ad hoc* interpreting or even contact interpreting or dialogue interpreting. In some countries community interpreting includes court interpreting. In others, court interpreting is regarded as a separate speciality. In the United States and Canada medical interpreting is fast becoming a specialised area too.

Social workers, doctors, nurses, probation officers, teachers, housing officers and the police in the developed world all come across more and more situations where their native language is not understood by the people they are dealing with. There is more movement of people nowadays than ever before. People within the European Economic Area (the EU plus Iceland, Liechtenstein and Norway) are free to live and work in any of the eighteen EEA countries. There has been a huge increase in tourism worldwide. If a tourist is involved in a car accident, he or she may as a result have dealings with the casualty department of a hospital and with the local police. The numbers of asylum seekers and refugees have also increased greatly. Asylum seekers are people who are seeking to be granted refugee status. Unlike the United States, Canada and Australia, the European Union does not have a policy of allowing people from outside to migrate legally to Europe. As most asylum seekers are from Eastern Europe, Africa and Asia and many do not speak mainstream languages such as English, French, German, Italian and Spanish, it may be difficult to locate suitable interpreters.

It is impossible for a judge or a lawyer or a doctor to know if an interpreter is providing a good service. Their only criterion is the interpreter's use of the language that they share. They have no idea if information is omitted or altered. Indeed, in some cases interpreters may give additional information. A number of administrations have come to the conclusion that it is not good enough just to exclude people who come from a different linguistic background, or pretend they do not exist or expect their children or friends to interpret. The challenge then is to give interested parties the opportunity to train as interpreters, to set up a system of accreditation and a register containing details such as interpreters' phone numbers, languages and specialities. It also becomes necessary to train other people in how to carry out their work with the help of interpreters. For example, judges, lawyers and court officials need to learn how to deal with interpreters and they should have a clear picture of the interpreter's role. The police also need to be trained as do doctors and health staff. The big problem is that interpreting services are expensive.

Some community interpreters find themselves interpreting for people in heartrending situations. For example, people who have been tortured, whose families have been killed, whose relations are untraceable. Some of the interpreters may have gone through similar experiences. It is important for interpreters to be able to discuss their feelings with other interpreters while still respecting the confidentiality of the interpreting situation. In a medical setting, interpreters may have to tell patients that they have cancer or are terminally ill. Some interpreters may not find this type of work at all upsetting but others may need access to counselling services. The Babelea Association for Community Interpreting has funded research in this area by Dr Karen Baistow of Brunel University in the United Kingdom. Dr Baistow analysed the causes of emotional and psychological trauma among community interpreters in six European countries and proposed strategies to help interpreters deal with this problem.

Sometimes the staff in a hospital for example may not know in what language interpreting is required. In Australia the interpreting services provide hospitals and police with a card containing the statement 'I need an interpreter' in a variety of languages. The person picks out his or her language and a request is then made for an interpreter in that language. There is an important translation issue here as well. Information leaflets and consent forms should be provided in various languages.

A great deal of this type of interpreting takes place face to face. However, if an interpreter in any large city has to attend a number of appointments at different locations he or she ends up spending far more time commuting than interpreting. Community interpreters may ask to be paid for a minimum amount of time or in some cases commuting time may be paid at a lower rate than interpreting time. Some interpreter providers have contracts with hospitals or post offices whereby an interpreter is made available one morning or afternoon each week.

Sometimes community interpreters are told at the last minute that their appointment has been cancelled or rescheduled. In some countries the interpreter is not compensated in any way despite the fact that he or she is available to work. In others the interpreter is paid the full fee if less than 24 hours notice is given, or half the fee if less than 48 hours notice is provided.

The police may require the help of an interpreter when investigating an accident, questioning a suspect, taking statements, charging a suspect etc. Interpreters are also needed in the courts. If an interpreter has interpreted at a police station and is asked to work on the same case in court, he or she should declare this to the judge.

Community interpreters use a combination of whispered simultaneous and consecutive interpreting. The latter may consist of short questions and answers or may require some notetaking for longer segments. Interpreters may also be asked to do sight translations of short texts – the interpreter is handed a text that he or she is asked to translate aloud.

People working with interpreters may need to be trained in how to deal with interpreting and what to expect from the interpreter. When public service interpreters work with people for the first time they should provide a brief explanation to both parties of what they are about. It is a good idea to remind clients to address each other rather than addressing the interpreter. Some interpreters in this situation make a point of looking down or writing in a notebook in order to encourage the participants to address each other directly.

The European based Babelea Association for Community Interpreting is doing some useful work and organized its first conference in Vienna in November 1999. Two representatives from JICS/SCIC, the Interpreting Section in the EU Commission attended the Conference, signalling some interest at EU level in the provision of community interpreting. The basic idea behind Babelea is that European countries should work together rather than separately and all state organizations in the European Union should use Babelea community interpreters by the year 2015.

There is enormous variation between countries in the provision, training and accreditation of community interpreters. Different countries have developed their own systems to provide training to community interpreters. In some countries this has been done at national level, in others at local level only. Some organizations such as Language Line in the United Kingdom are profit making. The provision of community interpreting varies widely both within and between countries. Some governments finance community interpreting directly whereas others do so indirectly. Some countries have worked out coherent strategies for organizing and providing community interpreting whereas others are only beginning to realise that they have a problem. Training is provided at local level in some countries and by universities in other countries. Perhaps in the future the European Union will provide leadership and legislation for what is going to be a very important sphere in the future. The following section provides readers with an idea of the situation prevailing around the world at the start of the year 2000. Australia probably provides the best example in that community interpreting has government support and interpreters are tested and accredited.

## AUSTRALIA

In Australia the Department of Immigration and Multicultural Affairs offers a round the clock telephone interpreting service and face to face interpreting. This is known as the Translation and Interpreting Service (TIS). Telephone interpreting is used for contact with government departments and some community organizations. Face to face interpreting is available for hospital appointments and with community organizations. About 2,000 interpreters and translators work for TIS in over 100 languages and dialects. They all adhere to the professional Code of Ethics of the Australian Institute of Interpreters and Translators Inc. (AUSIT). Interpreters who have been successful in the Australian accreditation system (see below) are preferred. Sixty per cent of TIS interpreters are women. Non English speaking women can ask for a woman interpreter. There is also an indigenous language interpreting service.

---

**Australian Department of Immigration and Multicultural Affairs**
Web site: www.immi.gov.au

---

The Australian National Accreditation Authority for Translators and Interpreters (NAATI) operates an accreditation system. Set up in 1977 it began by surveying the profession and then went on to set up testing and procedures for accreditation. The Authority operates a four level accreditation system for interpreters:

- Paraprofessional Interpreter
- Interpreter
- Conference Interpreter
- Senior Conference Interpreter

The languages offered at interpreter level in 2000 were Albanian, Arabic, Assyrian, AUSLAN (Australian Sign Language), Bosnian, Burmese, Chinese, Croatian, Dari, French, German, Greek, Hindi, Hungarian, Indonesia, Italian, Japanese, Korean, Lao, Macedonian, Persian, Polish, Portuguese, Romanian, Russian, Samoan, Serbian, Spanish, Tamil, Thai, Tongan, Turkish, Urdu and Vietnamese.

---

**NAATI**
ACT-Canberra Head Office, PO Box 40, Hawker ACT 2614, Australia
Web site: www.naati.com.au

---

## CANADA

The Critical Link is a Canadian initiative, basically consisting of conferences about community interpreting which take place every three years. The first one took place in 1995, the second in 1998 and the third is due to take place in Montreal in May 2001. The conference proceedings are published. A further initiative of the Critical Link was to launch a Web site in April 2000. The aim of the Web site is to build up connections between community interpreters in Canada and elsewhere. The Web site includes twelve papers that did not appear as part of the 1998 conference proceedings. The twelve papers cover:

- court interpreting
- sign language interpreting
- medical interpreting
- liaison interpreting

The Web site also features a quarterly newsletter with input from people involved in community interpreting all around the world.

---

**The Critical Link**
Web site: www.criticallink.org
Critical Link 3 Conference Web site: www.rrsss06.gouv.qc.ca/english/colloque/index2.html

---

## FRANCE

In France, the Paris based ISM Interprétariat was founded in 1971 and offers both face to face and over the phone interpreting in 80 languages and dialects. Face to face interpreting is provided for medical services, schools, social services and appointments with psychologists. New interpreters are assigned mentors for the first six months. Ongoing training is provided. Interpreting is provided in 3,000 institutions each year and adds up to about 110,000 hours a year. The hospitals and schools pay for the interpreting service. The telephone interpreting service has been available for emergencies day and night since 1990.

---

**Inter Service Migrants Interprétariat**
12, rue Guy de la Brosse, 75005 Paris, France
No Web site at time of writing

---

## ITALY

In Italy, a non-governmental organization called Cospe has developed training courses for interpreters who work face to face and over the phone with non-native Italian speakers. Cospe also plans to educate user institutions on how to work with interpreters and on the role of the interpreter. Cospe's brief is wider than just community interpreting as it is also involved in anti-racism programmes and in the education of migrant children.

---

**Cospe**
Via Slataper 10, 50134 Florence, Italy
Web site: www.Cospe.it (This site is in Italian).

---

## THE NETHERLANDS

In 1999 at the First Babelea Conference on Community Interpreting, Giuseppe B. Raaphorst of the Dutch Ministry of Justice provided a background report on the situation in his country. The Netherlands is one of the few countries where the government has taken responsibility for the provision of community interpreting services. The system is that there are six interpreter centres or *tolkencentra* that were set up by the government in the 1970s. The Ministry for Justice pays the interpreters. Interpreting is provided both face to face and over the phone with an even split between the two. About 85% of interpreting is related to justice and 10% to health. The Interpreter Centres operate from a register of 700 freelance interpreters covering 85 languages and dialects. In 1998 the Centres provided interpreters for 400,000 encounters. Seventy five per cent of interpreting encounters take place with asylum seekers. The minimum age for community interpreters in the Netherlands is 23 and they should have spent at least three years in the country.

Many of these positive developments took place because of the proactive approach of officialdom. In 1986, Dutch Members of Parliament demanded an enquiry into interpreting in the courts. More recently, they raised questions concerning the quality and remuneration of interpreters. The ruling of the European Court on Human Rights in the case of Kamasinski vs. Austria was interpreted as meaning that suspects in criminal investigations have a right to a qualified, registered interpreter. The Ombudsman drew up a critical report on interpretation provision in the immigration procedures. As a result, new guidelines were established for the selection of interpreters. A national working group was set up to assess the situation and improve the service.

The next step will be the establishment of an independent accreditation system for interpreters. From 2003 all interpreters will have to be accredited if they are to work for government services. Training courses are to be provided and ongoing training is to be a feature of the system even after accreditation, as certification will become void after a certain amount of time. It is also planned to change to one central interpreter centre rather than the six operating at present. Uniform rates for all interpreters have been proposed although this has aroused opposition from court interpreters who have postgraduate training.

**Tolkencentrum**
Noord en Oost Nederland, PO Box 695, 7550 AR Hengelo, Netherlands
Web site: www.tolkencentrum-non.nl (Note: this Web site is in Dutch)

## SWEDEN

Sweden is a very good example of what can be done to train and test community interpreters. The Institute for Interpretation and Translation Studies at Stockholm University is responsible for the training of community interpreters at high schools throughout the country. Interestingly, the Institute is also responsible for training programmes for sign language interpreters, interpreters for the deaf-blind and courses for sign language teachers. Between 1995 and 1996 the Institute provided 226 courses to 3,230 students in an amazing 53 languages. Some courses were bilingual whereas others were generic training courses provided only in Swedish. The Legal, Financial and Administrative Services Agency, known as *kammarkollegiet* in Swedish, organizes exams for interpreters. The authorisation test for community interpreters is available at basic and specialised levels. Candidates must pass the written section in order to proceed to the oral test. The written section tests knowledge of medicine, social welfare and law. A terminology section tests knowledge of 100 special terms. The oral test consists of role-plays and questions on ethics and interpreting know-how.

**Institute for Interpretation and Translation Studies (IITS)**
Stockholm University, S-106 91 Stockholm, Sweden
Web site: lisa.tolk.su.se (in English)

## UNITED KINGDOM

The system in the United Kingdom is quite different in that the initiative for change did not come from the government or from the universities but from the Institute of Linguists and Language Line. A number of colleges offer training for the Institute of Linguists Diploma in Public Service Interpreting (DPSI). The different colleges cover over 20 languages. South Tyneside College offers a distance learning scheme for the DPSI. A full list of colleges involved in providing training is available on the Institute of Linguists Web site. See Section 10 for more information on the Institute of Linguists.

Four areas of community interpreting are covered:

- English law
- Scottish law
- Health
- Local Government

The Local Government option includes council services, social services, housing, planning and economic development and education. The Legal option covers police procedures, procedures for the different courts and the different types of cases that can be taken to court. The Medical option deals with the many different professionals working in the area – from doctors to dentists to physiotherapists to speech therapists. It also covers many different health areas.

In the United Kingdom, Language Line provides an over the phone interpreting service which focuses principally on community interpreting. Its origins lie in a pilot interpreting project covering four languages at the Royal London Hospital in London in 1990. Word of the project spread to the local police force and Language Line began to operate twenty-four hours a day. In 1992 it became a limited company. AT&T Language Line Services in the United States and the Australian Telephone Interpreting Service provide additional cover in languages not covered by Language Line and when demand is high. Altogether, 100 languages are covered by the service, which is mainly used by the police, hospitals, charities and local authorities. These bodies subscribe to Language Line and are provided with a six-hour course on how to use the service. The course includes guidance on preparing calls in advance in order to save time and on how to put non-English speakers at their ease. Language Line interpreters are expected to be holders of the Institute of Linguists Diploma in Public Service Interpreting but exceptions have to be made in the case of languages not covered by the Institute of Linguists. Each year Language Line covers the costs of the DPSI for about twenty interpreters. Those born in the United Kingdom are expected to hold a university degree. Regular training sessions are provided to interpreters. Language Line has drawn up its own code of ethics and interpreters have to sign a legally binding confidentiality agreement.

**Language Line Ltd.**
Swallow House, 11–21 Northdown Street, NI 9BN London, United Kingdom
Web site: www.languageline.co.uk

The Cambridgeshire Interpreting and Translation Agency (CINTRA) was set up by Cambridge City Council, Cambridgeshire County Council and the Cambridge and Huntingdon Health Authority. Social services, the health authority and the local district council provided some funding, as did the Ethnic Minority Health Unit of the National Health Service. CINTRA interpreters are holders of the Institute of Linguists Diploma in Public Service Interpreting. They are provided with supplementary training in child protection, racial harassment, mental health and bereavement. CINTRA provides a 24-hour telephone interpreting service in 27 languages. There is no personal charge to individuals for using the service.

**CINTRA**
CPDC Foster Rd, Trumpington, Cambridge CB2 2NL, United Kingdom
No Web site at the time of writing.

Still in the United Kingdom, Staffordshire Social Services Department
provides a telephone interpreting service at each of its Area Services
Offices where people can access interpreters in over one hundred languages. Video conferencing facilities for British Sign Language interpreting are also available at seven locations.

**Staffordshire Social Services Department**
Web site: www.staffordshire.gov.uk/locgov/county/socserv/ssasoff.htm

## UNITED STATES

In the United States, the Texas Department of Human Services is another
example of public service interpreting over the phone. Ninety languages
are spoken in the Dallas – Fort Worth area and volunteers are sought
to interpret over the phone for people who are elderly, disabled or
marginalised.

**Texas Department of Human Services**
Web site: www.dhs.state.tx.us/regions/03

# Court Interpreting

As we have seen, interpreting is essential in a number of areas. But it is
particularly important in the case of court interpreting where so much
depends on what people say and whether they are perceived to be telling
the truth. There have been miscarriages of justice in cases where no foreign language was involved. There is greater potential for miscarriages
of justice when untrained, unqualified interpreters are at work. According
to the European Convention on Human Rights and Fundamental
Freedoms, adopted by the Council of Europe in 1950:

Article 6. Everyone charged with a criminal offence has the following **minimum**
rights:

To be informed promptly, in a language he understands and in detail, of the nature
and cause of the accusation against him;

To have adequate time and facilities for the preparation of his defence;

To defend himself in person or through legal assistance of his own choosing or, if he has not sufficient means to pay for legal assistance, to be given it free when the interests of justice so require;

To examine or have examined witnesses against him and to obtain the attendance and examination of witnesses on his behalf under the same conditions as witnesses against him;

To have the free assistance of an interpreter if he cannot understand or speak the language used in court.

In 1988 an American citizen called Theodore Kamasinski took a case against Austria under Articles, 6, 13 and 14 of the Convention. The case was taken on a number of grounds but one issue was interpreting. Mr Kamasinski claimed that the process of accreditation for court interpreters in Austria was inadequate. He also alleged that some court testimony was not interpreted for him and that he did not receive written translations of court documents. The Court agreed that important court documentation should be translated. It decided that it could not make a blanket judgement concerning accreditation because it is not specifically mentioned in the Convention. However, it did say:

In view of the need for the right guaranteed by paragraph 3e (article 6-3-e) to be practical and effective, the obligation of the competent authorities is not limited to the appointment of an interpreter but, if they are put on notice in the particular circumstances, may also extend to a degree of subsequent control over the adequacy of the interpretation provided.

In its judgement the Court rejected most of Mr Kamasinski's grounds of complaint. However, the case itself was useful in that the issues were aired in court. Clearly, the right to an interpreter is not the same as the right to a trained and qualified interpreter. The full text of the proceedings in Kamasinski vs. Austria is available on the European Court of Human Rights Web site at: www.dhcour.coe.fr

Some countries such as the Netherlands decided that this meant that they should accept the need for a proper provision of interpreting services. Others just ignored it. The result is that within Europe the provision of interpreting in the courts varies enormously from one country to another. Yet it is absolutely essential that court interpreters should be impartial, they should not take on the role of advocates and they should have an understanding of legal concepts. But if interpreters are not trained, how can they acquire these characteristics themselves?

There are two different legal systems. The civil law system is the system in English speaking countries such as Australia, Canada, Ireland, New Zealand, United Kingdom and the United States. The common law system is the system in mainland Europe. In the civil law or adversarial system the defendant and all witnesses appear in court before a judge and jury and give their version of events. An interpreter is present in order to render a foreign language into the language of the court and to inform the defendant of the proceedings. In the common law system a judge is appointed to a case when a crime is committed and he or she takes written statements from the defendant and the witnesses. Foreign language statements are translated. The court interpreter's role is closer to that of a translator in that he or she does mainly sight translation. For example, in Spain, there is a university qualification known as *traductor jurado* or *traductor público*. These people are trained legal translators. Despite this legal background, these translators may benefit from courses in court interpretation. The stenographer or court reporter records everything that is said in the language of the court i.e. everything except the foreign language. In some countries an audio recording is also made of the whole proceedings. In some jurisdictions the interpreter has to take a specific interpreter's oath to interpret to the best of his or her ability.

Court interpreters should always remember that their job is to interpret – not to question clients or tell them what their rights are or explain points to them. The court interpreter is not a lawyer. The interpreter must be neutral and should not supply extra information over and above what the clients actually say.

As for the types of interpreting provided in the courts, consecutive interpreting is provided in question and answer sessions. If statements are particularly long the interpreter may need to take notes. Accuracy is extremely important here because this is testimony that will appear in the court record. It is very easy for the interpreter to misrepresent the language of a defendant or a witness. Informal, uneducated speech can be interpreted into very correct, educated speech. The interpreter may censor bad language, thus making the speaker appear more polite than he or she really is. The interpreter may omit or add information.

Whispered simultaneous interpreting is provided to defendants so that they can understand the testimony that is heard in court. Some courts have equipment for simultaneous interpreting. In the United States some interpreters buy their own infrared equipment. The ideal is to ensure that the defendant understands everything that is going on in court. However, in some jurisdictions it may not be clear if the interpreter is to interpret everything or if he or she can interpret certain items and omit others.

## UNITED STATES

Court interpreting in the United States is particularly interesting. In the seventies there was a lot of discontent about court interpreting. In some cases janitors, local restaurant workers or bilingual attorneys were asked to interpret. The Federal Court Interpreters Act, which applies to cases taken under the Constitution or federal legislation, was passed in 1978. Under this Act, interpreters have to be certified as competent. An accreditation system known as the Federal Certification System was set up in 1986. As there are some 32 million Hispanics in the United States, Spanish was an immediate priority. From 1985 to 2000 the University of Arizona was contracted to develop and administer Spanish/English certification examinations to candidates across the United States. At the time of writing (September 2000) the Administrative Office of the US Courts had not yet announced if it intended to award the contract to the University of Arizona once again or not. There was some controversy about the level of difficulty of the exam and the small number of interpreters who were deemed successful. However, the examination is open to all candidates regardless of their level of education. The first section of the exam is written and the second is oral. Candidates need a thorough knowledge of both Spanish and English in order to pass the written section. If successful, they can then proceed to the oral section, which comprises consecutive interpretation, simultaneous interpretation (English–Spanish only) and sight translation. Candidates must pass both parts and a pass is 80%. In 1987 the pass rate was 4%. By the end of 1997, 751 Spanish-English interpreters had passed the examination. In 1988 Haitian Creole and Navajo were added to the contract. There is a need for certification in other languages too but this will be dependent on funding from Congress.

**National Center for Interpretation Testing, Research and Policy**
The University of Arizona, Department of English, Tucson, Arizona, 85721, USA
Web site: nci.arizona.edu

At state court level the National Center for State Courts administers the Consortium for State Court Interpreter Certification. Founded in 1995, the Consortium designs tests for interpreters and makes them available to member states. The system helps interpreter mobility: a pass in the California state certification exam will be accepted by all other states that are members of the Consortium. The test is available in ten languages: Arabic, Cantonese, Haitian Creole, Hmong, Korean, Laotian, Polish, Russian, Spanish and Vietnamese.

The twenty three members of the Consortium are Arkansas, California, Colorado, Delaware, Florida, Georgia, Hawaii, Idaho, Illinois, Maryland, Massachusetts, Michigan, Minnesota, Missouri, Nebraska, New Jersey, New Mexico, North Carolina, Utah, Oregon, Virginia, Washington and Wisconsin.

**The National Center for State Courts**
300 Newport Avenue, Williamsburg, VA 23185, USA
Web site: www.ncsc.dni.us/

Some states have introduced their own certification system for interpreters in the State Courts. For example the California State Certification
exam for interpreters is available in eight languages: Arabic, Cantonese,
Japanese, Korean, Portuguese, Spanish, Tagalog and Vietnamese. More
languages are spoken in California than in any other American state.
Nearly one person out of every ten has no English at all. The state certification exam is in two parts, one written and one oral. Interestingly,
the written section covers protocol and ethics as well as vocabulary range
and reading comprehension.

Interpreters for languages other than the eight certified languages can
do an English proficiency examination and a test of knowledge of court
procedure and ethics. If they are successful they are listed as 'registered
interpreters of nondesignated languages'.

---

**California courts**
Web site: www.courtinfo.ca.gov

---

**AT&T Language Line Services** provide services and contract interpreters
for the US Court Interpreting Project where interpreting for certain court
cases is provided over the phone. The main motivation is financial – it
is cheaper to employ an interpreter over the phone rather than pay for
travel and accommodation. So far, telephone interpreting is provided in
Spanish and English for short district court proceedings such as pre-trial
hearings, arraignments, initial appearances and for probation and pre-
trial interviews. David Mintz, President of the American National
Association of Judiciary Interpreters and Translators (NAJIT) and a member of the Federal Court Interpreters Advisory Subgroup, gives an interesting description of his experience of telephone interpreting in Las
Cruces in the winter 1998 edition of *Proteus*. The interpreter wears a head-
set with an attached microphone. Two telephone lines feed into the head-
set, one for English and one for Spanish. There is a side-tone suppresser
to prevent the interpreter hearing his or her own voice. Video teleconferencing could well be possible in the future for this type of procedure
and would have the advantage that the interpreter could actually see the
person for whom he or she is interpreting.

A number of universities in the United States offer courses in court
and medical interpreting. Every July there is a three-week course for
English-Spanish court interpreters at the Agnese Haury Institute for
Court Interpretation at the University of Arizona. The course is extremely
intensive and concentrates on simultaneous and consecutive interpretation along with sight translation. There are also lectures on law and
ethics.

**Agnese Haury Institute for Court Interpretation**
University of Arizona, Modern Languages Building, Room 445, PO Box 210067, Tucson,
AZ 85721–0067, USA
Web site: nci.arizona.edu/ahi.htm

The International Interpretation Resource Centre at the Monterey
Institute of International Studies provides courses in Spanish–English
court and medical interpreting. The court interpreting courses are available at introductory, intermediate and advanced levels and last between
one and four weeks. The introductory medical interpreting course lasts
two weeks. The Centre hopes to offer its course in Cantonese, Korean,
Russian and Vietnamese and indeed to offer some form of distance education courses.

**International Interpretation Resource Centre**
Monterey Institute of International Studies, 425 Van Buren Street, Monterey, CA 93940,
USA
Web site: www.miis.edu/iirc/iirc2.html

The University of Charleston, South Carolina, offers a two-year Master
of Arts in Bilingual Legal Interpreting. The M.A. consists of eleven core
courses, nine of which are available over two summers. There is also a
Certificate program that can be taken in eight weeks over one summer
or can be spread over two summers. The Certificate program covers the
Fundamentals of Interpreting, Legal Language and Consecutive and
Simultaneous Interpreting. Both the Graduate Program and the
Certificate are available in English–Spanish. The cost in 2000 for the
Certificate course was US$4436.

**University of Charleston**
South Carolina
Web site: www.cofc.edu/programs/legal-int.html

ACEBO is a company run by Holly Mikkelson that designs and sells
audiocassettes and other materials for court interpreting. A great deal of
the material is in Spanish but there are also audiocassettes for some items
in Cantonese, Korean, Mandarin, Polish, Russian and Vietnamese. The
resources available include some legal terminology glossaries in Spanish
and English. The Web site includes ten articles on interpreting by Holly
Mikkelson.

**ACEBO**
Post Office Box 7485, Spreckels, California 93962, USA
Web site: www.acebo.com

## AUSTRALIA

In New South Wales, Australia, the Cross Cultural Committee of the Law Society has drawn up a *Guide to Best Practice for Lawyers Working with Interpreters and Translators in a Legal Environment.* The Guide has been endorsed by the National Accreditation Authority for Translators and Interpreters and by the Australian Institute of Interpreters and Translators and is available online.

**Law Society of New South Wales**
170 Phillip Street,Sydney NSW 2000
Web site: www.lawsocnsw.asn.au/about/papers/translators_interpreters/

## Medical Interpreting

If a person with very little English is hospitalised in England for example, an interpreter should be made available to explain the doctor's diagnosis of the medical problem and the procedures that will be carried out. It is unfair to expect family members or friends to interpret in this type of situation. It is also unfair on the patient who should be entitled to the professional services of an impartial interpreter. The patient may not want his family or friend to know about his or her medical problems.

When a proper medical interpreting service is provided doctors can make their diagnoses faster. If medical professionals are unclear about exact symptoms they will refer their patients on to consultants or they will carry out procedures that could be unnecessary. In less serious cases, patients may return several times to a doctor unnecessarily. Language is the obvious problem but cultural differences can also be important. People from different cultures have different attitudes on a huge range of issues from illness and dying to blood transfusions to organ transplants. They may also have different attitudes towards the medical profession. Many of these issues are included on the Transcultural and Multicultural Health Links Web site, which is divided up into General Resources, Religious Groups, Ethnic Groups and Special Populations.

**Transcultural and Multicultural Health Links**
www.lib.iun.indiana.edu/trannurs.htm

Other problems can arise if people cannot read the instructions on when to take their medicine and how much to take. Anne Fadiman has written a fascinating book on the true story of a Hmong child living in California and suffering from epilepsy. Called *The Spirit Catches You and You Fall Down*, it gives an account of the language gap and especially the clash between two completely different cultures.

Medical Interpreting as a speciality has been developed in Canada and the United States in particular in the sense that a number of hospitals provide training to interpreters and in some cases employ staff interpreters. Interpreting in Mental Health settings is seen as a further speciality within medical interpreting.

## UNITED STATES

In the United States, under Title VI of the 1964 Civil Rights Act:

> 'No person in the United States shall, on ground of race, color, or national origin, be excluded from participation in, be denied the benefits of, or be subjected to discrimination under any program or activity receiving Federal financial assistance'.

Thus, limited English speakers have the right to equal treatment with English speakers. This is a federal regulation. However, there is no central training programme or accreditation system except for Washington State. In the eighties a number of court cases were taken against the Washington State Department of Social and Health Services (DSHS) on the grounds of inequality in access to health services. The DSHS agreed to provide and pay for interpreters and to administer a test for interpreters. The test is available in Cambodian, Cantonese Chinese, Korean, Laotian, Mandarin Chinese, Russian, Spanish and Vietnamese. The written section of the test consists of multiple choice questions on ethics, medical terminology, clinical procedures and English grammar. Candidates must pass the written section in order to proceed to the oral section, which consists of a sight translation and a consecutive interpretation. There is also a non-language specific test for languages other than the eight mentioned above.

---

**Language Interpreter Services and Translations (LIST)**
Department of Social and Health Services, PO Box 45820, Olympia, WA 98504–5820
Web site: www.wa.gov/dshs/index.html

This is the Web site of the Washington Department of Social and Health Services but at the time of writing it did not contain any information on LIST.

---

In April 2000 in Massachusetts an Emergency Room Interpreter Bill was signed into law. The law will come into force on 1st July 2001. From that date all hospitals in the state will be required to hire competent interpreters to interpret for patients in casualty and at acute care psychiatric services. Depending on the language involved, interpreting could be over the phone or face to face. State insurers such as Medicaid will be billed for the service. More details are available at: Web site: www.health-law.org/pubs/Alert000426.html

In 2000 preparatory work on certification was being carried out in Minnesota and in parts of New York State and California. Elsewhere, provision varies from one state to the next and indeed from one hospital to the next.

In August 2000 President Clinton signed Executive Order 13166 which stipulates that all federal agencies are obliged to have written policies on the provision of service to people with limited English.

The **National Council on Interpretation in Health Care** (NCICH) was set up in the United States in 1998 to 'promote culturally competent professional medical interpretation as a means to support equal access to health care for all individuals with limited English proficiency'. This council brings together medical interpreters, coordinators of interpreter services, interpreting trainers and researchers. The goals of NCICH include:

- Defining and supporting standards of quality health care for limited English proficient individuals
- Supporting standards and code of ethics for interpreters in health care
- monitoring the development of policies , research and model practices
- sponsoring a dialogue of diverse voices and interests on related issues

Resources for Cross Cultural Health Care has a Web site called Diversity Rx, which is maintained with the help of funding from the Henry J. Kaiser Family Foundation. This is an excellent site containing a huge amount of very useful information on medical interpreting. Those interested in developments in medical interpreting in the United States can subscribe to the Diversity Rx mail list or listserv.

---

**Resources for Cross Cultural Health Care**
8915 Sudbury Road, Silver Spring, MD 20901, USA
Web site: www.diversityrx.org
Mail list: NCICH-list@diversityRx.org

---

Remote interpreting has been tried out in some hospitals in America. The interpreter is based in the hospital and interprets simultaneously over the phone. A report by journalist Edward Wong in *The New York Times* gave an account of the use of wireless transmission technology at Gouverneur Hospital in Manhattan. Both doctors and patients wear headphones and what they say is sent via a receiver along a fibre optic line to the interpreter. The interpreters at Gouverneur are either blind or partially sighted.

In Seattle the Cross Cultural Health Care Program (CCHCP) provided interpreters for 33,000 medical or medical related meetings in 1998. There were eight staff interpreters, over forty contract interpreters and a number of interpreters provided by six agencies. Between them the interpreters covered a total of 52 languages. The CCHCP offers a forty-hour training course for medical interpreters. This programme has trained over a thousand interpreters in eight different states across America.

On the Web site Links and Resources include items such as books for sale. There is a list of recommended books with brief summaries of each. There are twelve community profiles.

**Cross Cultural Health Care Program**
1200 12th Ave. S, Seattle, WA 98144, USA
Web site: www.xculture.org

The University of Minnesota began its Community Interpreter Training Program in 1991. This is a generic course with common classes for all interpreters and separate interpreting practice classes for different language groups. The main languages in demand for interpreting in Minneapolis and St. Paul are Cambodian, Hmong, Lao, Russian, Somali, Spanish and Vietnamese.

The staff at the University of Minnesota have done some very useful work on producing resources for community interpreting. The resources, which are available for purchase, include:

- A video about Health Care Interpreting
- A video on Interpreting in Refugee Mental Health Settings.
- *An Instructor's Manual*

**University of Minnesota**
2nd Floor Nolte Hall, 315 Pillsbury Dr. SE, Minneapolis, MN 55455, USA
Web site: cla.umn.edu/pti

## CANADA

The Hospital for Sick Children in Toronto, Canada, provides an interpreting service in Chinese, French, Italian, Portuguese and Spanish. Arrangements can also be made for other languages such as Greek, Somali, Vietnamese and Sign Language. About 6,000 encounters are catered for each year.

**Hospital for Sick Children**
555 University Avenue, Toronto, Ontario, M5G 1X8 Canada
Web site: www.sickkids.on.ca

## AUSTRALIA

In New South Wales, Australia, the Multicultural Health Communication Service provides online information in a number of languages on a range of health issues including asthma, cancer, parenting and nutrition. It also acts as an advisor on how to deal with cultural issues. The Service works with medical staff to ensure that a full range of information is available in different languages. This is more in the field of translation than interpreting.

**NSW Multicultural Health Communication Service**
PO address: Locked Bag 1156, Waterloo Delivery Centre NSW, Australia
Web site: www.mhcs.health.nsw.gov.au

# **5** Ethics

---

Nowadays most professions have their own code of ethics or code of conduct. These have evolved because people realised that it is important to be explicit about what is acceptable and what is not acceptable. Some aspects of these codes may appear to be based simply on common sense but it is important to spell out what exactly is expected of any professional. Interpreters have a privileged situation regarding access to confidential information. Their clients have to be able to trust them not to pass on information whether it is about a new product, new plans for policing or about someone who is hospitalised.

A number of organizations in different countries have drawn up guidelines or codes of conduct for interpreters. It is clear that interpreters should not take on work that they may not be able to complete. When contacted about an assignment they should check the language and the situation to ensure that it is within their capabilities. The more information the interpreter has the better he or she can prepare him or herself. In certain situations such as hospital appointments the authorities may be reluctant to provide details about a patient. However, the interpreter needs to know what area of terminology he or she should prepare. The interpreter should obviously be punctual and should behave professionally at all times. Breaks are essential for interpreters in all situations. People are aware that conference interpreters need breaks but other interpreters involved in long interviews with asylum seekers or suspected criminals need breaks too. In some cases of community and court interpreting more than one interpreter may be required for lengthy assignments.

Guidelines for other professionals who work with interpreters are also important because many people are not aware of the role of the interpreter. The police, lawyers, judges, teachers, doctors and nurses may well need training in how to deal with interview situations which include an interpreter. Ideally, all these groups should have a language policy. In some cases the interpreter may have to lay down the ground rules for his or her dealings with other professionals. Often the interpreter decides whose turn it is to speak.

Below you will find different codes of conduct or professional guidelines for interpreters working in different areas. They appear in the following order:

▦  The AIIC Professional Guidelines for Conference Interpreters
▦  The American Association of Language Specialists (TAALS)
   Standards of professional practice for conference interpreters
▦  The National Register for Public Service Interpreters (NRPSI) Code
   of Conduct for Public Service Interpreters
▦  The Vancouver Health Care Interpreter Standards of Practice
▦  Code of Ethics of the Registry of Interpreters for the Deaf in the
   United States

The five codes are similar in a lot of ways. The AIIC guidelines have a
dual purpose – to ensure professional conduct among conference interpreters and that the Association is held in good stead. The TAALS standards are quite similar to the AIIC guidelines but the emphasis is on
interpreting as a business.

The NRPSI code contains a great deal of detail on the complaints procedure. This is particularly useful for clients because they know that if a
problem arises there is a system in place. The Vancouver Health Care
Interpreters Standards of Practice were developed in 1995–1996 by a col-
laborative group of health organizations in Vancouver, British Columbia.
Ruth Coles, Director of Diversity at Providence Health Care, led the
group. The Code of Ethics of the Registry of Interpreters for the Deaf is
a very detailed one but it throws up interesting points for all interpreters.

**The 1994 AIIC Code of Professional Ethics** lays down guidelines for
conference interpreters:

## AIIC Code of Professional Ethics

*I – Purpose and Scope*
**Article 1**
a)  This Code of Professional Ethics (hereinafter called the "Code") lays
    down the standards of integrity, professionalism and confidentiality
    which all members of the Association shall be bound to respect in
    their work as conference interpreters;
b)  Candidates shall also undertake to adhere to the provisions of this
    Code;
c)  The Council, acting in accordance with the Regulation on
    Disciplinary Procedure, shall impose penalties for any breach of the
    rules of the profession as defined in this Code.

*II – Code of Honour*
**Article 2**
a)  Members of the Association shall be bound by the strictest secrecy,
    which must be observed towards all persons and with regard to all
    information disclosed in the course of the practice of the profession
    at any gathering not open to the public;

b) Members shall refrain from deriving any personal gain whatsoever from confidential information they may have acquired in the exercise of their duties as conference interpreters.

## Article 3
a) Members of the Association shall not accept any assignment for which they are not qualified. Acceptance of an assignment shall imply a moral undertaking on the member's part to work with all due professionalism;
b) Any member of the Association recruiting other conference interpreters, be they members of the Association or not, shall give the same undertaking;
c) Members of the Association shall not accept more than one assignment for the same period of time.

## Article 4
a) Members of the Association shall not accept any job or situation which might detract from the dignity of the profession.
b) They shall refrain from any act which might bring the profession into disrepute.

## Article 5
For any professional purpose, members may publicise the fact that they are conference interpreters and members of the Association, either as individuals or as part of any grouping or region to which they belong.

## Article 6
It shall be the duty of members of the Association to afford their colleagues moral assistance and collegiality;

Members shall refrain from any utterance or action prejudicial to the interests of the Association or its members. Any complaint arising out of the conduct of any other member or any disagreement regarding any decision taken by the Association shall be pursued and settled within the Association itself;

Any problem pertaining to the profession which arises between two or more members of the Association, including candidates, may be referred to the Council for arbitration.

### III – Working Conditions
## Article 7
With a view to pursuing the best quality interpretation, members of the Association:

■ shall endeavour always to secure satisfactory conditions of sound, visibility and comfort, having particular regard to the Professional Standards as adopted by the Association as well as any technical standards drawn up or approved by it;

- shall not, as a general rule, when interpreting simultaneously in a booth, work either alone or without the availability of a colleague to relieve them should the need arise;
- shall try to ensure that teams of conference interpreters are formed in such a way as to avoid the systematic use of relay;
- shall not agree to undertake either simultaneous interpretation without a booth or whispered interpretation unless the circumstances are exceptional and the quality of interpretation work is not thereby impaired;
- shall require a direct view of the speaker and the conference room. They will thus refuse to accept the use of television monitors instead of this direct view, except in the case of videoconferences;
- shall require that working documents and texts to be read out at the conference be sent to them in advance;
- shall request a briefing session whenever appropriate;
- shall not perform any other duties except that of conference interpreter at conferences for which they have been taken on as interpreters.

**Article 8**

Members of the Association shall neither accept nor, a fortiori, offer for themselves or for other conference interpreters recruited through them, be they members of the Association or not, any working conditions contrary to those laid down in this Code or in the Professional Standards.

*IV Amendment Procedure*

**Article 9**

This Code may be modified by a decision of the Assembly taken with a two-thirds majority of votes cast, provided a legal opinion has been sought on the proposals.

International Association of Conference Interpreters

# The American Association of Language Specialists (TAALS) Standards of Professional Practice for Conference Interpreters

- In the interest of ensuring professional standards of quality, TAALS recommends that its members always endeavor to ensure that physical conditions not hinder them in the performance of their tasks. They must be able to see and hear properly. Simultaneous interpretation without a booth may lead to deterioration in sound quality and to such a level of ambient noise as to disturb both participants and interpreters.
- Interpreting teams should be organized so as to avoid the systematic use of relay.

- All engagements should be covered by a written contract which stipulates the fee, the duration of the appointment, the working languages, the hours of work, the name of the coordinating interpreter, briefing sessions and/or study days. Travel time and travel arrangements, accommodations, per diem, etc., as appropriate.
- Contracts may also include provisions for compensating the interpreter when the proceedings are recorded (see Recording below).
- Since a contract creates a firm and binding commitment and prevents an interpreter from accepting any other offer for the same period of time, a cancellation clause should be considered by the parties.
- There may be provision for a coordinating interpreter, to serve as liaison between the conference organizer and the interpreters. If the coordinating interpreter cannot be present throughout the conference, he or she should designate another interpreter as team leader and acquaint that person with all necessary information.
- Whispered interpretation is not generally recommended but may be used to work from one or two languages into a single language and for a small number of listeners.

**Preparation & Briefing**
- Since the interpreter must be well prepared, background material should be provided sufficiently in advance. In the case of technical and scientific conferences, interpreters may request a briefing session at the conference or an equivalent period of independent study.

**Recording**
Under some circumstances the work produced by interpreters may become their intellectual property thus protected by the Bern Convention for the Protection of Literary and Artistic Works (Paris Text, 1971) Whenever this may have economic or commercial significance, the rights of the interpreter and of the employer to the work product should be specified in the contract of employment.

The NRPSI is the National Register for Public Service Interpreters in the United Kingdom. The Register is administered by the Institute of Linguists.

## NRPSI Code of Conduct for Public Service Interpreters

*1. Introduction*
Public Service Interpreters appearing in the National Register are

expected to abide by the Code of Conduct to which they are signatories. The standards in the Code set a framework for interpreting in the public services, upheld if necessary by professional and impartial disciplinary procedures. The objective of the Code of Conduct is to make sure that communication across language and culture is carried out consistently, competently and impartially, and that all those involved in the process are clear about what may be expected from it.

This Code of Conduct is registered with the Office of Fair Trading under the Restrictive Practices Act 1976.

### 2. Competence
Interpreters admitted to the register are expected to:

2.1 have a written and spoken command of both languages, including any terminology, current idioms and dialects;
2.2 possess the ability to interpret and translate accurately and fluently between both languages using the correct interpreting techniques;
2.3 understand the relevant procedures of the particular discipline they are working in;
2.4 maintain and develop their written and spoken command of English and the other language;
2.5 be familiar with the cultural backgrounds of both parties

### 3. Procedure
Interpreters will:

3.1 interpret truly and faithfully what is said, without anything being added, omitted or changed; in exceptional circumstances a summary may be given if requested, and consented to by both parties;
3.2 disclose any difficulties encountered with dialects or technical terms, and if these cannot be satisfactorily remedied, withdraw from the assignment;
3.3 not enter into the discussion, give advice or express opinions or reactions to any of the parties;
3.4 intervene only
3.4.1 to ask for clarification;
3.4.2 to point out that a party may not have understood something;
3.4.3 to alert the parties to a possible missed cultural reference;
3.4.4 to ask for accommodation for the interpreting process and inform all parties present of the reason for the intervention;
3.5 not delegate work, nor accept delegated work, without the consent of the client;
3.6 be reliable and punctual at all times;
3.7 must state (in a criminal trial) if they have been involved in interpreting at the police station on the same case.

*4. Ethical and Professional Issues*
Interpreters will:

4.1 respect confidentiality at all times and not seek to take advantage of any information disclosed during their work;
4.2 act in an impartial and professional manner;
4.3 not discriminate against parties, either directly or indirectly, on the grounds of race, colour, ethnic origin, age, nationality, religion, gender or disability;
4.4 disclose any information, including any criminal record, which may make them unsuitable in any particular case;
4.5 disclose immediately if the interviewee or immediate family is known or related;
4.6 disclose any business, financial, family or other interest which they might have in the matter being handled;
4.7 not accept any form of reward, whether in cash or otherwise, for interpreting work other than payment by the employer;
4.8 not engage in any behaviour likely to discredit the NRPSI (including impairment through drugs or alcohol, sexual misconduct, violence, intimidation or abusive behaviour).

*5. Disciplinary Procedures*
Any complaint against an interpreter thought to be acting contrary to this Code may be referred by the Institute of Linguists to the National Register Disciplinary Panel as specified in the NRPSI Disciplinary Procedures.

5.1 Principles.
    The NRPSI is responsible only for the administration of the NRPSI (list of interpreters). It asks to be advised of all complaints and issues arising in respect of services provided by listed interpreters that may be in breach of the NRPSI Code of Conduct.

    Interpreters are engaged on a freelance basis. The NRPSI is not party to any contracts of service or contracts for service, and the engagement of interpreters by any client agency will not imply any such contract between the NRPSI and interpreters. Such contractual disputes as may arise will therefore principally be between the interpreter and the commissioning agency and not the NRPSI, but they might involve a Disciplinary Procedure element.

    The NRPSI is committed to the early resolution of substantiated complaints.

    Complaints about individuals providing interpreter services can either be linguistic or non-linguistic and may arise from a variety of sources, including persons directly requiring interpreter assistance or the agency hiring the interpreter. The following principles will govern how complaints are handled:

▓ matters will be handled fairly and openly
▓ wherever possible, complaints will be speedily resolved
▓ all matters will be recorded
▓ the individual subject of the complaint will be informed of the nature of the complaint and given a copy of it
▓ in linguistic matters, advice will be sought from sources of linguistic expertise

5.2    Structure for handling complaints.

All notifications of complaint or concern should preferably be made immediately and in writing (and in any case not more than three months after the event or first knowledge of it) and will be subject to further enquiry. This will normally entail a written communication to the interpreter concerned, seeking further information about the incident and offering a right of reply. The interpreter's response, if any, will be directed back to the complainant for further comment, if appropriate, along with any comment from the NRPSI. The complaint may rest here and no further action will be taken. Alternatively, the procedure(s) indicated below may be activated. The absence of a response from an interpreter will not normally prevent further action under the disciplinary procedures.

5.3    Disciplinary procedures.

*If a complaint is to progress to any of the disciplinary stages outlined below, statements will be sought from the complainant and other parties involved and penalties only imposed if, on the balance of probabilities, the interpreter is found to be at fault.*

The NRPSI Disciplinary Panel (see below) will be convened as soon as possible.

The Panel may consider documentation alone or representation from any interested parties, or a mixture of both.

5.3.1  Warning.

For minor indiscretions (such as inappropriate dress or lateness), a warning will be given in writing, which will offer advice and guidance on the interpreter's future conduct.

5.3.2  Suspension pending further enquiry.

In certain circumstances, for example, failure to improve after several warnings or an alleged major breach of the Code, the interpreter will be suspended pending conclusion of enquiries. This suspension will be for an indeterminate period while further details are gathered from interested parties and considered. The interpreter should not undertake interpreting under the NRPSI scheme whilst suspended from the NRPSI. It may be that the information gathered warrants no further action or it may require action at one of the following penalty levels.

5.3.3  Demotion.

Where the circumstances of the breach are serious and proven on a balance of probabilities, but which do not call for suspension or expulsion, the interpreter may be given a warning and demoted from Full to Interim category on the NRPSI for a period determined by the Disciplinary Panel. (The circumstances may include, for instance, isolated lapses in interpreting accuracy, persistent lateness, and persistent failure to turn up.) The demotion may require the interpreter to undergo recognised in-service training or to pass an appropriate examination before being considered for reinstatement to the Full category.

5.3.4    Suspension from the NRPSI for a determined period.

Suspension for a limited period of time may be necessary in situations where the breach of the Code of Conduct is of grave concern to the NRPSI but where there may be acceptable mitigating circumstances that would preclude expulsion from the NRPSI. Such circumstances may include first-time major breaches, lack of judgement in isolated incidents or swapping assignments without authorisation. It may be that in appropriate cases, the period of suspension served pending enquiry is of itself deemed discipline enough and that no further penalty is warranted. The interpreter should not undertake interpreting under the NRPSI scheme while suspended from the NRPSI.

5.3.5    Expulsion from the NRPSI.

Interpreters may be expelled from the NRPSI for a major breach of the Code, for further serious breaches for which the interpreter has previously been suspended or for repeated less serious infringements of the Code. In addition, automatic expulsion will result where an interpreter has been found to be working as an NRPSI interpreter whilst serving a period of suspension as outlined above.

*Major breaches of the Code include:*
Unprofessional conduct likely to discredit the NRPSI (including impairment through drugs or alcohol, sexual misconduct, violence, intimidation or abusive behaviour); substantiated allegations of incompetence such as major lapses in interpreting accuracy; serious negligence causing unacceptable loss/damage/injury. (The above is not meant to be exhaustive).

5.4    Appeals.

The right of appeal to the Appeals Panel will depend on material fact/s coming to light after a Disciplinary Panel hearing and not previously considered by the Disciplinary Panel. A request for an appeal should normally be received in writing within 28 days of receiving notification of the Disciplinary Panel's decision and has to provide details of the material fact/s not previously heard by the Disciplinary Panel.

The Appeals Panel Chairman decides whether to convene the Appeals Panel on the basis of the material fact/s presented. The new material fact/s will be communicated to the complainant with a request for comment and the Appeals Panel is convened as soon as possible thereafter if it is decided to go ahead with the appeal hearing. The appeal hearing is held on the basis of documentation alone. The result will be final.

5.5     General.

5.5.1   Past conduct.

Each complaint will be judged on its merits for the purposes of deciding, on a balance of probabilities, whether a breach has been substantiated. However, an overall view will be taken of past conduct and performance under the NRPSI scheme when deciding on the penalty administered by the Disciplinary Panel.

5.5.2   Information on progress and notification of result.

In all cases the interpreter will be kept informed, on request, of the progress of any complaint made and will be notified in writing of the outcome.

The result will also be communicated to the complainant and, in the case of the severest penalty (expulsion), to the entire NRPSI user clientele.

Records will be kept for a reasonable time of all complaint investigations and their results.

5.5.3   Re-admission.

Applications will not be considered from an interpreter who has been removed from the NRPSI as a result of the complaints procedure.

5.5.4   Out of pocket expenses.

Panel members' reasonable expenses will be reimbursed from NRPSI funds.

Reasonable out of pocket expenses incurred by an interpreter subject to disciplinary procedures will only be reimbursed if the disciplinary hearing finds that there were absolutely no grounds whatever for the complaint.

A complainant's expenses will not normally be reimbursed from NRPSI funds.

5.6     Disciplinary panel.

Comprises: Institute of Linguists (IoL) Director of Examinations as manager of the NRPSI

    plus

two practising interpreters from a recognised interpreting institution

    plus

one representative of interpreter users (e.g. LSAG member)

5.7     Disciplinary appeals panel.

Comprises: IoL Chief Executive as the ultimate salaried officer responsible for the NRPSI

    plus

one senior officer from another interpreting institution or interpreter client agency

plus
an interpreter from a recognised interpreting institution.

© National Register of Public Service Interpreters, Institute of Linguists, 1999

## Vancouver Health Care Interpreter Standards of Practice

### STANDARDS FOR HEALTH CARE INTERPRETING

*(from Vancouver, BC. Health Interpreter Standards Initiative 1995/96)*
The purpose of Health Care Interpreting is to overcome language barriers that impede access to Health Care services. The function of interpreting is to transfer a message spoken in one language into another without distorting meaning. The values from which the standards are based, derive from this understanding. No governing body currently exists to uphold these standards. They were developed as the framework for training curricula. The concepts represented by these standards will be expanded in training programs. It will be the responsibility of the instructor to interpret the document for the learners.

### STANDARDS OF PERFORMANCE

*A. Confidentiality*

| Value Statement | Demonstrated Performance |
|---|---|
| 1. Confidentiality is accepted as an element of ethical practice by all Health Care Professionals. A Health Care interpreter who becomes part of this practice is governed by the same ethic in order to uphold the trust of both parties and allow uninhibited transfer of information. | a) Nothing said within the interpreting session will be communicated <u>out side</u> the session. <br> b) Everything <u>within</u> the session is communicated to all parties. <br> c) The Health Care Interpreter articulates a reporting obligation statement[1] at the time of every introduction. The reporting commitment relates only to the information revealed after the person is introduced as an interpreter. |

| | |
|---|---|
| 2. Health Care Professionals work in the best interests of the patient. Information which may have an impact on patient care is shared with the appropriate Health Care Professionals in extenuating circumstances where the safety of the patient is concerned. | |

[1] This statement cautions the patients against disclosing information they do not wish revealed and reassures that all information revealed is shared.

## B. Respect for Individuals

| Value Statement | Demonstrated Performance |
|---|---|
| The Health Care Interpreter recognizes that a spirit of respect and care pervades Health Care practise and this quality must be reflected in Health Care interpreting. | a) The Health Care Interpreter responds in a supportive and empathic manner within the parameters of the role. b) The Health Care Interpreter uses rapport building skills. |

## C. Accuracy

| Value Statement | Demonstrated Performance |
|---|---|
| Accuracy preserves the meaning of the message | a) The Health Care Interpreter transmits the source language message into the target language without omission, addition, or embellishment, including obscenities. b) The Health Care Interpreter does not provide any opinion or answer that does not come from either of the parties. c) The Health Care Interpreter uses the same level of language sophistication as the original speaker and does not make it more acceptable or complete than the original (Refer to Demonstrated Performance (f) under the value "Clear Role Boundaries"). d) The Health Care Interpreter reveals |

|  | and corrects any errors made in interpreting.<br><br>e) The Health Care Interpreter verifies meanings and understandings, when there is incompatibility of accent, dialect, and language form. If accuracy is threatened, the Health Care Interpreter offers to withdraw from the assignment. If the offer is refused by either party, the Health Care Interpreter requests that the Health Care Practitioner document the refusal on the patient's chart. |
| --- | --- |

## D. Proficiency

| Value Statement | Demonstrated Performance |
| --- | --- |
| Language proficiency expedites the transfer of meaning. Lack of language proficiency impedes the transfer of meaning. | a) The Health Care Interpreter passes the required language proficiency assessments at the appropriate level in English and the language of specialty.<br><br>b) Health Care Interpretation conveys an understanding of medical terminology. |

## E. Objectivity/Impartiality

| Value Statement | Demonstrated Performance |
| --- | --- |
| Objectivity is essential to prevent distortion of the message. | a) The Health Care Interpreter shows no preference or bias towards either party involved in the interpretation.<br><br>b) The Health Care interpreter declines to interpret when there is a conflict, or perception of conflict of interest, or a factor or belief that may influence objectivity.<br><br>c) The Health Care Interpreter discloses to the Health Care |

| | Professional any prior acquaintance with the patient.<br><br>d) The Health Care Interpreter maintains composure.<br>e) The Health Care Interpreter does not accept gratuities, favours, or bribes from any part involved in the interpretation. |
|---|---|

## F. Clear Role Boundaries

| Value Statement | Demonstrated Performance |
|---|---|
| Respect for the Health Care Interpreter's role and its boundaries minimizes the risk of misunderstandings and enhances the process of communication | a) The Health Care Interpreter facilitates verbal communication between, but not on behalf of, two people who do not share a common language.<br>b) The Health Care Interpreter refrains from advice giving, expressing opinions, problem solving, mediating, and advocating.<br>c) The Health Care Interpreter refrains from personal, political, or potentially controversial topics in informal conversation with patients and families.<br>d) The Health Care Interpreter refers questions or issues raised by the patient or family to the appropriate Health Care Professional with consent.<br>e) The Health Care Interpreter maintains decorum.<br>f) The Health Care Interpreter informs the parties of actual or potential miscommunications and suggests the speaker reframe the message. |

## G. Cultural Sensitivity

| Value Statement | Demonstrated Performance |
|---|---|
| Since language can not be separated from culture, cultural sensitivity enhances the transfer of the meaning of the message. | a) The Health Care Interpreter alerts the parties to potential cultural misunderstandings without contributing stereotypes or perceptions of their own.<br>b) The Health Care Interpreter observes, and after verifying, conveys relevant cultural practises to both parties.<br>c) The Health Care Interpreter assists the Health Care Professional to reframe culturally inappropriate questions or statements in an appropriate manner. |

## H. Standardized Interpreting Format

| Value Statement | Demonstrated Performance |
|---|---|
| Health Care interpreting is conducted in a standardized format, in order to reduce confusion and achieve consistency of style. | a) The Health Care Interpreter explains the structure of the session, when this is new to either party.<br>b) Consecutive mode[2] is the accepted method for Health Care Interpreting.<br>c) The Health Care Interpreter uses techniques which will enhance direct communication between parties. |

[2] The interpreter conveys meaning of speaker's message in a sequential manner after speaker has completed a phrase or statement.

## STANDARDS FOR DELIVERY OF SERVICE

### A. Availability

| Value Statement | Demonstrated Performance |
|---|---|
| Health Care Interpreters are available to meet emergent[3], urgent[4], and elective[5] needs. | a) The Health Care Interpreter responds to emergent calls within 15 minutes.<br>b) The Health Care Interpreter responds to urgent calls within 12 hours.<br>c) The Health Care Interpreter responds to elective calls within 48 hours. |

[3] Emergent: needs immediate attention, a time delay is harmful to the patient.
[4] Urgent: condition requires attention within a few hours; possible danger in the absence of attention.
[5] Elective: non-acute, a delay of hours to days will not be harmful.

### B. Accessibility

| Value Statement | Demonstrated Performance |
|---|---|
| To be useful within a Health Care setting, the process of accessing a Health Care Interpreter must be simple, convenient, and efficient. | a) The process of accessing a Health Care Interpreter involves one step one time.[6] |

[6] One action requiring no follow-up.

### C. Efficiency

| Value Statement | Demonstrated Performance |
|---|---|
| Health Care resources are limited. Efficient interpreting services conserve resources. | a) The skills of the Health Care Interpreter match the needs of the situation.<br>b) Cancellations are communicated to all parties in a timely fashion.<br>c) All parties are punctual within 5–10 minutes.<br>d) Interpreter requests are made appropriately.<br>e) Health Care agencies using the Interpreting service consider the service worth the price. |

## D. Expediency

| Value Statement | Demonstrated Performance |
|---|---|
| Expediency influences usefulness in the Health Care system. Interpreting procedures must balance expedience against other values. | a) Planning and rapport building which requires only 2 of the 3 parties occurs outside of the interpreting session.<br>b) A clear statement of the agreed process and time allotted for the interpreting session is required.<br>c) Appropriate adaptation of the accepted interpreting process is permitted to accommodate emergencies.<br>d) When appropriate and feasible, the same Health Care Interpreter is used for the same patient/family and Health Care Professional. |

# Code of Ethics of Registry of Interpreters for the Deaf

*1. Interpreters/transliterators shall keep all assignment-related information strictly confidential.*

**Guidelines:** Interpreters/transliterators shall not reveal information about any assignment, including the fact that the service is being performed.

Even seemingly unimportant information could be damaging in the wrong hands. Therefore, to avoid this possibility, interpreters/transliterators must not say anything about any assignment. In cases where meetings or information become a matter of public record, the interpreters/transliterators should first discuss it with the person involved. If no solution can be reached, then both should agree on a third person who could advise them. When training new trainees by the method of sharing actual experiences, the trainers shall not reveal any of the following information:

- name, sex, age, etc., of the consumer
- day of the week, time of the day, time of the year the situation took place;
- location, including city, state or agency; other people involved;
- unnecessary specifics about the situation.

It takes only a minimum amount of information to identify the parties involved.

*2. Interpreters/transliterators shall render the message faithfully, always conveying the content and spirit of the speaker using language most readily understood by the person(s) whom they serve.*

**Guidelines:** Interpreters/transliterators are not editors and must transmit everything that is said in exactly the same way it was intended. This is especially difficult when the interpreter disagrees with what is being said or feels uncomfortable when profanity is being used. Interpreters/transliterators must remember that they are not at all responsible for what is said, only for conveying it accurately. If the interpreter's/transliterator's own feelings interfere with rendering the message accurately, he/she shall withdraw from the situation.

While working from spoken English to sign or non-audible spoken English, the interpreter/transliterator should communicate in the manner most easily understood or preferred by the deaf or hard-of-hearing person(s), be it American Sign Language, manually coded English, fingerspelling, paraphrasing in non-audible spoken English, gesturing, drawing, or writing. It is important for the interpreter/transliterator and deaf or hard-of-hearing person(s) to spend some time adjusting to each other's way of communicating prior to the actual assignment. When working from sign or non-audible spoken English, the interpreter/transliterator shall speak the language used by the hearing person in spoken form, be it English, Spanish, French, etc.

*3. Interpreters/transliterators shall not counsel, advise or interject personal opinions.*

**Guidelines:** Just as interpreters/transliterators may not omit anything that is said, they may not add anything that is said, they may not add anything to the situation, even when they are asked to do so by other parties involved.

An interpreter/transliterator is only present in a given situation because two or more people have difficulty communicating and thus the interpreter's/transliterator's only function is to facilitate communication. He/she shall not become personally involved because in so doing, he/she accepts some responsibility for the outcome, which does not rightly belong to the interpreter/transliterator.

*4. Interpreters/transliterators shall accept assignments using discretion with regard to skill, setting, and the consumers involved.*

**Guidelines:** Interpreters/transliterators shall only accept assignments for which they are qualified. However, when an interpreter/transliterator shortage exists and the only available interpreter/transliterator does not possess the necessary skill for a particular assignment, this situation should be explained to the consumer. If the consumer agrees that services are needed regardless of skill level, then the available interpreter/

transliterator will have to use his/her best judgment about accepting or rejecting the assignment.

Certain situations, due to content, consumer involvement, the setting or other reasons, may prove so uncomfortable for some interpreters/transliterators and/or consumers that the facilitating task is adversely affected. An interpreter/transliterator shall not accept assignments which he/she knows will be adversely affected.

Interpreters/transliterators shall generally refrain from providing services in situations where family members or close personal or professional relationships may affect impartiality, since it is difficult to mask inner feelings. Under these circumstances, especially in legal settings, the ability to prove oneself unbiased when challenged is lessened. In emergency situations, it is realized that the interpreter/ transliterator may have to provide services for family members, friends, or close business associates. However, all parties should be informed that the interpreter/transliterator may not become personally involved in the proceedings.

*5. Interpreters/transliterators shall request compensation for services in a professional and judicious manner.*

**Guidelines:** Interpreters/transliterators shall be knowledgeable about fees that are appropriate to the profession, and be informed about the current suggested fee schedule of the national organization. A sliding scale of hourly and daily rates has been established for interpreters/transliterators in many areas. To determine the appropriate fee, interpreters/transliterators should know their own level of skill, level of certification, length of experience, nature of the assignment, and local cost of living index.

There are circumstances where it is appropriate for interpreters/transliterators to provide services without charge. This should be done with discretion, taking care to preserve the self-respect of the consumers. Consumers should not feel that they are recipients of charity. When providing gratis services, care should be taken so that the livelihood of other interpreters/transliterators will be protected. A freelance interpreter/transliterator may depend on this work for a living and therefore must charge for services rendered, while persons with other full-time work may perform the service without feeling a loss of income.

*6. Interpreters/transliterators shall function in a manner appropriate to the situation.*

**Guidelines:** Interpreters/transliterators shall conduct themselves in such a manner that brings respect to themselves, the consumers, and the national organization. The term "appropriate manner" refers to:

dressing in a manner that is appropriate for the skin tone and is not distracting, and

- conducting oneself in all phases of an assignment in a manner befitting a professional.

*7. Interpreters/transliterators shall strive to further knowledge and skills through participation in workshops, professional meetings, interaction with professional colleagues, and reading of current literature in the field.*

*8. Interpreters/transliterators, by virtue of membership in or certification by the RID, Inc., shall strive to maintain high professional standards in compliance with the Code of Ethics.*

© The RID Code of Ethics is Copyright the Registry of Interpreters for the Deaf.

# 6 The European Union

## Interpreting in the European Union

With 720 staff interpreters and over 1,300 temporary and freelance interpreters, the European Union (EU) employs more interpreters than any
other organization in the world. Unlike most other international organizations, the EU has decided to treat all languages equally. This means
that interpretation has to be provided for all official EU languages. The
fifteen members of the EU are Austria, Belgium, Denmark, Finland,
France, Germany, Greece, Ireland, Italy, Luxembourg, Netherlands,
Portugal, Spain, Sweden and the United Kingdom. In the current 15 member Union, interpreting is provided in eleven languages – Danish, Dutch,
English, Finnish, French, German, Greek, Italian, Portuguese, Spanish
and Swedish. If the EU continues with the present system of treating all
languages equally, its interpreting needs will increase enormously with
enlargement. The following table lists the countries that have applied to
join:

| Country | Language(s) | Year of Application to join European Union |
|---------|-------------|---------------------------------------------|
| Bulgaria | Bulgarian | 1995 |
| Cyprus | Greek and Turkish | 1990 |
| Czech Republic | Czech | 1996 |
| Estonia | Estonian | 1995 |
| Hungary | Magyar/Hungarian | 1994 |
| Latvia | Latvian/Lettish | 1995 |
| Lithuania | Lithuanian | 1995 |
| Malta | English and Maltese | 1990 and 1998 |
| Poland | Polish | 1994 |
| Romania | Romanian | 1995 |
| Slovakia | Slovak | 1995 |
| Slovenia | Slovenian | 1996 |
| Turkey | Turkish | 1987 |

**Table 2** *The thirteen candidate countries*

Switzerland is a special case: it is a member of the European Free Trade Association (EFTA) which also includes Iceland, Liechtenstein and Norway. Established in 1960, EFTA was originally a much larger organization but over a period of twenty-two years Austria, Denmark, Portugal, Sweden and the United Kingdom defected to the European Union.

The EU and three EFTA members (Iceland, Liechtenstein and Norway) established the European Economic Area (EEA) in 1991, which came into effect on the 1st January 1994. The EEA allows for the free movement of goods, services and peoples throughout all 18 countries. It also requires Iceland, Liechtenstein and Norway to adopt EU policies to do with company mergers, state aid to industry, consumer protection, labour markets and the environment. The Swiss people voted against joining the EEA in 1992. Consequently, it would appear unlikely that Switzerland will join the European Union. Norway applied to join the EU on two occasions but the people voted against membership in 1972 and again in 1994. Malta applied in 1990, withdrew its application in 1996 and after a change of government, reapplied in 1998.

Turkey applied to join the European Union in 1987 but the process has been very slow due to concern about human rights and the economy there. Since 1996 there has been a customs union between Turkey and the EU.

At the Helsinki summit in December 1999 it was agreed that the thirteen countries in Table 2 would all be put on an equal footing and would become members over ten to fifteen years. The main surprise was the decision that Turkey would be accorded the same treatment as the other states. Thirteen new members will mean eleven new languages or double the present number to a new total of 22 languages. With eleven languages there are 110 possible language combinations. With 22 languages there will be an amazing 462 different language combinations. For the EU to continue with its policy of treating all languages equally a huge investment will be necessary in terms of translation and interpretation. No decisions have been made yet and in fact there has been very little discussion to date within the EU concerning these issues. There will have to be some kind of rationalisation. Some of the new countries such as Estonia, Latvia and Slovenia have small populations – Estonia 1.5 million, Latvia 2.6 million and Slovenia just under 2 million. Their languages are not spoken anywhere else. However, the attitude within the European Parliament in particular is that candidates should be elected on merit, not based on their knowledge of languages. In practical terms the possible language combinations will mean that there will probably be far greater reliance on relay. There will also be problems recruiting qualified staff. Most universities in Western Europe provide courses in English, French, German, Italian and Spanish. Interpreters usually interpret into their own language. Clearly there will be problems when Members of the European Parliament from Poland, Hungary or Romania speak – interpreters may have to work both in and out of their mother tongue as happened in the Finnish booth when there were problems finding interpreters with Finnish. Knowledge of East European languages will be a plus when it comes to recruitment of interpreters in the future.

There are three sections within the European Union, which are responsible for organizing everything to do with interpreting requirements. They are:

- The **Joint Interpreting and Conference Service (JICS)**, also known by its French title **Service Commun Interprétation-Conférences (SCIC)**. This is part of the European Commission.
- The **Interpretation Directorate** at the European Parliament.
- The **Interpretation Division** at the European Court of Justice.

The usual requirements for European Union interpreters are as follows:

- University degree in conference interpreting **or**
- University degree **and** experience of conference interpreting (200 days during the past three years) **or**
- Certified training as an interpreter **and** experience of conference interpreting (100 days during the past two years) **or**
- Experience of conference interpreting (500 days during the past five years).
- Perfect command of mother tongue.
- Thorough command of a specified EU language and two other official EU languages. Knowledge of a fifth EU language is desirable.
- EU national.

## THE JOINT INTERPRETING AND CONFERENCE SERVICE (JICS/SCIC)

JICS or SCIC as it is more commonly referred to, provides interpreting for the European Commission, the Council of the European Union, the Economic and Social Committee, the Committee of the Regions, the European Investment Bank and for the following EU agencies:

- European Agency for the Evaluation of Medicinal Products, London
- European Environment Agency, Copenhagen, Denmark
- European Training Foundation, Turin, Italy
- European Centre for the Development of Vocational Training, Thessaloniki, Greece
- European Monitoring Centre for Drugs and Drug Addiction, Lisbon, Portugal
- European Monitoring Centre on Racism and Xenophobia, Vienna, Austria

▓   European Foundation for the Improvement of Living and Working
    Conditions, Dublin, Ireland
▓   Office for Harmonization in the Internal Market, Alicante, Spain
▓   Community Plant Variety Rights Office, Angers, France
▓   European Agency for Health and Safety at Work, Bilbao, Spain

SCIC employs 530 staff interpreters and provides interpreting services
for between 50 and 60 meetings per day. For example, in 1997 SCIC organized over 10,000 meetings. This was the equivalent of 138,000 interpreter
days. To cope with this huge demand, about 150 temporary and freelance
interpreters are also hired each day from a pool of 1,700 freelancers.
Despite the large numbers of interpreters on this panel, SCIC sometimes
has difficulties finding interpreters. Temporary interpreters are recruited
for special or urgent needs. SCIC covers interpreting needs at meetings
outside the EU. The same rate is charged regardless of location.

   In October 1999 the European Commission advertised the posts of
interpreter and assistant interpreter. Candidates were expected to have a
degree or a diploma in law, economics, auditing, finance, languages, natural sciences or technology. A qualification in interpreting was a requirement. The text of the advertisement was as follows:

---

**Conditions of admission:**

• You should have completed a full course of university study and obtained a university-level degree or diploma (in law, economics, auditing, finance, languages,
  natural science, technology).
• You must have been born after 16 November 1953.
• You must be a citizen of one of the Member States of the European Union.

**Assistant Interpreters (grade LA8)**
**Open competition**
**Training and experience required**: Candidates must have completed a course of
training as a conference interpreter and obtained a university-level diploma, **or**
completed a course of university studies and obtained a degree or diploma giving
access to doctoral studies, **together with** training as a conference interpreter or certified experience as a conference interpreter. You must have acquired the first
degree or diploma qualifying you for the competition or, alternatively, the diploma
in interpreting, after 16 November 1996.

**Working languages required:** Active language: English. Other working languages: at
least two of the other ten official languages of the European Union.

**Interpreters (grade LA7/LA6)**
**Open competition**
**Training and experience required**: Candidates must have completed a course of
training as a conference interpreter and obtained a university-level diploma, **or**

---

completed a course of university studies and obtained a degree or diploma giving access to doctoral studies, **together with** training as a conference interpreter. You must have acquired university-level professional experience after graduating of at least two years, of which twelve months must have been spent as a conference interpreter.

**Working languages required**: Active language: English. Other working languages: at least two of the other ten official languages of the European Union. **Or** active languages: English **and one** of the other ten official languages of the European Union. Other working languages: at least two of the other ten official languages of the European Union, of which one is your second active language.

Place of employment: Brussels, Luxembourg or any other place of European Commission activity.

Staff interpreter vacancies are advertised in all EU countries and in the *Official Journal* of the European Communities. Open competitive examinations are held annually. Candidates are required to do consecutive interpretation of a 7–10 minute speech and simultaneous interpretation of a 15–20 minute speech from each of the three passive languages into their mother tongue. There is also an interview to assess general and EU knowledge and motivation. Candidates may also sit optional interpreting tests in their fifth language. The whole process of recruitment is very lengthy.

Freelance interpreters are a special case in that they do not have to be EU nationals and SCIC may be interested in any languages worldwide, not just the official EU languages. However, freelance interpreters will need to be able to interpret into a widely used EU language. Candidates must pass a professional SCIC test in order to be included on the freelance list. The test, which is organized twice or three times a year, includes consecutive and simultaneous interpreting and general knowledge. Successful candidates may be offered a guaranteed minimum number of working days per year.

There is also a scheme for 'young interpreters', young meaning under 45 years of age. Candidates for these posts are expected to have a qualification in conference interpreting. They are not expected to have much working experience as interpreters – a maximum of 20 days in an EU institution or in another international organization or forty days elsewhere. They should have at least one active and two passive languages, all of which should be official EU languages. Tests are organized at least twice a year. They are not advertised in national newspapers but rather at those universities that teach conference interpreting. The test consists of an interview to assess general knowledge particularly with regard to the EU. There are two five-minute consecutive tests and two ten-minute simultaneous tests into the candidate's active language. Candidates also have the option of doing a consecutive or simultaneous test into one of their passive languages or from a third passive language into their active language. Successful candidates are guaranteed 100 days of work as an interpreter for one year. A close eye is kept on the young interpreters. They receive a written evaluation of their work after six months. Three negative reports from different people can mean that their services are no longer required. If they are to progress to a freelance position at the end of their year as a young interpreter, they will need a third passive language or a 'retour' into one of their passive languages in both consecutive and simultaneous modes.

As many staff interpreters were recruited in the seventies the average age of interpreters is rather high. For example, the average age of interpreters in the French booth in 1999 was 49 years. New interpreters need to be good, but unusual or difficult to find language combinations are an asset.

Along with the Interpretation Directorate of the European Parliament, SCIC is involved in promoting conference interpreting. To this end it organizes three-day visits to Brussels so that students can see interpreters in action. Students have the opportunity to sit in a dummy booth and try out their interpreting skills. Interpreter trainers cooperate with universities. Financial aid is available for courses with unusual language combinations. In 1998 a European Master's Diploma in Conference Interpreting was piloted in eight universities. The programme was extended to six other universities in the academic year 1999–2000. A number of other universities have also expressed interest. Emphasis is placed on less widely used or less taught languages. A list of universities involved in the programme is included in the Appendix to this volume. Up to date information is also available on the SCIC Web site.

A European Master's in Congress Management began in 1999 at four universities. This is largely the result of cooperation between SCIC and the European Association for Tourism and Leisure Education (ATLAS). The aim of this postgraduate qualification is to move away from the traditional training provided on the job to professional training in all aspects of conference organization including for example the compilation of programmes and organization of accommodation and travel.

SCIC has its own internal Internet or Intranet where interpreters can access information on their assignments and lists of meetings in Brussels and elsewhere. TIARA or Terminology Interface and Research Application is specifically designed for use by interpreters.

**Eurodicautom** is the terminology database of the Translation Service of the European Commission. At the start of 1998 it contained five million entries. Twelve languages are covered, the eleven EU languages plus Latin. The database is mainly concerned with areas of interest to the European Union. Two teams of terminologists worked on setting up the database.

**Eurodicautom**
Web site: eurodic.ip.lu

**Joint Interpreting and Conference Service (JICS/SCIC)**
rue de la Loi 200, B-1049 Brussels, Belgium
Web site: europa.eu.int/comm/scic/index_en.htm

## THE INTERPRETATION DIRECTORATE AT THE EUROPEAN PARLIAMENT

The Interpretation Directorate provides interpreters for European Parliament sessions and associated meetings and committees in Strasbourg and Brussels. It also provides interpreters to the Court of Auditors and the Commission services in Luxembourg. The Directorate employs 180 staff interpreters and has a list of over 1,000 freelance interpreters. The services of 200–400 freelance interpreters are required each day. In 1996 this represented 61,500 interpreter days for the European Parliament alone.

Staff interpreter vacancies are advertised in national newspapers throughout the European Union. Interpreters should have a university degree in any field, training or experience as a conference interpreter and at least three EU working languages. Interpreting tests are also held for freelance interpreters who, if successful, work as session auxiliaries. Grants are sometimes awarded to trainee conference interpreters who have a qualification in interpreting but are lacking in experience or who are willing to learn new languages.

The Interpretation Directorate offers traineeships to graduate interpreters and advanced traineeships to freelance interpreters. A Director, with the aid of two Linguistic Counsellors, is in charge of organization and the Directorate budget. Staff interpreters are divided up into eleven groups according to language and a Head of Division or Head of booth is in charge of each group. The Heads of Division organize schedules and check on quality control of staff and freelance interpreters.

**Secretariat of the Interpretation Directorate**
European Parliament, Room 538, BAK Building, L-2929 Luxembourg
Web site: www.europarl.eu.int/interp/public/en/default.htm

## THE INTERPRETATION DIVISION AT THE COURT OF JUSTICE OF THE EUROPEAN COMMUNITIES

The Court of Justice employs 40 staff interpreters and between 100 and 150 freelance interpreters. As well as a university degree and interpreting experience, staff interpreters are usually expected to have three passive languages although exceptions may be made in the case of unusual language combinations. Legal knowledge and interpreting ability are tested at the recruitment stage. Cases can be taken in any of the official EU languages or in Irish.

Interpreters interested in freelance work who submit their CVs may be employed on a trial basis at the Court. They must however have interpreting experience, preferably within the European Union. Experience in the legal field is considered to be an asset. The Court never takes on total beginners because of the difficulty of the subject matter and the speed and complexity of the pleadings. A considerable amount of preparation is required for interpreting at the Court: there are documents to be studied and terminology to be prepared.

---

**The Interpretation Division**
Court of Justice of the European Communities, Palais de la Cour de Justice, L-2925 Luxembourg
Web site: europa.eu.int/cj

At the time of writing the European Court of Justice site did not contain any information on interpreting.

---

## The European Union – Past and Present

The European Union has undergone a number of transformations, which have come about through the steady increase in membership over the years and through the ratification of a number of treaties. The origins of the EU date back to the Treaty of Paris and the establishment in April 1951 of the six-member European Coal and Steel Community (ECSC). As with so many other international organizations, the ECSC was established shortly after the end of the Second World War. The original members were neighbours – Belgium, France, Germany, Italy, Luxembourg and the Netherlands. Around this time there was some interest in setting up a European Defence Community. However, in 1954 the French National Assembly voted against this idea.

In 1957 the Treaties of Rome established the European Economic Community and the European Atomic Energy Community (Euratom). These treaties came into force the following year and represented a broadening of interests outside the original core areas of coal and steel. The Common Agricultural Policy began in 1962. In 1968 customs duties on manufactured products were eliminated. The United Kingdom, at the time a member of the European Free Trade Association, was interested in joining the Community but was prevented by France under General de Gaulle. When Georges Pompidou became President of France he was more favourable to expansion and negotiations got underway with the United Kingdom, Denmark, Ireland and Norway. The UK, Denmark and

Ireland joined in 1973. The people of Norway voted against membership.

The establishment of a European exchange rate system known as the snake in 1972 was the first concrete step towards monetary union. France, Italy and the UK left the exchange rate system and as a result it was no longer viable. The European Monetary System (EMS) came into being in 1979. The EMS was the dawn of the ECU, exchange rates were fixed in bands and central banks had the power to intervene to ensure that bilateral exchange rates did not exceed a threshold of 15%. Greece joined what was then the European Economic Community in 1981, followed by Spain and Portugal in 1986. A decision was taken in 1989 to introduce a single currency to the EU.

The different treaties have been essential to changing the focus of the EU down through the years. In order to change the treaties, Intergovernmental Conferences are held where governments negotiate amendments to the treaties. Regular meetings are held over a year or more. The European Parliament is consulted and proffers its views.

The 1986 Single European Act, to create the single market and allow the free movement of people, goods, services and capital, came into force in 1987.

The most wide-ranging treaty however was the 1992 Treaty on European Union or Maastricht Treaty, which came into force in 1993. Two referendums had to be held in Denmark to gain a majority in favour. Indeed, voting was very close in France also. New treaties have to be ratified either by referendum, which is usually the case in Denmark, France and Ireland, or by the national parliament. Under the Maastricht Treaty the European Economic Community was renamed the European Union. The aim of the Treaty was to establish economic and monetary union and to allow for the establishment of a single European currency, the euro, which will come into circulation on 1st January 2002. The Treaty laid down conditions that had to be fulfilled if member states were to be allowed become part of monetary union. These conditions included:

- low inflation and interest rates
- national budget deficits below 3% of Gross National Product
- public debt under 60% of GNP
- no devaluation of national currency

Denmark, Sweden and the United Kingdom declined to enter the euro zone and Greece was deemed ineligible. However, the Greeks succeeded in bringing their inflation rate down to 2% and public debt to 1.98% of Gross National Product and as a result it was agreed at the June 2000 EU summit that Greece could join the euro zone from 1st January 2001. A referendum was held on the issue in Denmark on 28th September 2000 when the majority of the people (53.1%) voted against formal participation in the euro. Denmark already had a fixed exchange rate policy anyway dating back to 1982 and in January 1999 the Danish krone was linked to the euro in a band of plus or minus 2.25%.

The Maastricht Treaty established three pillars:

| First Pillar | Second Pillar | Third Pillar |
|---|---|---|
| **The European Community** | **Common Foreign & Security Policy** | **Justice & Home Affairs** |
| ECSC, EC and Euratom treaties<br>Agricultural policy<br>Economic & Monetary Union<br>Regional policy<br>EU institutions | Safeguard peace and promote international security<br>Promote democracy and the rule of law<br>Respect for human rights<br>Build up the Western European Union<br>Possible common defence policy in the future | Asylum seekers<br>Immigration policy<br>Customs and police cooperation |

**Table 3** *The three pillars of the Maastricht Treaty*

The Maastricht Treaty represents a move away from purely economic concerns to the adoption of common policies in the areas of foreign and security policy and concerning Justice. Previously, these issues had been considered purely national issues. The European Parliament was granted new powers under the Maastricht Treaty, the most significant of which was codecision with the Council of the European Union. Citizens of the EU were given the right of petition and the right to appeal to the European Ombudsman.

Austria, Finland and Sweden joined the EU in 1995.

The Amsterdam Treaty was signed in 1997 and came into force on 1st May 1999. Basically, it is a revision of the Maastricht Treaty on European Union and it covers a large number of areas. For example, immigration and the crossing of external and internal borders and judicial cooperation on civil matters are to be transferred to the First Pillar. This process will take place over five years. The Amsterdam Treaty created a new post, that of High Representative for the Common Foreign and Security Policy, who is also the Secretary General of the Council of Ministers and unofficially known as Mr CFSP. The first appointee was Javier Solana, former Secretary General of NATO. Mr Solana was also appointed Secretary General of the Western European Union. The Schengen Agreement whereby 13 member states, with the exception of Ireland and the UK, have abolished internal border checks, has been incorporated into the Union framework. Changes have been made in European Parliament procedures and to the brief of the Court of Justice. A cap of 700 has been put on the number of MEPs and this will apply even after enlargement. Qualified majority voting at the Council of the European Union now also includes public health, customs cooperation and the fight against social exclusion.

In early 2000 a group was set up to draft an EU charter of fundamental rights. This group was made up of 15 representatives of heads of state or government, one representative of the European Commission, 16 MEPs and, unusually, 30 members of national parliaments. The chairman is Roman Herzog of Germany.

A seventh Intergovernmental Conference is taking place in 2000. Its brief is preparation for enlargement and includes the size and make up of the Commission, the weighting of votes in the Council and the possible extension of qualified majority voting in the Council to other areas of interest.

The following table details the different accessions to the European Union (or its incarnations) in chronological order:

| Country | Language | Joined in |
|---------|----------|-----------|
| Belgium | French | 1951 (ECSC) |
| France | French | 1951 |
| Germany | German | 1951 |
| Italy | Italian | 1951 |
| Luxembourg | German | 1951 |
| the Netherlands | Dutch | 1951 |
| Denmark | Danish | 1973 (EEC) |
| Ireland | English | 1973 |
| United Kingdom | English | 1973 |
| Greece | Greek | 1981 |
| Portugal | Portuguese | 1986 |
| Spain | Spanish | 1986 |
| Austria | German | 1995 (EU) |
| Finland | Finnish | 1995 |
| Sweden | Swedish | 1995 |

**Table 4** *The fifteen EU members*

The budget of the European Union comes from four different sources:

- Agricultural levies on products imported from non-member countries and sugar levies on sugar companies.
- Customs duties applied to goods imported from non-member countries.
- VAT resource – 1% of VAT collected in member states goes to the EU.
- Gross National Product – each country makes a contribution in proportion to its GNP. This is subject to a cap – in 1999 the ceiling was 1.27% of total Community GNP.

Eighty per cent of the EU budget is spent in the member states. Slightly less than half of the budget is absorbed by the Common Agricultural Policy. This figure represents a reduction compared to the high 1985 figure of 68%. About a third of the budget is allocated to Structural Funds. This figure has increased in recent years. The Structural Funds finance regional and social policies aimed at increasing employment and reducing the disparity in wealth between different member countries.

So, the European Union has come a long way. Over fifty years it has developed from a six-member community focused on coal and steel to a far more ambitious 15-member Union. The next step will be enlargement. The fall of Communism in Central and Eastern Europe has meant that a further thirteen countries are interested in becoming members. New members will have to meet the political and economic conditions laid down by the EU. Political conditions cover such areas as democracy and the rule of law, human rights, freedom of expression and respect for minorities. Economic conditions include the existence of a market economy and the ability to compete within the EU. A further condition is that all new members will have to take on board all the obligations of membership including political, economic and monetary union – in Eurospeak this is known as the *acquis communautaire*.

Agenda 2000 detailed the changes that will have to be carried out in both the EU and the applicant countries in order to bring about enlargement. The Common Agricultural Policy in particular will require adjustment. **Sapard** was set up to help the farming community of the candidate countries to prepare for EU membership. Under Sapard, 529 million euros are allocated to structural and rural development programmes. **ISPA**, a fund for the environment and transport, was also established as part of Agenda 2000.

The EU is investing a lot of money in the candidate countries, particularly through **PHARE** (Poland–Hungary Aid for Economic Restructuring) begun in 1989 and which now also includes Albania, the Czech Republic, Bulgaria, Estonia, Latvia, Lithuania, Romania, Slovakia and Slovenia. The Phare programme aims to help these countries to eventually become EU members. The areas targeted include the restructuring of state enterprises, the reform of social services, education and health, the development of infrastructures in the areas of energy, transport and telecommunications, the environment and nuclear safety.

The **Tempus** programme was established in 1990 and extended for the third time to run from 1999 to 2006 to contribute to the development of higher education in Central and Eastern Europe, in the Commonwealth of Independent States (CIS – Armenia, Azerbaijan, Belarus, Georgia, Kazakhstan, Kyrgyzstan, Moldova, Russia, Tajikistan, Turkmenistan, Ukraine and Uzbekistan) and in Mongolia.

The **TACIS** programme was set up to help Mongolia and the Commonwealth of Independent States (CIS). The aim of TACIS is to facilitate change to a market economy. Support is provided to the problem areas of nuclear safety and the environment and assistance is provided for the establishment of new businesses. There is also an agreement to set up a free trade area between the EU and Russia and the Ukraine.

The **Meda** programme is directed at Algeria, Cyprus, Egypt, Israel, Jordan, Lebanon, Malta, Morocco, the Palestinian Authority, Syria, Tunisia and Turkey. Its purpose is to help ensure stability in the Mediterranean. By 2010 it is expected that there will be a free trade area between the EU and these countries.

The EU signed the Lomé Convention with the 71 African, Caribbean and Pacific States (ACP) in 1975, 1979, 1984, 1989, 1995 and 2000. This covers financial aid to these countries and trade agreements. In January 2000 a development aid package was agreed whereby the ninth European Development Fund was established. The European Union provided a development aid package of 13.5 billion euros over five years. A European Investment Bank loan of 1.7 billion euros was part of the package also. Under the terms of the agreement the EU gives tariff free access to 95% of ACP exports in exchange for more limited access to ACP markets. In the long term, the aim is to establish free trade zones between the EU and regions within the ACP zone.

In April 2000 the heads of state and government of the European Union met with the leaders of the 53 countries of the Organization of African Unity in Cairo to bring the African problems of development and AIDS to the forefront of discussion.

Framework agreements have been developed with Mercosur, the South American economic community made up of Argentina, Brazil, Paraguay and Uruguay, with Bolivia and Chile as associate members. In March 2000 the EU and Mexico agreed to reduce tariffs on industrial products over a number of years and eventually to establish a free trade area.

There has been an increase in police cooperation in recent years. In July 1999 the European Police Office or **Europol** came into operation. The Office is based in The Hague where it works on developing police cooperation between the forces in the 15 EU member states in order to combat organized crime, terrorism, drug trafficking, money laundering and counterfeiting.

---

**Europol**
PO Box 90850, NL-2509 LW The Hague, The Netherlands
Web site: www.europol.eu.int/home.htm

---

By 2003 the European Union will have a rapid response force called EUROFOR made up of some 60,000 troops and 5,000 police. In this way, the EU will no longer have to rely on the United States to take action as occurred in Kosovo. An Interim Military Committee is to be established within the Secretariat of the European Council. This section will brief the Council of Ministers on crisis situations. EUROFOR will act in cases that come under the umbrella of the so-called Petersberg Tasks, which were included in the Amsterdam Treaty. These are:

- humanitarian and rescue tasks
- peace-keeping tasks
- tasks of combat forces in crisis management, including peacemaking.

Any future extension of the role of EUROFOR beyond the Petersberg Tasks could have implications for traditionally neutral countries such as Austria, Finland, Ireland and Sweden.

The European Union is changing at a very rapid rate. Each new Treaty brings complex changes. Most quality national newspapers provide good coverage of what is happening in Europe. However, *The European Voice* is particularly useful as it is a weekly newspaper exclusively about the European Union, published by *The Economist* group and also available online.

---

**The European Voice**
Web site: www.european-voice.com

---

The European Policy Centre (EPC) was established in 1997 as a think tank that would bring together people from EU governments, business and the professions to debate what is happening in Europe. The chairman is Peter Sutherland. The Centre provides political briefings for corporate members as well as monthly breakfast meetings. The EU also contributes funding. The EPC has an online journal called *Challenge Europe* containing articles by politicians, journalists and lawyers on the future of the European Union.

---

**European Policy Centre**
42 Boulevard Charlemagne, B-1000 Brussels, Belgium
Web site: www.theepc.be

**Challenge Europe**
Web site: www.theepc.be/Challenge_Europe/top.asp
or access directly from the European Policy Centre Web site.

---

## The Institutions of the European Union

The three most important institutions within the European Union are the Commission, the Council and the Parliament. Unfortunately, their working arrangements are unnecessarily complicated. Most of their work involves introducing new legislation and agreeing on the annual budget.

---

**European Union**
Web site: europa.eu.int

## THE EUROPEAN COMMISSION

The European Commission has 16,000 staff (3,000 of whom work as translators or interpreters) and twenty Commissioners – two from France, Germany, Italy, Spain and the United Kingdom and one from each of the other member states. The heads of state or government agree on a new President at the European Council. This is done in consultation with the European Parliament. Romano Prodi was appointed President in 1999. The remaining 19 Commissioners are nominated by their governments in consultation with the incoming President. They also have to appear before the European Parliament. They are appointed for a five-year term and are expected to act in the interests of Europe. Before the Commission can take office, it has to be approved by Parliament, which also has the power to pass a motion of censure and force the Commission to resign. This occurred for the first time in March 1999 when President Jacques Santer and the entire Commission were obliged to resign because of allegations of fraud and mismanagement.

The EU Commission appointed in July 1999 by member governments in consultation with Romano Prodi was made up as follows:

| | Commissioner | Country |
|---|---|---|
| President, Secretariat, legal affairs, media relations, Inter-governmental Conferences | Romano Prodi | Italy |
| Vice President – EU reform | Neil Kinnock | United Kingdom |
| Vice President – transport, energy and relations with European Parliament | Loyola de Palacio | Spain |
| Agriculture, Rural Development & Fisheries | Franz Fischler | Austria |
| Enlargement | Gunter Verheugen | Germany |
| Budget | Michaele Schreyer | Germany |
| Justice & Home Affairs | Antonio Vitorino | Portugal |
| Regional Policy | Michel Barnier | France |
| Trade | Pascal Lamy | France |
| Internal Market | Frits Bolkestein | Netherlands |
| Economic & Monetary Affairs | Pedro Solbes Mira | Spain |
| External Relations | Christopher Patten | United Kingdom |
| Research | Philippe Busquin | Belgium |
| Development & Humanitarian Aid | Poul Nielson | Denmark |
| Enterprise & Information Society | Erkki Liikanen | Finland |
| Employment & Social Affairs | Anna Diamantapoulou | Greece |
| Health & Consumer Protection | David Byrne | Ireland |
| Education & Culture | Viviane Reding | Luxembourg |
| Environment | Margot Wallstrom | Sweden |
| Competition | Mario Monti | Italy |

**Table 5** *The European Commission*

The Directorates used to be referred to by numbers – DGV, DGX etc. but Mr Prodi very sensibly decided that they should be referred to by name rather than number.

The Commission, which is based in Brussels, meets on a weekly basis. It draws up the annual budget and passes it to the Council of the EU and Parliament for approval. It also proposes new laws that are similarly passed on to the Council of the EU and the European Parliament for approval. The three conditions of European interest, consultation and subsidiarity apply to all new laws. In other words, any new laws must be in the interest of Europe as a whole, they must be proposed in consultation with other bodies and they must be judged necessary at EU level and not just at national level. The Commission ensures that existing Treaties are observed in all member states. Moreover, it acts as a policy maker and manages the EU budget. It negotiates trade and cooperation agreements with the countries of Africa, Caribbean and the Pacific (ACP), with the Commonwealth of Independent States and with the countries of Central and Eastern Europe.

English and French are the official languages of the Commission.

---

**European Commission**
rue de la Loi 200, B-1049 Brussels, Belgium
Web site: europa.eu.int/comm/index_en.htm

---

## COUNCIL OF THE EUROPEAN UNION

The Council of the European Union, usually referred to as the Council of Ministers, is made up of the ministers of the 15 member states. The Council meets in the Justus Lipsius Building in Brussels where the Council Headquarters is located. In April, June and October it meets at the Kirchberg European Centre in Luxembourg. The High Representative for the Common Foreign and Security Policy is the Secretary General of the Council and attends its meetings. Different meetings are held on a regular basis – for example, all Ministers for Finance meet once a month in the General Affairs Council. The Ministers for Economy and for Finance also meet once a month at the Economic and Financial Affairs Council. The Transport and Industry Councils meet less often, between two and four times a year.

Informal ministerial meetings in the areas of culture, education, housing and industry are held in three languages – English, French and the language of the Presidency. In July 1999 the Germans objected to Finnish being used during the Finnish presidency saying that German should be accepted as a working language.

A Committee made up of ambassadors and deputies from each of the member states prepares the Council's work. This is the Permanent Representatives Committee, known as COREPER.

Each member state holds the Presidency of the Council for six months. The Presidency entails arranging and presiding over all meetings of the Council, problem solving and ensuring consistency in decision-making. When a country holds the Presidency it is a boom time for interpreters.

| 2000 | Portugal | France |
|------|----------|--------|
| 2001 | Sweden | Belgium |
| 2002 | Spain | Denmark |
| 2003 | Greece | Italy |
| 2004 | Ireland | the Netherlands |
| 2005 | Luxembourg | United Kingdom |
| 2006 | Austria | Germany |
| 2007 | Finland | Portugal |

**Table 6** *Presidency of the Council of the European Union*

Along with the European Parliament, the Council is involved in the process of codecision where it can reject proposals from the Commission. In 1996 the European Commission proposed that codecision should apply to all areas of Community decisions concerning legislation. Clearly, this would make a lot of sense. However, this has not happened and codecision applies to 38 areas. Under the Maastricht Treaty, codecision applies to the free movement of workers, services, the internal market, incentive measures for education and health, consumer policy, trans-European networks, the environment, culture and the framework programme for research. Under the Amsterdam Treaty, codecision was extended to social exclusion, public health and the fight against fraudulent use of EU funds.

The Council reaches decisions either by qualified majority voting or by unanimity. Unanimous decisions are required for taxation, industry, culture, and regional and social funds. Unanimity is also required for the Common Foreign and Security Policy and for Justice and Home Affairs (Pillars Two and Three of the Treaty on European Union). This means that one particular country can veto a proposed change in law. Some people believe that the areas of taxation, welfare and labour laws should be dealt with under the qualified majority voting system.

Qualified majority voting applies to agriculture, fisheries, the internal market, environment and transport. Under the Amsterdam Treaty qualified majority voting will also apply to job initiatives, equal opportunities for men and women, public health, framework programmes for research and customs cooperation.

| France<br>Germany<br>Italy<br>United Kingdom | 10 votes each | 40 |
|---|---|---|
| Spain | 8 votes | 8 |
| Belgium<br>Greece<br>The Netherlands<br>Portugal | 5 votes each | 20 |
| Austria<br>Sweden | 4 votes each | 8 |
| Denmark<br>Finland<br>Ireland | 3 votes each | 9 |
| Luxembourg | 2 votes | 2<br>87 votes in total |

**Table 7** *Qualified majority voting at the Council of the European Union*

At least 62 votes are required in favour of a proposal from the Commission. In other cases there is an additional proviso that a minimum of 10 member states must vote in favour. However, the Council favours consensus whenever possible. EU enlargement will necessitate change in the arrangements for voting.

Confusingly, there is also a **European Council** made up of the heads of state or government and the President of the Commission. This is not an EU institution, but a summit, which meets at least twice a year, usually in June and December. The meetings are held in the country that holds the six-month presidency of the Council of the European Union. Eleven interpreting booths are required, with three interpreters per booth. Usually, the head of state or government of the country that holds the presidency visits each member state for discussions with his or her counterparts before the summit. The President of the European Parliament addresses each meeting of the European Council but does not attend the actual discussions. The European Council agrees on the new Commission President every five years. It deals with issues that the Council of the European Union has been unable to agree on and it reports to the European Parliament after each meeting. In turn, the European Parliament debates the outcome of the summit in its plenary session. The Commission also submits its reports to the European Council. Agreement at European Council level is by consensus.

**Council of the European Union**
rue de la Loi, 175, B-1048 Brussels, Belgium
Web site: ue.eu.int

## THE EUROPEAN PARLIAMENT

The European Coal and Steel Community included a Parliamentary Assembly from the beginning. The members were delegates from the national governments of the member states. The first direct elections to the European Parliament were held in 1979.

The European Parliament has 626 Members for 15 countries. The numbers are not strictly based on population; rather they are weighted in order to give a greater say to smaller countries such as Ireland and Luxembourg. Luxembourg for example has one MEP for every 64,000 inhabitants. If this rate were applied to Germany it would have 1,296 MEPs. Similarly, if Germany's rate of one MEP for every 840,000 people were applied to Luxembourg it would not even be entitled to one MEP. Because there was concern that the Parliament would be unworkable if it continued to mushroom, under the Treaty of Amsterdam the maximum number of MEPs will be 700. The new Louise Weiss Parliament building in Strasbourg, opened in 1999, contains only 700 seats. With enlargement to include thirteen incoming countries with a population of over 110 million, it is clear that a lot of adjustments will have to be made to the present system of allocating seats to each country.

| Country | Number of MEPs | Population |
|---------|----------------|------------|
| Austria | 21 | 7.8 million |
| Belgium | 25 | 10 million |
| Denmark | 16 | 5.2 million |
| Finland | 16 | 5 million |
| France | 87 | 58 million |
| Germany | 99 | 83 million |
| Greece | 25 | 10 million |
| Ireland | 15 | 3.5 million |
| Italy | 87 | 57 million |
| Luxembourg | 6 | 386,000 |
| The Netherlands | 31 | 15.5 million |
| Portugal | 25 | 9.9 million |
| Spain | 64 | 38.8 million |
| Sweden | 22 | 8.9 million |
| United Kingdom | 87 | 58.5 million |

**Table 8** *Members of the European Parliament*

MEPs are elected to a five-year term. Monthly plenary sessions are held in the last week of each month in Strasbourg, while committee meetings and additional sittings are held in Brussels. The General Secretariat and its 4,000 officials are based in Luxembourg. MEPs spend a considerable amount of time commuting between Brussels, Luxembourg and their home countries. The Parliament represents 370 million people. MEPs join one of the EP political groups:

| Political Group | Number of MEPs elected June 1999 |
|---|---|
| European People's Party (Christian Democrats) and European Democrats | 232 |
| Party of European Socialists (PES) | 180 |
| European Liberal Democrats (ELDR) | 51 |
| Greens/European Free Alliance | 48 |
| European United Left /Nordic Green Left | 42 |
| Union for a Europe of Nations | 30 |
| Europe of Democracies and Diversities (EDD) | 16 |
| Independents | 26 |

**Table 9** *The political groups at the European Parliament*

Some 30% of MEPs elected in 1999 were women. The European Parliament elects its own President, fourteen Vice Presidents and the Chairmen of the seventeen EP committees which make up a sort of shadow commission and deal with all aspects of EU affairs, from security and defence policy to budgetary control to fisheries and women's rights. However, the EP Committees do not correspond exactly to the twenty Commissioners' portfolios. Nicole Fontaine was elected President in 1999. The term of office is two and a half years. Together, the President and Vice Presidents make up the Bureau of Parliament, which is in charge of the administration of the parliament. A further five MEPs are elected Quaestors. They deal with any administrative issues that concern their fellow MEPs.

The seventeen European Parliament Committees are:

- Foreign Affairs, Human Rights, Common Security and Defence Policy
- Budgets
- Budgetary Control
- Citizens' Freedoms and Rights, Justice and Home Affairs
- Economic and Monetary Affairs
- Legal Affairs and the Internal Market
- Industry, External Trade, Research and Energy
- Employment and Social Affairs
- The Environment, Public Health and Consumer Policy
- Agriculture and Rural Development
- Fisheries
- Regional Policy, Transport and Tourism
- Culture, Youth, Education, the Media and Sport
- Development and Cooperation

- Constitutional Affairs
- Women's Rights and Equal Opportunities
- Petitions. The European Parliament receives more than 1,200 petitions each year from EU citizens. Some of these complaints are passed on to the European Ombudsman. In other cases, the European Commission is requested to contact the national authorities mentioned in the petition in order to ascertain more information.

Depending on the subject, the European Parliament may be asked for its assent, it may be consulted or it may have the power of codecision along with the Council of the European Union. When the European Commission makes proposals for new laws and for the budget, these proposals are sent to the EP President who allocates them to the appropriate committees. There are between 25 and 50 MEPs from the various parliamentary groupings on each committee. One MEP acts as Rapporteur and writes a draft report which then goes through to the plenary session of the European Parliament.

Each year the Commission sends the draft budget to the Budget Committee of the Parliament. The Budget Committee proposes changes that are voted on at Plenary Sessions. The amended draft budget goes to the Council for a second reading and then back to the Parliament, which can reinstate any amendments rejected by the Council.

The European Parliament approves the EU budget each year. It can decide on such issues as economic and social cohesion, transport, research and development but not on the Common Agricultural Policy, where the Council of Ministers has the final say. The President of the Parliament signs the budget into law. The EP Committee on Budgetary Control checks that funds are put to proper use. Parliament supervises the putting into practice of EU policy.

Every five years the EP is involved in approving the President and members of the European Commission. MEPs put a series of written and oral questions to each potential Commissioner. A power struggle has been going on in recent years between the Commission and the Parliament, with Parliament fighting for more power. This reached its height in March 1999 when Parliament forced the resignation of all twenty Commissioners. There is ongoing contact with the Commissioners who report to Parliament and to the committees during each Plenary Session. MEPs submit written questions to the Commission and the answers are published in the *Official Journal*.

The Amsterdam Treaty strengthened Parliament's powers. The European Commission drafts new laws, which the Council of Ministers and the Parliament examine. Under the latest system of codecision, the Parliament and the Council of Ministers both have the power to reject a proposed law. A Conciliation Committee made up of Parliament and Council members works to find a compromise in cases where Parliament and Council do not agree. If agreement is impossible at that stage,

Parliament can reject the proposal definitively. The codecision procedure covers 38 areas of law making including employment, the environment, public health and consumer protection. Parliament can also propose amendments to proposed legislation.

Parliament's assent must be obtained before any new countries can join the EU. MEPs believe that EU internal structures must be reformed before any enlargement can take place. Parliament's assent is also required for Structural and Cohesion Funds destined for regional development. The assent procedure also applies to association agreements with third countries, new international agreements, EP election procedures, rules governing the rights of residence for EU citizens and the tasks and powers of the European Central Bank.

When European Parliament committees meet, interpretation is provided towards the most common languages of the committee members where possible. When this approach proves impossible, interpretation is provided towards English, French and German only.

---

**European Parliament General Secretariat**
L-2929 Luxembourg
Web site: www.europarl.eu.int

---

## COURT OF JUSTICE OF THE EUROPEAN COMMUNITIES

Each member state appoints a judge to the Court of Justice for a six-year renewable term. The judges elect the President of the Court to a three-year term. The nine advocates general are also appointed by the member states. Their job is to deliver objective, independent opinions on cases brought before the Court. Under the Amsterdam Treaty, the brief of the Court of Justice has been extended to include the safeguarding of fundamental rights, EU action on asylum and immigration, and cooperation in police and judicial matters.

The Court ensures that individuals, institutions and member states observe Community law. Member states, institutions, individuals and companies also have the option of bringing cases before the Court. For example at the end of 1999 the European Commission decided to take France and Germany to court for refusing to allow British beef to be imported. In March 2000 Germany changed its stance and agreed to allow imports of British beef.

**The Court of First Instance** also has 15 judges appointed by member states for six years. It deals with cases brought by individuals and companies against decisions made by EU institutions and agencies. Appeals lodged against decisions of the Court of First Instance are heard in the Court of Justice.

**Court of Justice of the European Communities**
Palais de la Cour de Justice, L-2925 Luxembourg
Web site: europa.eu.int/cj

## EUROPEAN COURT OF AUDITORS

The Court of Auditors is not actually a court. It keeps a close eye on everything to do with the spending of EU money. This means all European, regional, national and local administrations must document all their spending and make all necessary information available to the Court of Auditors. Audits can be carried out at any time. Any irregularities are reported. The Court can also signal areas where management could be improved. The Court publishes an Annual Report in the *Official Journal*, which is scrutinised by Parliament. Each member state of the European Union appoints a Member to the Court of Auditors for a six-year renewable term. The European Parliament has to approve each nomination. The Members elect a President to a three-year renewable term. Jan O. Karlsson was elected President in January 1999. The President presents the Court's annual report on the previous financial year to the European Parliament. This information is central to the Parliament's decision on whether to discharge the Commission or not. Five hundred people work at the Court.

**European Court of Auditors**
12, rue Alcide De Gasperi, L-1615 Luxembourg
Web site: www.eca.eu.int

## EUROPEAN INVESTMENT BANK

Founded in 1958, the European Investment Bank (EIB) lends money both within the European Union and outside it. The EIB borrows money on the world's capital markets where it has an AAA credit rating. These long-term loans are made at a low rate of interest and are guaranteed by the EU. Within the EU the EIB prioritises certain areas: the less favoured regions, transport and telecommunications, Small and Medium-sized Enterprises, environmental protection, architectural heritage and energy supplies. The Bank works closely with the Commission when deciding which projects it should help finance. At the Amsterdam Summit the Amsterdam Special Action Programme was set up to help create jobs in Europe and the EIB was asked to help by investing money in the areas of education and health and in Small and Medium sized Enterprises, particularly those in the high technology sector.

In 1999 the EIB lent 31.8 billion euros. Ninety per cent of EIB loans are for projects within the EU. Outside the European Union, loans have been given in over 100 countries. These include the ten EU applicant countries in Central and Eastern Europe, the African, Caribbean and Pacific (ACP) countries and the Republic of South Africa. Reconstruction projects in the Lebanon have received loans, as have schemes in Gaza and the West Bank. Loans have been provided to the Southern Mediterranean countries and to finance projects in Asia and Latin America.

The Board of Governors of the EIB is made up of the Ministers of Finance of the EU member states. This Board appoints a President and eight Vice Presidents to form the Management Committee, which looks after the day to day running of the Bank. Four Vice Presidents are from France, Germany, Italy and the United Kingdom, the major shareholders in the EIB.

The Board of Governors also appoints 25 directors and 13 alternates to the Board of Directors. Member states nominate 24 directors and 12 alternates and the European Commission nominates one of each. The Board of Directors meets ten times per year to make sure that the Bank is being managed in accordance with EU Treaties and to approve loans. Philippe Maystadt of Belgium began a six-year term as President and Chairman of the Board of Directors on the 1st January 2000.

---

**European Investment Bank**
100, Boulevard Konrad Adenauer, L-2950 Luxembourg
Web site: eib.eu.int

---

## EUROPEAN CENTRAL BANK

The European Central Bank was established in 1998 when the President, Vice President and four other members were appointed to the Executive Board. On 1st January 1999 the exchange rates of Austria, Belgium, Finland, France, Germany, Ireland, Italy, Luxembourg, the Netherlands, Portugal and Spain were irrevocably linked in preparation for the advent of the euro on 1st January 2002. The European Central Bank took over the development of a single monetary policy on behalf of these eleven countries. Denmark, Sweden and the United Kingdom decided not to enter the euro zone and Greece was originally deemed ineligible. However, Greece is to become a member of the euro zone from 1st January 2001 and Denmark held a referendum on membership on 28th September 2000 when 53.1% of voters said no to formal participation in the euro. Sweden and the United Kingdom are expected to hold referendums on the euro at some stage.

The Governing Council consists of the members of the Executive Board plus the governors of the national central banks. The General Council consists of the President, Vice President and the governors of the national central banks. The President is Wim Duisenberg. The remaining four members of the Executive Board may participate in the General Council but do not have a vote.

English is the working language of the European Central Bank.

---

**European Central Bank**

Kaiserstrasse 29, D-60311 Frankfurt am Main, Germany

Web site: www.ecb.int

---

## COMMITTEE OF THE REGIONS

Set up under the 1992 Treaty on European Union, the Committee of the Regions met for the first time in Brussels in 1994. There are 222 members.

| Country | Number of Representatives |
|---------|---------------------------|
| France | 24 |
| Germany | 24 |
| Italy | 24 |
| United Kingdom | 24 |
| Spain | 21 |
| Austria | 12 |
| Belgium | 12 |
| Greece | 12 |
| the Netherlands | 12 |
| Portugal | 12 |
| Sweden | 12 |
| Denmark | 09 |
| Finland | 09 |
| Ireland | 09 |
| Luxembourg | 06 |

**Table 10** *National representation at the Committee of the Regions*

Each representative is appointed for a four-year term. The membership is made up of city mayors and chairpersons of cities and councils. Members are paid a travel and accommodation allowance only. The thinking behind the establishment of the Committee is that regions should be more involved in policy design and implementation.

The Committee of the Regions, which meets in plenary session five times a year, must be consulted about employment, the environment, vocational training, public health, education, youth, culture, trans-European networks and economic and social cohesion. The Committee can also give its opinions on other areas such as agriculture and the environment. Within the Committee there are eight standing commissions and four sub-commissions. There is also a Special Commission on Institutional Affairs, which is concerned with EU institutional reform.

All eleven EU languages are the working languages of the Committee of the Regions.

---

**Committee of the Regions**
rue Belliard 79, B-1040 Brussels, Belgium
Web site: www.cor.eu.int

---

## ECONOMIC AND SOCIAL COMMITTEE

The Economic and Social Committee was set up under the 1957 Treaties of Rome.

Representation at the Economic and Social Committee is organized on the same basis as in the above mentioned Committee of the Regions. There are 222 members drawn this time from employers, workers and various interests (farmers, consumers, professionals and cooperatives). The members are recommended by their respective governments and then appointed by the Council of the European Union to a four-year term. They are paid a travel and accommodation allowance only. Every two years the members elect a Bureau made up of 21 members. A President and two Vice Presidents are chosen from each constituency of employers, workers and various interests. Monthly plenary sessions are held in Brussels. The Economic and Social Committee is a consultative body that gives opinions on legislation to the European Commission, the Parliament and the Council of the EU. The Committee must be consulted on regional policy, the environment, employment, social matters, public health, economic policies, combating social exclusion and at the request of the European Parliament. These opinions appear in the *Official Journal* of the EU. The Committee also has the right to issue opinions on any EU related matter.

---

**Economic and Social Committee**
rue Ravenstein 2, B-1000 Brussels, Belgium
Web site: www.esc.eu.int

---

The following four offices are part of the European Commission:

**ECHO** is the European Community Humanitarian Office and comes under the brief of the Commissioner for Development and Humanitarian Aid. ECHO was set up in 1992 to help non-member countries in emergency situations caused by natural disasters or by war. ECHO also finances the clearance of landmines. The actual operations are carried out by non-governmental organizations and by specialised agencies. ECHO signs Framework Partnership Agreements with humanitarian organizations. Its funds come from the European Community budget and from humanitarian aid allocated under the terms of the Lomé Convention to the ACP countries (Africa, Caribbean and Pacific). There is also an emergency fund. There are 114 staff at ECHO headquarters in Brussels who liaise with seventy experts in the field.

The European Union together with its fifteen member states is the world's biggest donor of humanitarian aid. However, it has been criticised for the slowness of its response to emergency situations.

**European Community Humanitarian Office**
Web site: europa.eu.int/comm/echo/en/index_en.html

**Eurostat** collects data from the national statistics offices in the eighteen EEA countries and in Switzerland. It also collects data on the United States of America and Japan. It employs about 720 staff and is often mentioned in newspaper articles. It dates back to 1953. Eurostat comes under the authority of the Commissioner for the Budget.

**Eurostat**
Statistical Office of the European Communities, Jean Monnet Building
rue Alcide de Gasperi, L-2920 Luxembourg
Web site: europa.eu.int/comm/eurostat/

The Food and Veterinary Office (FVO) was set up in 1997. It purpose is 'to monitor the observance of food hygiene, veterinary and plant health legislation within the European Union and elsewhere and to contribute towards the maintenance of confidence in the safety of food offered to the European consumer'. The FVO carries out inspections both within the European Union and in other countries around the world which export food to the EU.

**Food and Veterinary Office**
Belfield Office Park, Dublin 4, Ireland

**OLAF**, the European Anti Fraud Office, was established by a Commission decision in April 1999 to replace the Task Force for Coordination of Fraud Prevention. The Office investigates fraud within the European Union and works on new legislation to protect EU financial interests. A supervisory committee steers the work of the Office. This committee is made up of five independent outsiders who are appointed with the agreement of the European Parliament, the Council of the European Union and the Commission. OLAF forms part of the brief of the Commissioner for the Budget.

**OLAF**
Web site: europa.eu.int/comm/anti_fraud/index_en.htm

**Others**

The **European Ombudsman** deals with complaints by members of the public or by businesses concerning administrative problems such as discrimination, unnecessary delay, abuse of power, lack or refusal of information, by the institutions and bodies of the European Community. The Ombudsman receives about 1,000 complaints each year but only one third of these come within his brief. The Ombudsman's decisions are not legally binding. The European Parliament elected Jacob Soderman to the post of Ombudsman in 1995 and again in 1999.

---

**The European Ombudsman**

1 avenue du Président Robert Schuman, BP 403, F-67001 Strasbourg Cedex, France

Web site: www.euro-ombudsman.eu.int

---

## Agencies and Bodies of the European Union

The following agencies are autonomous bodies that were established after decisions taken by the European Commission or the European Council. There is a deliberate policy to spread these around the different countries of the EU. The interpreting needs of the agencies are covered by the Joint Interpreting and Conference Services (JICS/SCIC) in Brussels, which sends interpreters on site.

In January 2000 David Byrne, Commissioner for Health and Consumer Protection, proposed the introduction of an independent **European Food Authority** (EFA) in which scientists would gather information on food and food safety. This followed a number of major problems such as BSE, dioxin in the food chain in Belgium and the controversy over genetically modified food.

### COMMUNITY PLANT VARIETY RIGHTS OFFICE

The **Community Plant Variety Rights Office (CPVO)** is a self-financing centralised EU system for the registration of new plants. Community protection lasts for 25 years for most plants or for 30 years in the case of potatoes, trees and vines. The Administrative Council is made up of a representative from each member state and a representative of the European Commission. The Council decides on policies and is the budget authority for CPVO. The Council of the European Union nominates the President. There are three units within the CPVO. These are the Technical Unit, the Financial and Administrative Unit and the Legal Unit. If a grower wishes to appeal a decision of the CPVO it can do so to an independent Board of Appeal and, if necessary, subsequently to the European Court of Justice.

**Community Plant Variety Rights Office (CPVO)**
CPVO-OCVV, BP 2141, F-49021 Angers Cedex 02, France
Web site: www.cpvo.fr/

## EUROPEAN AGENCY FOR THE EVALUATION OF MEDICINAL PRODUCTS (EMEA)

The EMEA employs 200 staff and authorises medicinal products for human and veterinary use. It also fixes maximum residue levels of medicinal products in animals destined for human consumption. Since 1995 there have been two systems for authorising products. The central EU system applies to products derived from biotechnology and on request to other new products. Companies submit a product to the EMEA. The Scientific Committee evaluates the submission over seven months and issues an opinion. The European Commission can then authorise the product for the European Union. The second system is a decentralised one where a product is authorised in a member state and that authorisation is extended to other EU countries. If the different countries cannot come to an agreement on authorisation, the EMEA steps in. The European Commission's Standing Committee helps the Commission adopt a decision. As a last resort, the Council of the European Union has the final say. The EMEA is also involved in harmonising agreements on medicinal products with other countries outside the European Union.

**European Agency for the Evaluation of Medicinal Products (EMEA)**
7 Westferry Circus, Canary Wharf, London E14 4HB, United Kingdom
Web site: www.eudra.org/emea.html

## EUROPEAN AGENCY FOR HEALTH AND SAFETY AT WORK

The European Agency for Health and Safety at Work was established in 1995 and began work the following year. Its purpose is to provide up to date information to all levels of the EU (institutions, member states, people on the ground) concerning health and safety at work. A Director oversees the Agency's operations. There is also an Administrative Board made up of representatives of governments, employers and employees from the member states as well as representatives of the European Commission.

**European Agency for Health and Safety at Work**
Gran Vía 33, E-48009 Bilbao, Spain
Web site: agency.osha.eu.int

## EUROPEAN CENTRE FOR THE DEVELOPMENT OF VOCATIONAL TRAINING

The **European Centre for the Development of Vocational Training**, also known by its French acronym, CEDEFOP or *Centre Européen pour le Développement de la Formation Professionnelle* and based in Greece, is a vocational training think tank for the European Economic Area. Established in 1976, the Centre does not provide any training itself. Instead, it advises policymakers on vocational training for young people and continuing training for adults. The director and deputy are proposed by the Management Board and appointed by the European Commission to a five-year renewable term of office. The Council and the European Parliament decide on the CEDEFOP budget.

**European Centre for the Development of Vocational Training**
PO Box 27, GR- 55102 Thessaloniki (Finikas), Greece
Web site: www.cedefop.gr

## EUROPEAN ENVIRONMENT AGENCY

The **European Environment Agency (EEA)** and the **European Environment Information and Observation NETwork (EIONET)** were established in 1994. They collect information on the environment and make predictions about future developments. EIONET is the Extranet of Europe, comprising 34 server computers across Europe in the 18 EEA countries and in the Phare countries in Central and Eastern Europe. The Extranet includes National Environment Agencies in each of the countries involved. It includes the EU institutions, non-governmental organizations, scientists and the public.

**European Environment Agency (EEA)**
Kongens Nytorv, 6, DK-1050 København, Denmark
Web site: www.eea.eu.int/

**EIONET**
Web site: www.eionet.eu.int

## EUROPEAN FOUNDATION FOR THE IMPROVEMENT OF LIVING AND WORKING CONDITIONS

Founded in 1975 under a regulation of the Council of Ministers and based in Dublin, the European Foundation for the Improvement of Living and Working Conditions researches ways of improving conditions and advises the EU institutions. The Board of the Foundation represents trade unions and the national administration of all EU member states as well as the European Commission.

**European Foundation for the Improvement of Living and Working Conditions**
Loughlinstown House, Shankill, Co. Dublin, Ireland
Web site: www.eurofound.ie

## EUROPEAN MONITORING CENTRE FOR DRUGS AND DRUG ADDICTION (EMCDDA)

The EMCDDA was set up in 1993. Its purpose is to collect information about drugs and drug addiction in Europe. The Centre coordinates the European Information Network on Drugs and Drug Addiction (REITOX).

**European Monitoring Centre for Drugs and Drug Addiction (EMCDDA)**
Palacete Mascarenhas, Rua da Cruz de Santa Apolónia No 23/25, P-1149-045 Lisboa
Web site: www.emcdda.org

## EUROPEAN MONITORING CENTRE ON RACISM AND XENOPHOBIA (EUMC)

The EUMC is an independent body funded by the European Union. The Centre compiles data on racism, xenophobia and anti-Semitism and provides examples of good practice. The Management Board is made up of one member from each of the 15 EU states and one member from the European Parliament, the Council of Europe and the European Commission. The Centre produces an annual report and issues a newsletter called *Equal Voices* four times a year.

**European Monitoring Centre on Racism and Xenophobia**
Rahlgasse 3, 1060 Vienna, Austria
Web site: www.eumc.at

## EUROPEAN TRAINING FOUNDATION

The **European Training Foundation** was set up in 1995. It works with the countries of Central and Eastern Europe, the CIS, Mongolia and the Mediterranean countries in the Meda programme in promoting cooperation in the area of the reform of vocational training. It also provides technical assistance for the implementation of the Tempus programme in the area of higher education. The Governing Board meets twice a year and is made up of representatives appointed by the EU member states and the European Commission.

**European Training Foundation**
Villa Gualino, Viale Settimo Severo 65, I-10133 Torino, Italy
Web site: www.etf.eu.int

## OFFICE FOR HARMONIZATION IN THE INTERNAL MARKET

The **Office for Harmonization in the Internal Market** is a central registration system for trademarks and designs. Community trademarks are issued for a renewable ten-year term and are valid in all fifteen EU countries. The office is self-financing from fees for registration and renewal.

**Office for Harmonization in the Internal Market (OHIM)**
Avenida de Aguilera 20, AC 77, E-03080 Alicante, Spain
Web site: www.oami.eu.int

## TRANSLATION CENTRE FOR BODIES IN THE EU

The **Translation Centre for Bodies in the European Union** was set up in 1994. It carries out translation work for eight of the ten agencies and bodies that precede this entry. The two exceptions are CEDEFOP and the European Foundation for the Improvement of Living and Working Conditions.

**Translation Centre for Bodies in the European Union**
Nouvel Hémicycle, niveau –4, 1, rue du Fort Thüngen, L-1499 Luxembourg
Web site: www.cdt.eu.int

# 7 War and Peace

## Introduction

Europe's defence organizations were founded in response to the situation that existed at the end of the Second World War. Germany was occupied by Great Britain, France, the United States and the Union of Soviet Socialist Republics. The Soviet-occupied section became East Germany. Europe and America were concerned at Communist expansion throughout Eastern Europe. It was felt that West Germany was a weak link that should be allowed to rearm and join a defence organization. This option was preferable to the possibility that West Germany could be taken over by the Russians and become part of the Eastern Bloc. These circumstances led to the establishment of NATO and the Western European Union.

Belgium, France, Luxembourg, the Netherlands and the United Kingdom signed the Brussels Treaty in 1948. They agreed that if any one of them were attacked, the others would come to its aid. A defence plan was organized whereby air defences would be coordinated and a joint command established. The United States and Canada were impressed and decided to join forces with these five European countries, and also with Denmark, Iceland, Italy, Norway and Portugal, thus forming the North Atlantic Treaty Organization (NATO) in 1950. Military responsibility was thereby transferred to NATO. France suggested a European Army but the French National Assembly rejected this idea. Instead, it was proposed that Germany and Italy join the five Brussels Treaty countries in the Western European Union, founded in 1955. As it happened, Germany was recognised as an independent nation and joined NATO in the same year. In reaction to German membership of NATO, seven Communist countries (Albania, Bulgaria, Czechoslovakia, East Germany, Hungary, Poland, Romania and the USSR) signed the Warsaw Pact in 1955. This was the era of the Cold War.

Defence issues were taken over by NATO, social and cultural issues by the Council of Europe and economic issues by the then European Economic Community.

However, the whole situation in Central and Eastern Europe changed dramatically at the end of the 1980s and at the start of the 1990s. The year 1989 was very eventful. The Berlin Wall fell, Poland, Hungary and Romania ousted the Communist regimes and in November the

Communist Government was ousted from Czechoslovakia. East and West Germany became the Federal Republic of Germany in 1990. In 1993 Czechoslovakia split up into two countries, the Czech Republic and the Slovak Republic or Slovakia.

The former Union of Soviet Socialist Republics collapsed in 1991 breaking up into fifteen independent states. Twelve of these – Armenia, Azerbaijan, Belarus, Georgia, Kazakhstan, Kyrgyzstan, Moldova, Russia, Tajikistan, Turkmenistan, Ukraine and Uzbekistan – formed the Commonwealth of Independent States (CIS). The other three independent states are Estonia, Latvia and Lithuania, also known as the Baltic States. There were new conflicts in the new states – civil war in Tajikistan from 1992 to 1996, war between Armenia and Azerbaijan over Nagorno-Karabakh, independence campaigns in Chechyna and Dagestan. The Warsaw Pact was dissolved in 1991.

In 1991 and 1992, four Yugoslav republics declared their independence. These were Bosnia and Herzegovina, Croatia, Macedonia and Slovenia. Serbia and Montenegro declared themselves the Federal Republic of Yugoslavia in April 1992. There was a ten-day war in Slovenia, a seven month one in Croatia, a war between Croats, Muslims and Serbs in Bosnia, ongoing problems in the Kosovo region of Serbia.

There were so many changes so quickly in Europe that the organizations that had concentrated all their energies on Cold War strategies were suddenly out of date. Other issues became important. A new approach had to be found in Europe. All the organizations took the decision to expand so as to include the countries of Central and Eastern Europe. As a result of German reunification the former East Germany automatically became a member of all the international organizations to which West Germany belonged.

## Council of Europe

The main point to remember about the Council of Europe is that it is not a European Union institution. In fact, the Council of Europe is a much bigger organization in terms of member countries – there are 41 members including all fifteen EU members, and four more countries have applied for membership. The United States, Canada and Japan have observer status while over 350 non-governmental organizations have consultative status.

Unfortunately, one of the main missions of the Council of Europe appears to be confusion. The Council of Europe and the European Union share the same flag (a circle of twelve gold stars against a blue background). Both their parliaments used to meet at the Palais de l'Europe in Strasbourg – a new building was opened for the European Parliament in summer 1999. They both have courts: the EU has the European Court of Justice to deal with EU Treaties while the Council of Europe has the European Court of Human Rights.

The Council of Europe was founded in 1949 under the articles of the Brussels Treaty, which provided for social and cultural cooperation. The Brussels Treaty was also the basis for the founding of NATO. The Council of Europe is an intergovernmental organization that aims to protect human rights, democracy and the rule of law. It is concerned with issues such as racism, the environment and drugs. In fact it has an interest in every facet of society apart from defence. Each member country holds the presidency for six months.

The Council of Europe operates on three levels:

The **Committee of Ministers** is made up of the Foreign Ministers of each member state. This Committee makes decisions. A different member country chairs the Committee every six months.

National parliaments appoint members to the **Parliamentary Assembly**, which debates issues. The number of members per country varies according to population. The total number was 286 in 1998. Assembly members are drawn from the main political parties of each member country. The Assembly elects a Secretary General to a five year term. Walter Schwimmer is the Secretary General.

The **Congress of Local and Regional Authorities** (CLRAE) represents local and regional authorities. An annual plenary session is held in Strasbourg. The Congress consists of the Chamber of Local Authorities and the Chamber of Regions. Between the two Chambers, there are 291 titular members and the same number of substitute members who represent over 200,000 regional and local authorities throughout the Council of Europe.

The Council of Europe's most important work has been on European conventions and agreements. Nearly 170 conventions have been drawn up, mainly concerning human rights. The best known is the 1950 European Convention for the Protection of Human Rights and Fundamental Freedoms. Under the terms of the Convention, individuals and states can take cases to the European Court of Human Rights. All sorts of issues have been dealt with from laws on homosexual activities to laws on abortion to property rights.

The governments of member states propose candidates for the position of judge at the European Court of Human Rights. The Parliamentary Assembly then elects the judges. The judges meet in varying numbers depending on the case. For example, if it is decided that a plaintiff does not have a case, then a committee of three judges can throw out the case. If an application goes ahead, it is heard by seven judges. The Chamber usually strives to find an amicable solution. If this proves impossible the Chamber gives its judgement. Occasionally cases are heard by a seventeen judge Grand Chamber. The Committee of Ministers ensures that the Court's judgements are adhered to.

In 1999 a new post of Council of Europe Commissioner for Human Rights was created. Alvaro Gil-Robles was the first appointee. As the European Court of Human Rights deals with individual cases, the Commissioner's role is political. His first project was to set up a human rights office in Chechnya. The office would document complaints on alleged abuses and act as mediator between the Russian authorities and the people of Chechnya. The Human Rights Commission also intends to work alongside the Northern Ireland Human Rights Commission, which is to draft a Charter of Rights for the people of all of Ireland. This work will be done through a joint committee made up of members of both Commissions.

The war in Chechnya posed particular problems for the Council of Europe because Russia is of course a member of the Council and yet human rights abuses were clearly taking place in Chechnya. Russia's response was that they were trying to eliminate terrorism.

The European Committee for the Prevention of Torture ensures that the European Convention of the same name is enforced. The Committee visits prisons, police stations and mental health institutions. It writes up reports on what it sees and makes recommendations for change.

The Secretariat has a permanent staff of about 1,300. The 1998 budget of the Council of Europe amounted to £144 million. Member states' contributions are based on wealth and population.

The official languages of the Council of Europe are English and French. However, German, Italian and Russian are working languages at the Parliamentary Assembly. On occasion, other languages may also be interpreted at debates. There are six staff interpreters and approximately 600 freelance interpreters. Vacancies are advertised in the *AIIC Bulletin, Le Monde, Le Soir, Tribune de Genève, The Guardian* and in certain cases in Interpreting Schools such as ESIT, ISIT, ETI and Westminster. The Council of Europe has experienced some difficulty in recruiting interpreters with some Eastern European languages – for example Russian with German and Italian.

---

**Council of Europe**
F-67075 Strasbourg cedex, France
Web site: www.coe.fr

---

*Council of Europe Members*: Albania, Andorra, Austria, Belgium, Bulgaria, Croatia, Cyprus, Czech Republic, Denmark, Estonia, Finland, France, Georgia, Germany, Greece, Hungary, Iceland, Ireland, Italy, Latvia, Liechtenstein, Lithuania, Luxembourg, Malta, Moldova, Netherlands, Norway, Poland, Portugal, Romania, Russia, San Marino, Slovakia, Slovenia, Spain, Sweden, Switzerland, the former Yugoslav Republic of Macedonia, Turkey, Ukraine, United Kingdom.

*Candidates for Membership*: Armenia, Azerbaijan, Belarus, Bosnia and Herzegovina.

*Observers*: Canada, Japan, United States of America.

# European Bank for Reconstruction and Development

The European Bank for Reconstruction and Development (EBRD) was set up by the countries of the European Union and the G7 industrialised nations and was endorsed in December 1989 by the European Council in Strasbourg. The G7 nations are Canada, France, Germany, Italy, Japan, United Kingdom and United States. Their heads of state or government meet once a year to discuss global issues. In 1991, the EBRD was established. Based in London, the Bank is a multinational institution which invests in and provides loans to 26 countries in central and Eastern Europe and to the Commonwealth of Independent States (CIS). The purpose of this investment is to help these countries change over to market economies. The shareholders include the 26 countries of operations, the European Community, the European Investment Bank and other countries around the world. The EBRD provides loans that other financial institutions might not be prepared to offer. The EBRD has an AAA credit rating that facilitates borrowing on the international capital markets.

The Board of Governors meets at an annual meeting that is held in a different location each year.

A great deal of the bank's work is carried out in English. Interpretation is provided at Board of Governor sessions for English, French, German and Russian. Both staff and freelance interpreters are employed.

---

**European Bank for Reconstruction and Development**
One Exchange Square, London EC2A 2JN, United Kingdom
Web site: www.ebrd.org

---

*Countries of operations*: Albania, Armenia, Azerbaijan, Belarus, Bosnia and Herzegovina, Bulgaria, Croatia, Czech Republic, Estonia, FYR Macedonia, Georgia, Hungary, Kazakhstan, Kyrgyzstan, Latvia, Lithuania, Moldova, Poland, Romania, Russian Federation, Slovak Republic, Slovenia, Tajikistan, Turkmenistan, Ukraine and Uzbekistan.

# North Atlantic Treaty Organization

Belgium, France, Luxembourg, the Netherlands and the United Kingdom signed the Brussels Treaty in 1948. Under the Treaty, the five countries agreed to defend themselves collectively and to cooperate in economic, social and cultural matters. They realised that they were not strong enough on their own so decided that they needed to involve more countries. The North Atlantic Treaty was signed in 1949 by twelve countries – the five original signatories plus Canada, the United States, Denmark, Italy, Iceland, Norway and Portugal. Iceland does not have an army. According to the NATO Treaty, the purpose of the Organization is 'to safeguard the freedom and security of all its members by political and military means in accordance with the principles of the United Nations Charter'.

For many years NATO was preoccupied with the Cold War. It wanted to show the Eastern Bloc that it would act in defence of any of its member countries. NATO had its ups and downs over the years: in 1966 France withdrew from the integrated military command structure of NATO. France under President Charles de Gaulle felt that NATO was dominated by the United States. De Gaulle objected to the large international staff based in France. As a result the staff moved to Belgium. France retained its seat on the NATO council but remained outside the integrated military command of NATO until December 1995.

Greece and Turkey joined NATO in 1952 and West Germany in 1955. Spain joined in 1982 and this decision was upheld by the 1986 referendum. Spanish membership was conditional on a partial withdrawal of US troops stationed in Spain. On 1st January 1999 Spain joined the NATO Integrated Military Command.

NATO's *raison d'être* changed totally with the end of the Cold War. The Warsaw Pact was dissolved in 1991. Suddenly, NATO had no purpose. The alternatives were to disband or to expand. NATO chose expansion. Partnership for Peace was founded in 1994 and became a means of attracting potential NATO members. In the mid 1990s NATO forces participated in peacekeeping operations in Bosnia and Herzegovina and launched air strikes against Bosnian Serb forces. The Czech Republic, Hungary and Poland joined NATO in 1999. This left Austria in the unusual situation of being neutral but surrounded by NATO members apart from Switzerland.

In March 1999 NATO, concerned at the treatment of Albanian Kosovars by the Serbs, began bombing Kosovo despite the fact that UN Security Council members China and Russia had exercised their veto concerning action against Serbia. The 78-day 'operation' represented a significant change in NATO policy. NATO subsequently led KFOR, a multinational peacekeeping force made up of 49,000 people and based in Kosovo.

NATO policy in recent years has involved working with Russia, Ukraine and some of the Mediterranean countries. In 1995 dialogue began with Egypt, Israel, Jordan, Mauritania, Morocco and Tunisia. In 1997 NATO and Russia signed an agreement on their future relations and established the NATO-Russia Permanent Joint Council. In the same year the NATO-Ukraine Charter was signed and the NATO-Ukraine Commission was established. The Commission meets twice a year. NATO is also working on establishing a European Security and Defence Identity (ESDI) along with the countries of the European Union. NATO frequently works with the Organization for Security and Cooperation in Europe (OSCE).

There are very close links between NATO and the Western European Union (WEU), the European pillar of NATO. The NATO and WEU Councils meet at least four times a year, their subordinate bodies hold joint meetings, WEU is allowed to use NATO's integrated telecommunications system and the Secretariats and military staff from both organizations hold regular joint meetings. However, as the WEU comes to play a more central role within the European Union through the Common Foreign and Security Policy, it remains to be seen whether WEU and NATO continue to have such a close relationship.

## CIVILIAN STRUCTURE

The NATO Secretary General is nominated by member governments. Former British Minister for Defence Lord Robertson was appointed in 1999.

The **North Atlantic Council**, which takes all major decisions and controls the budget, is made up of permanent members, headed by the Secretary General. Each member state is represented by an Ambassador or a permanent representative and has the assistance of a national delegation.

The **North Atlantic Assembly** is an interparliamentary organization based in Brussels. It meets twice a year in plenary session. Members are appointed by national parliaments. The nineteen NATO members and associate countries have representation at the Assembly.

The **Euro-Atlantic Partnership Council** (EAPC) is made up of all 19 NATO members along with Partnership for Peace members.

NATO Headquarters in Brussels employ about 2,600 full time staff. English and French are the official languages. There are 42 staff interpreters and about 100 freelance interpreters. All interpreters are bilingual. As a result there can be difficulties finding suitable staff. Vacancies are advertised in newspapers and in the *AIIC Bulletin*.

## MILITARY STRUCTURE

ACE or Allied Command Europe is the Military Command in Europe and extends from the tip of Norway to Turkey's eastern frontier. Established in 1951 by General Eisenhower, **SHAPE** or Supreme Headquarters of the Allied Powers in Europe is the military headquarters of ACE based near Mons in Belgium since 1967. The SACEUR is the Supreme Allied Commander Europe. There are over 2,000 staff at SHAPE including officers, other ranks and civilians. A further 1,800 staff are National Military Representatives. Each member of staff spends three to four years at SHAPE.

The Headquarters of Allied Command Atlantic (ACLANT) is in Norfolk, Virginia.

*NATO members*: Belgium, Canada, Czech Republic, Denmark, France, Germany, Greece, Hungary, Iceland, Italy, Luxembourg, the Netherlands, Norway, Poland, Portugal, Spain, Turkey, United Kingdom, United States.

The **Atlantic Treaty Association** is a grouping of voluntary national organizations in NATO member countries.

**Partnership for Peace (PfP)** was begun in 1994. Members are allowed share defence information and take part in peacekeeping operations and in joint exercises. PfP members have worked with NATO members in peacekeeping operations in Bosnia and Kosovo. PfP includes Austria, Finland, Ireland and Sweden, all of which are members of the European Union but not of NATO. PfP stretches into Asia to include such countries as Tajikistan and Turkmenistan.

*Partnership for Peace members*: Albania, Armenia, Austria, Azerbaijan, Belarus, Bulgaria, Estonia, Finland, Georgia, Ireland, Kazakhstan, Kyrgyzstan, Latvia, Lithuania, Moldova, Romania, Russian Federation, Slovakia, Slovenia, Sweden, Switzerland, the Former Yugoslav Republic of Macedonia, Tajikistan, Turkmenistan, Ukraine, Uzbekistan.

---

**NATO Office of Information and Press**
1110 Brussels, Belgium
Web site: www.nato.int/

**SHAPE Supreme Headquarters Allied Powers Europe**
B-7010 SHAPE, Belgium

---

## Organization for Security and Cooperation in Europe

Readers may recall seeing people with the acronym OSCE on their jackets or on their helmets on news items concerning Kosovo in 1999. From 1975 to 1994 this was CSCE, C being for Conference, rather than Organization. It organized conferences and meetings between the West and the Eastern bloc. There were no permanent bodies within the CSCE. The CSCE became the OSCE in 1994. Its main functions are early warning of potential flashpoints, conflict prevention, crisis management and post-conflict rehabilitation. The thinking here is that war anywhere in Europe threatens all European countries. Another aim of the Organization is to promote cooperation among economies, and to do with the environment, science and technology.

The OSCE sends Verification Missions to areas of conflict. The missions are made up of civilians or military seconded by their countries. The OSCE works with many international organizations including the United Nations, the International Organization for Migration and the International Committee of the Red Cross. The OSCE has assisted in monitoring UN sanctions against several countries.

All member countries have equal status and decisions are reached by consensus.

The OSCE holds summits every two years when heads of state or government meet to decide priorities.

The **Ministerial Council** is made up of Foreign Ministers of participating states. It considers issues, review OSCE activities and takes decisions.

The **Senior Council** meets once a year as the economic forum. It can also convene meetings in emergency situations. Each member state is represented.

The **Permanent Council** is based in Vienna. Its members are permanent representatives to the OSCE and they meet on a weekly basis at the Hofburg Congress Centre in Vienna.

The **Forum for Security Cooperation** also meets every week in Vienna. It is concerned with arms control and disarmament and aims to increase confidence and trust between participating countries.

The **Parliamentary Assembly** is based in Copenhagen and meets once a year.

The **Office for Democratic Institutions and Human Rights** is in Warsaw. It has been involved in election monitoring in most of the member states of the Commonwealth of Independent States and in Estonia and Latvia.

The **Court of Conciliation and Arbitration** is in Geneva.

The Offices of the High Commissioner for National Minorities are in The Hague.

The Secretariat is based in Vienna and includes a Department for Conference Services. In 1996 there were about 35 language staff, including interpreters. The official languages of the OSCE are English, French, German, Italian, Russian and Spanish.

*OSCE Members*: Albania, Armenia, Austria, Azerbaijan, Belarus, Belgium, Bosnia and Herzegovina, Bulgaria, Canada, Cyprus, Croatia, Czech Republic, Denmark, Estonia, Finland, France, Georgia, Germany, Greece, Holy See, Hungary, Iceland, Ireland, Italy, Kazakhstan, Kyrgyzstan, Latvia, Liechtenstein, Lithuania, Luxembourg, the former Yugoslav Republic of Macedonia, Malta, Moldova, Monaco, Netherlands, Norway, Poland, Portugal, Romania, Russian Federation, San Marino, Slovak Republic, Slovenia, Spain, Sweden, Switzerland, Tajikistan, Turkmenistan, Turkey, Ukraine, United Kingdom, United States, Uzbekistan, Yugoslavia (suspended since 1992).

*Mediterranean Partners for Cooperation*: Algeria, Egypt, Israel, Jordan, Morocco and Tunisia.

*Asian partners*: Japan and the Republic of Korea (i.e. South Korea).

---

**OSCE Secretariat**
Kärntner Ring 5–7, A-1010 Vienna, Austria
Web site: www.osce.org

## Western European Union

The WEU was founded in 1955 by the signatories of the 1948 Brussels Treaty (Belgium, France, Luxembourg, the Netherlands and the United Kingdom) along with Germany and Italy. The WEU did very little for thirty years but got a new lease of life when the European Union Ministers for Foreign Affairs and for Defence met in Rome in 1984. Three years later, in 1987, the Council of Ministers agreed on the Platform on European Security Interests. In 1991 in Maastricht it was decided that the Treaty on European Union should establish a Common Foreign and Security Policy.

In 1992 at Petersberg in Germany, it was agreed that military units of WEU member states could be deployed under the authority of the WEU for certain tasks known as the Petersberg Tasks. These are:

- humanitarian and rescue tasks
- peacekeeping tasks
- tasks of combat forces in crisis management, including peacemaking

The Petersberg Tasks were incorporated into the European Union framework under the Amsterdam Treaty.

In his foreword to *WEU Today*, the former WEU Secretary General, José Cutileiro, wrote in 1998 that the primary role of the WEU is:

> to enable Europeans to undertake the politico-military management of crises in which the North Americans would not wish to become directly involved. WEU will probably act following a political decision by the European Union and may, depending on the circumstances, call on NATO assets and capabilities.

In effect, the WEU is the European pillar of NATO. It is concerned with political control and strategic direction in any crisis. On 3 June 1999 at the Cologne EU summit, European leaders agreed that by the end of the year 2000 the WEU would be assimilated into the European Union. Javier Solana, former Secretary General of NATO, was nominated as the first High Representative for the Common Foreign and Security Policy of the European Union and took office in December 1999. He also became Secretary General of the Western European Union.

Examples of the work of the WEU include the following: in 1993 the WEU monitored the Adriatic embargo on the Former Republic of Yugoslavia (Serbia and Montenegro). Also in 1993, the WEU helped enforce UN sanctions on the River Danube. From 1994 to 1996 the WEU sent a police contingent to Mostar in Bosnia-Herzegovina. In 1997 it sent a mission to Albania to train the police force there.

In the future the WEU will be at the centre of European Union policy. A European rapid response force called EUROFOR and consisting of

60,000 soldiers, is to be set up. This force will act on the Petersberg Tasks mentioned above. An EU Interim Military Committee and an Interim Political and Security Committee met for the first time in March 2000. The European Council Secretariat will include a military staff section, which will draw up reports on potential crises. It remains to be seen how exactly relations between WEU and NATO will develop.

In 1992 the Western European Armaments Organization (WEAG) was set up. Its purpose is to encourage cooperation among member countries in producing new fighter planes for example.

The WEU **Council** looks after all security and defence issues.

The **Council of Ministers** is made up of the Ministers for Defence and for Foreign Affairs and usually meets twice a year, in the country holding the WEU presidency (the same country as holds the EU presidency if it is a member of both organizations).

The **Permanent Council** is made up of permanent representatives along with military delegates. It meets each week.

The **Assembly** and the **Institute for Security Studies** are based in Paris. Under the 1954 Paris Agreement, member states have the same representatives here as at the Council of Europe Parliamentary Assembly.

The Satellite Centre is in Torrejón, Spain.

The Western European Union employs about 200 staff. About 88 freelance interpreters are employed per day. The working languages are English and French. All interpreters have to be cleared by security and this is a lengthy process. No training is provided and posts in interpreting are not advertised. Simultaneous Interpreting is carried out at high-level ministerial meetings and at meetings of armaments experts.

*Member states*: Belgium, France, Germany, Greece, Italy, Luxembourg, Netherlands, Portugal, Spain, and United Kingdom.

*Associate members*: Iceland, Norway and Turkey.
Observers: Austria, Denmark, Finland, Ireland, Sweden.

*Associate partners*: Bulgaria, Czech Republic, Estonia, Hungary, Latvia, Lithuania, Poland, Romania, Slovakia, Slovenia (all prospective EU members).

**WEU Secretariat-General**
4, rue de la Régence, 1000 Brussels, Belgium
Web site: www.weu.int

# 8 The United Nations

The League of Nations, founded in 1920, was the forerunner of the United Nations. It had 63 members but came to an end in 1946 having failed to prevent the Second World War. The United Nations was founded in 1945. It employs under 9,000 people and includes 189 countries, or practically every independent state in the world. A full list of UN member states is included in the appendix to the present volume. The whole UN system with its various specialised organizations and programmes employs some 52,000 people. The federated states of Serbia and Montenegro opted to retain the name of Federated Republic of Yugoslavia. According to the *CIA World Factbook*, in 1999 there was a total of 191 independent states worldwide. East Timor became independent from Indonesia in the same year, thus bringing the total up to 192. The Holy See, Palestine Liberation Organization and Switzerland are observers at the UN. As the Swiss people voted against UN membership as recently as 1986, Switzerland is not a UN member but is a member of thirteen UN organizations including the International Monetary Fund and the World Health Organization. Swiss troops do not take part in UN peacekeeping operations. Ten UN programmes and seven specialised agencies are based in Geneva. UN Headquarters is in New York, built on land donated by John D. Rockefeller. Taiwan was expelled from the UN in 1971 and its seat was given to the People's Republic of China. Taiwan is claimed by China as a province of the People's Republic of China. Since 1992, Taiwan has applied each year for UN membership but China has objected.

Finance is a very important issue in the United Nations. Member countries contribute to the United Nations budget according to their means. The General Assembly reassesses the rates every three years. According to a UN factsheet, the main contributors are the United States (25%), Japan (17.98%), Germany (9.63%), France (6.49%), Italy (5.39%) and the United Kingdom (5.07%). These six countries contribute 69% of the UN budget of US$1.08 billion per annum. The United States contribution is capped at 25% – strictly speaking, it should be higher. However, by 1999 the United States owed US$1.69 billion. The reasons for this debt are various: the United States Department of State claims that it is in part due to different assessment terms. The United Nations works on a calendar year basis whereas the United States works from the beginning of each October. Since the 1980s there has been a deliberate policy on the part of the Republican Party and the Republicans in the United States Congress to withhold funding whenever it objected to UN policy. The Republicans and particularly Senator Jesse Helms, chairman of the Foreign Relations Committee, claim that the UN is inefficient, overstaffed and bureaucratic. The UN has acted to combat these claims: staffing levels have been cut by 1,000, an inspector general has been appointed and a rationalisation programme has been put into operation. Under Secretary General Kofi Annan, administrative costs were cut from 38% to 25% of the total budget. Although the US Administration under President Bill Clinton is in favour of paying arrears, Congress wants the American assessment to be reduced to 20%.

According to Article 19 of the United Nations Charter:

> A Member of the United Nations which is in arrears in the payment of its financial contributions to the Organization shall have no vote in the General Assembly if the amount of its arrears equals or exceeds the amount of the contributions due from it for the proceeding two full years. The General Assembly may, nevertheless, permit such a Member to vote if it is satisfied that the failure to pay is due to conditions beyond the control of the Member.

At any given time a number of countries are not allowed vote under Article 19. Most of these countries are poorer nations. The minimum assessment is 0.001% of UN costs. If the US were to be suspended it would still hold its seat on the Security Council. US policy has meant that the United Nations has been obliged to manage its budget very carefully. On many occasions the UN has been forced to borrow money from peacekeeping funds in order to stay afloat. As a result, at the end of 1998 the UN owed 73 countries US$872 million. It has also obtained interest free loans from a number of countries including Canada, France, Italy, United Kingdom and even Fiji and Pakistan.

In December 1999 the United States paid US$100 million in arrears to the United Nations. This was the first tranche of a three-tranche programme over three years. However, payment was subject to conditions to satisfy the US Congress. For example, Tranche Two required that the US contribution to the UN budget be reduced to 22% and that contributions to peacekeeping be reduced to 25%. Tranche Three (US$244 million payable to the UN specialised agencies) was to be conditional on the Food and Agricultural Organization, the International Labour Organization and the World Health Organization not increasing their budgets.

Many people associate the United Nations with peacekeeping. The Annual Peacekeeping Assessment is US$789,507,155. Of this the United States pays 31%, Japan 20%, Germany 10%, France 8%, Italy 5% and the UK 6%. The other member states pay 20%. The US Congress refuses to pay peacekeeping costs above the 25% rate. It refused to pay for peacekeeping missions in the Sahara and in Haiti. In early 2000 there were seventeen UN peacekeeping operations around the world. The Middle East operation dates back to 1948 and the India/Pakistan operation to 1949. Twelve operations began in the 1990s. Peacekeeping is funded separately from the regular UN budget. UN member states pay an agreed share of costs. The permanent Security Council members pay at a higher rate than other members. Peacekeeping costs reached an all time high in 1993 at US$4.6 billion due to interventions in the former Yugoslavia and in Somalia. Since then the trend has been steadily downwards. In 1996 peacekeeping costs came to US$1.4 billion, in 1997 US$1.3 billion and in 1998 it was hoped that US$900 million would be sufficient. However, by September 1998 member states owed US$1.75 billion for 1998 and previous years. Those countries that volunteer personnel continue to pay their staff while they are on peacekeeping duty. The UN pays an extra US$1,000 per soldier per month. Given the large number of different UN agencies it is amazing that there is no single peacekeeping agency. The process of organizing a peacekeeping force is a lengthy one because agreement has to be reached between the different countries involved before a peacekeeping operation can commence. A clear example of this phenomenon occurred after the 1999 independence referendum in East Timor when it was clear to the international community that an outside peacekeeping force was an urgent priority. However, a number of days elapsed before an Australian led force was put in place.

Enforcement operations differ from peacekeeping operations. In these cases the Security Council agrees to allow member states to take action to achieve an objective. However, enforcement is not under the control of the UN. Enforcement has been applied in the Gulf War, Somalia, Rwanda, Haiti, Bosnia and Herzegovina and Albania.

The International Tribunals are financed separately at a rate that combines the scales for the regular budget and the peacekeeping assessment. The Annual Tribunal Assessment is US$154,849,695. The US rate is 29%, Japan 20%, Germany 10%, France 7%, Italy 5%, UK 6% and the remaining countries pay 24%.

The official languages of the UN are Arabic, Chinese, English, French, Russian and Spanish. English and French are the working languages. Interpreting is provided at all UN meetings.

The United Nations Web site is www.un.org. As well as information about the United Nations it contains links to the constituent UN organizations.

The official Web site Locator for the United Nations System of Organizations is at www.unsystem.org. This Web site contains an alphabetical list of UN organizations and a list according to official classification.

There are fifty United Nations Information Centres (UNIC) around the world, some of which have Web sites.

There is a Vacancy Announcement Bulletin for vacancies arising in the UN system on the World Wide Web at: www.un.org/Depts/icsc/vab/index.htm

## General Assembly

Each member country is represented in the General Assembly in New York where each has one vote. A tiny state like Nauru (population 9,000) has one vote, just as China (population 1.25 billion) has one vote. A majority vote will secure procedural decisions for example. More significant issues such as the budget, peace and security require a two-thirds majority. The Assembly meets in session from mid September to mid December each year. It also meets in special sessions. The work of the Assembly continues on through the rest of the year in the form of six committees, each of which is charged with a particular area of concern:

- Disarmament and International Security Committee
- Economic and Financial Committee
- Social, Humanitarian and Cultural Committee
- Special Political and Decolonisation Committee
- Administrative and Budgetary Committee
- Legal Committee

The Assembly appoints the Secretary General who has never been a citizen of a major world power. It elects the non-permanent members of the Security Council to two-year terms. The Assembly approves the UN budget including peacekeeping operations around the world. It also decides UN policies. General Assembly resolutions are not binding on the member states. The fifty-fourth session of the General Assembly began in September 1999. The President was Dr Theo Ben Gurirab of Namibia. The President is chosen from a different regional grouping (Africa, Asia, Eastern Europe, Latin America and the Caribbean, Western Europe) each year.

Anyone speaking at the General Assembly has the option of using a non-working language if they either organize interpretation or provide a written translation in one of the six official languages. If they choose to provide a written translation they must ensure that the interpreter is guided so that the speech and the interpretation are synchronised.

## Security Council

The Security Council consists of fifteen members. Five are permanent and ten are elected to a two-year term by the General Assembly. The five permanent members are China, France, Russian Federation, United Kingdom and the United States. Of the ten elected members, five are from African and Asian states, one from Eastern Europe, two from Latin America and the Caribbean and two from Western Europe and other states. The members up to the end of 2002 are Columbia, Ireland, Mauritius, Norway, Singapore. The members to the end of 2001 are Bangladesh, Jamaica, Mali, Tunisia and Ukraine. Each member of the Council holds the Presidency for one month. Each member has one vote. At least nine members must vote affirmatively on procedural matters. Nine votes are also required on serious issues and all five permanent members must vote in agreement. In other words, each of the five permanent members has the power to veto any proposal. A number of countries have objected to this system saying that Africa for example is not a permanent member on the Security Council. Others have objected to the right to veto proposals. Of course the Security Council has vetoed all proposed changes. The power of veto also applies to the choice of Secretary General. For example, in 1996 the United States exercised its veto in the case of a renewal of the term of then Secretary General Boutros Boutros Ghali.

However, according to the United States Department of State the United States is in favour of allowing Germany and Japan to become permanent members of the Security Council. It would also accept three permanent regional seats, one each for Africa, Asia and Latin America. However, the United States is not in favour of any change to the present right to veto of permanent members of the Security Council.

---

**United States Department of State**
Web site: www.state.gov/www/issues/fs-unsc_expan_000105.html

---

The Security Council's task is to ensure international peace and security. In the case of a dispute, it will first of all seek agreement by peaceful means. It may also mediate in a dispute and set out principles for peaceful settlement. Sometimes it asks the Secretary General or a representative to mediate.

If fighting breaks out the Security Council may call for a ceasefire, allocate peacekeeping forces, impose economic sanctions or call for collective military action. For example the Security Council authorised military action when Iraq invaded Kuwait and in Somalia, Rwanda and Haiti. The country or countries involved in an armed conflict may be suspended from the General Assembly or expelled from the United Nations. Sanctions have been used against a large number of countries including Iraq and Libya.

The Iraqi army invaded oil rich Kuwait in August 1990 and the six-week Gulf War began in January 1991. Economic sanctions were imposed on Iraq immediately after the war and in accordance with UN resolution 687, will remain in place until the United Nations certifies that Iraq no longer has weapons of mass destruction. In December 1996, the United Nations agreed to a system whereby Iraq could export limited quantities of oil in return for food. Thirty per cent of earnings are earmarked for war reparations. United Nations arms inspectors were expelled in 1998. Bombing of the air exclusion zones in northern and southern Iraq by the US and British airforces has continued since 1991.

## Economic and Social Council (ECOSOC)

ECOSOC has 54 members, each of which has one vote. Eighteen members are elected by the General Assembly to the Council each year. Voting within ECOSOC is by simple majority. It meets for five weeks each year – one year in Geneva, the next in New York. Ministers and senior officials attend a special meeting during the session to discuss important economic and social issues. Commissions and committees carry out the Council's work during the remainder of the year.

ECOSOC aims to improve standards of living, to encourage full employment and to promote economic and social progress. It encourages international cooperation in such areas as housing, environmental protection and the prevention of crime. It coordinates the activities of the UN specialised agencies. ECOSOC was responsible for setting up the five regional Economic and Social Commissions for Europe, Latin America and the Caribbean, Western Asia. Asia and the Pacific and for Africa. ECOSOC elects members to the Commission on Human Rights, the Commission on Narcotic Drugs, the International Narcotics Control Board and to the Committees on Sustainable Development, the Status of Women, Crime Prevention and Criminal Justice, Social Development and Population and Development. The following five organizations are subsidiary bodies of ECOSOC:

- the Children's Fund
- the UN High Commission for Refugees
- UN Development Programme
- UN Population Fund
- the World Food Programme

## Secretariat

The working languages of the Secretariat are English and French. The Secretariat in New York, Geneva and Vienna employs 8,700 people (compared to 12,000 in 1984) from over 170 countries. It administers peacekeeping operations, acts as a mediator in international disputes, keeps an eye on social problems, organizes international conferences and coordinates interpretation and translation requirements. The Secretary General is the head of the Secretariat and is appointed by the General Assembly with the agreement of the Security Council for a five year renewable tenure. Kofi Annan of Ghana was appointed Secretary General in 1997. The previous secretaries general were Trygve Lie of Norway (1946 to 1953), Dag Hammarskjöld of Sweden (1953 to 1961), U Thant of Burma (1961 to 1971), Kurt Waldheim of Austria (1972 to 1982), Javier Pérez de Cuellar of Peru (1982 to 1991), and Boutros Boutros Ghali of Egypt (1992 to 1996). In 1997 Louise Fréchette of Canada was appointed to the new post of Deputy Secretary General.

The United Nations Office in New York (UNHQ NY) employs 4,700 staff including 110 staff interpreters. There is also a roster of 350 freelance interpreters, not all of whom are active. Vacancies are advertised at Interpretation Schools, in the world press and on the UN Web site. Interpretation is provided at all meetings of official UN bodies that require it. When conferences or meetings are held elsewhere, for example on the invitation of a member state, the inviting host country pays any additional costs such as travel and accommodation expenses.

Language examinations for interpreting posts are administered by the Office of Human Resources Management at UN Headquarters in New York. The examination consists of simultaneous interpreting from two official UN languages into a third, which should be the candidate's main language. Candidates are of course expected to have a university degree and interpreting experience.

---

**Languages Examinations**
Professional Staffing Service, Recruitment and Placement Division, Room S-2535, United Nations New York, NY 10017, USA

---

The United Nations Office at Geneva (UNOG) looks after recruitment of personnel for all sections of the United Nations based in Geneva. It covers the interpreting needs of all Geneva based UN organizations with the exception of the specialised agencies. That is to say it does not supply interpreters to the ILO, ITU, UPU, WHO, WIPO or WMO. It does supply interpreters to UNECE, UNCTAD, UNHCHR and UNHCR. Geneva is the largest conference centre in the UN. There are about 3,000 staff altogether but many extra staff are employed during conferences. As many as 300 conferences take place each year in the Palais des Nations in Geneva. In 1999 there were 84 staff interpreters and an average of 30 to 40 freelance interpreters in any given week. Temporary interpreters may be taken on in Geneva if they pass a language test administered by the Training and Examinations Section there. The UNOG recruits locally for these posts.

Interpreting posts in Geneva are advertised in such newspapers as *El País, Le Monde, Jeune Afrique,* and *The New York Times,* depending on which language is being sought. Examinations are held in Geneva, New York and in other cities if there is a sufficient number of candidates.

---

**Recruitment and Placement Section**
Room 245, Palais des Nations, 8–14 Avenue de la Paix, 1211 Geneva 10, Switzerland
Web site: www.unog.ch

---

The United Nations in Vienna looks after the interpreting requirements of those agencies based in Austria, in other words the International Atomic Energy Agency, United Nations Industrial Development Organization, the Drug Control Programme and the Comprehensive Test

Ban Treaty, which is not part of the United Nations but for which interpreting is provided. In 1999 there were 13 staff interpreters and up to 60
freelance interpreters at peak times.

---

**United Nations Vienna**
PO Box 500, A-1400 Vienna, Austria
Web site: www.un.or.at

---

A fourth United Nations Office was opened in Nairobi, Kenya, in 1988.
Web site: www.unon.org

# UN Programmes

The heads of UN programmes and funds are appointed by the Secretary
General of the United Nations.

The UN Economic and Social Council (ECOSOC) has established five
Economic or Economic and Social Commissions which cover most of the
world. The Economic Commission for Europe and the Economic and
Social Commission for Asia and the Pacific were both founded in 1947
with the aim of rebuilding after the Second World War. The Economic
Commission for Latin America was founded the following year and sub-
sequently extended to include the Caribbean. Ten years later, in 1958, the
Economic Commission for Africa was established. In 1973 the Economic
and Social Commission for Western Asia – basically the countries of the
Middle East – was established.

## ECONOMIC COMMISSION FOR AFRICA

Founded in 1958, the ECA is composed of all 53 African countries, each
of which is represented by its Minister of Finance. The ECA proposed
the establishment of the African Development Bank. It aims to encourage economic and social development in Africa. It promotes trade and
the development of information technology. It is concerned at the problems caused by a combination of rising population, reduced agricultural
production per capita and increasing damage to the environment. At the
end of 1996 the Commission employed 800 staff. The UN General
Assembly votes on the two year ECA budget. There is a UN Conference
Centre in Addis Ababa, Ethiopia where the ECA is based. Arabic, English
and French are the three official UN languages in Africa. The Executive
Secretary is K.Y.Amoako.

*Members:* Algeria, Angola, Benin, Botswana, Burkina Faso, Burundi,
Cameroon, Cape Verde, Central African Republic, Chad, Comoros,
Republic of the Congo, Democratic Republic of the Congo, Côte d'Ivoire,

Djibouti, Egypt, Equatorial Guinea, Eritrea, Ethiopia, Gabon, The Gambia, Ghana, Guinea, Guinea-Bissau, Kenya, Lesotho, Liberia, Libya, Madagascar, Malawi, Mali, Mauritania, Mauritius, Morocco, Mozambique, Namibia, Niger, Nigeria, Rwanda, Sao Tome and Principe, Senegal, Seychelles, Sierra Leone, Somalia, South Africa, Sudan, Swaziland, Tanzania, Togo, Tunisia, Uganda, Zambia, Zimbabwe.

*Associate members:* France, United Kingdom.

---

**Un Economic Commission for Africa**
PO Box 3001, Addis Ababa, Ethiopia
Web site: www.un.org/depts/eca

---

## ECONOMIC COMMISSION FOR EUROPE

The Economic Commission for Europe (ECE) was established in 1947 by the Economic and Social Council of the United Nations to help rebuild Europe after the Second World War. This was the first UN Economic Commission to be established. Its purpose nowadays is to promote cooperation on an economic level between Europe and North America. It develops international agreements on trade, transport and the environment. The Commission is involved in helping Eastern European states change over to a market economy. It organizes seminars and conferences on relevant issues. There are 55 members – all European countries plus Canada, Israel and the United States.

The ECE meets each April to decide on its programme for the coming year. The UN General Assembly and the UN Economic and Social Council can propose approaches or measures to ECE. The ECE cooperates closely with other organizations such as the Organization for Security and Cooperation in Europe (OSCE) and the European Union. Danuta Hübner was appointed Executive Secretary in the year 2000.

The United Nations Office at Geneva provides conference services to the UNECE. Some 150 ECE meetings are held in Geneva each year.

*Members:* Albania, Andorra, Armenia, Austria, Azerbaijan, Belarus, Belgium, Bosnia and Herzegovina, Bulgaria, Canada, Croatia, Cyprus, Czech Republic, Denmark, Estonia, Finland, France, Georgia, Germany, Greece, Hungary, Iceland, Ireland, Israel, Italy, Kazakhstan, Kyrgyzstan, Latvia, Liechtenstein, Lithuania, Luxembourg, Malta, Monaco, Netherlands, Norway, Poland, Portugal, Republic of Moldova, Romania, Russian Federation, San Marino, Slovakia, Slovenia, Spain, Sweden, Switzerland, Tajikistan, the former Yugoslav Republic of Macedonia, Turkey, Turkmenistan, Ukraine, United Kingdom, United States, Uzbekistan, Yugoslavia.

**UN/ECE Information Office**
Palais des Nations, CH-1211 Geneva 10, Switzerland
Web site: www.unece.org

## ECONOMIC COMMISSION FOR LATIN AMERICA AND THE CARIBBEAN

ECLAC was founded in 1948 by the Economic and Social Council of the United Nations. It was originally intended for Latin America and was subsequently extended to include the Caribbean. At present it includes all the countries of Latin America and the Caribbean. Other countries with historical and economic links to the region such as Canada, Spain, Portugal, the United Kingdom and the United States are also members. There are seven associate members. Representatives meet every second year to discuss social and economic issues, review progress and set objectives. The Secretariat, headed by an Executive Secretary, employs 500 staff. The Central American headquarters is in Mexico and the Caribbean headquarters is in Trinidad and Tobago. There are also National Offices in Argentina, Brazil, Colombia, Uruguay and the United States. The Commission aims to promote economic development and to increase trade both within the region and with the wider world. José Antonio Ocampo is the Executive Secretary.

*Members:* Antigua and Barbuda, Argentina, The Bahamas, Barbados, Belize, Bolivia, Brazil, Canada, Chile, Colombia, Costa Rica, Cuba, Dominica, Dominican Republic, Ecuador, El Salvador, France, Grenada, Guatemala, Guyana, Haiti, Honduras, Italy, Jamaica, Mexico, Netherlands, Nicaragua, Panama, Paraguay, Peru, Portugal, Saint Kitts and Nevis, Saint Lucia, Saint Vincent and the Grenadines, Spain, Suriname, Trinidad and Tobago, United Kingdom, United States, Uruguay, Venezuela.

*Associate members:* Anguilla, Aruba, British Virgin Islands, Montserrat, Netherlands Antilles, Puerto Rico, United States Virgin Islands.

**Economic Commission for Latin America and the Caribbean**
Casilla, 179-D, avenida Dag Hammarskjöld, Santiago, Chile
Web site: www.eclac.cl

## ECONOMIC AND SOCIAL COMMISSION FOR ASIA AND THE PACIFIC

The Economic and Social Commission for Asia and the Pacific or ESCAP was established in 1947 to help with economic reconstruction after the

Second World War. It has 51 members and 9 associate members. It is the largest of the UN Economic Commissions and represents 60% of the world's population. It is the only intergovernmental organization in Asia that covers all the countries of Asia and the Pacific. The Commission proposed the establishment of the Asian Development Bank. It has been involved in HIV and AIDS prevention programmes and in reducing the demand for drugs in certain areas. It has organized three conferences on the Environment and Development, in 1985, 1990 and 1995. Each year it publishes an Economic and Social Survey of the region and a document on the State of the Environment in Asia and the Pacific. Seven hundred people are employed at the ESCAP Secretariat. Kim Hak-Su assumed the post of executive secretary in July 2000.

The official languages of ESCAP are Chinese, English, French and Russian. There are seven permanent and two freelance interpreters. Unusually, all the interpreters are male. All the regular interpreters must have passed the UN examination for interpreters. They must have a perfect command of one official language and excellent knowledge of at least two other official languages. ESCAP has experienced some difficulty in finding interpreters with active English and passive Russian. Interpreting is provided at legislative meetings and at regular UN conferences.

*Members:* Afghanistan, Armenia, Australia, Azerbaijan, Bangladesh, Bhutan, Brunei, Burma, Cambodia, China, Fiji, France, India, Indonesia, Iran, Japan, Kazakhstan, Kiribati, North Korea, South Korea, Kyrgyzstan, Laos, Malaysia, Maldives, Marshall Islands, Federated States of Micronesia, Mongolia, Nauru, Nepal, Netherlands, New Zealand, Pakistan, Palau, Papua New Guinea, Philippines, Russia, Samoa, Singapore, Solomon Islands, Sri Lanka, Tajikistan, Thailand, Tonga, Turkey, Turkmenistan, Tuvalu, United Kingdom, United States, Uzbekistan, Vanuatu, Vietnam.

*Associate members:* American Samoa, Cook Islands, French Polynesia, Guam, Hong Kong, Macau, New Caledonia, Niue, Northern Mariana Islands.

---

**Economic and Social Commission for Asia and the Pacific**
UN Building, Rajdamnern Avenue, Bangkok 10200, Thailand
Web site: unescap.org

---

## ECONOMIC AND SOCIAL COMMISSION FOR WESTERN ASIA

The Economic and Social Commission for Western Asia or ESCWA employs 72 people in Beirut. Established in 1973, it is part of the UN Secretariat and reports to the Economic and Social Council. The

Ministerial Session, which is the governing body, meets every second year. It is assisted by the Standing Committee for the Programme. Six intergovernmental committees report to the Technical Committee. The Commission works closely with the governments of Western Asia and with other organizations. It collects information and carries out studies. It is a source of expertise and is a link between the UN and the region. Hazem Abdel-Azis El-Beblawi wa appointed executive secretary in 1995.

The languages of ESCWA are Arabic, English and French.

**Economic and Social Commission for Western Asia**
PO Box 11–8575, Riad el-Solh Square, Beirut, Lebanon
Web site: www.escwa.org.lb

## UNITED NATIONS CENTRE FOR HUMAN SETTLEMENTS (HABITAT)

The United Nations Conference on Human Settlements took place in 1976 and the Centre (UNHCS aka Habitat aka The City Agency) was founded two years later. The Second UN Conference on Human Settlements took place in Istanbul in 1996. The Conference was attended by mayors, local authorities and members of non-governmental organizations. The participants agreed on a global plan of action that is known as the Habitat Agenda. The Global Urban Observatory was subsequently set up to over-see and report on progress.

The Habitat work programme includes the following:

- shelter and social services
- urban management
- environment and infrastructure
- assessment, information and monitoring

The United Nations Commission on Human Settlements is the Governing Body of Habitat. In 1999 Habitat had 235 projects in 80 countries. It works closely with other UN organizations such as the United Nations Development Programme, the Children's Fund (UNICEF) and the World Health Organization. Habitat has also been involved in reconstruction programmes in Angola, Iraq, Rwanda and Somalia. The 1996–1997 biennial expenditure was US$100 million.

**UNCHS/Habitat**
PO Box 30030, Nairobi, Kenya
Web site: www.unchs.org

## UNITED NATIONS CHILDREN'S FUND (UNICEF)

The acronym stands for the United Nations International Children's Emergency Fund, which was established in 1946 immediately after the Second World War. The General Assembly has delegated the task of protecting children's rights to UNICEF, which concentrates on the most vulnerable children, as well as responding to children's needs in emergency situations. Children's immediate needs have to be met but they should also have the opportunity to reach their full potential. The Convention on the Rights of the Child is UNICEF's benchmark.

The Executive Board is the Fund's governing body. The Economic and Social Council of the UN elects states to sit on the Board. The 36 members are drawn from 8 African states, 7 Asian states, 5 Latin American or Caribbean states and 12 Western European states. They serve a three-year term. One annual session and two to three regular sessions are held in New York each year. All formal meetings of the Board are interpreted in the six official UN languages. The Executive Director is Carol Bellamy.

UNICEF employs 5,594 people, of whom 86% are working in the field. There are eight regional offices and 125 country offices. Thirty-seven National Committees for UNICEF support the Fund and aid with fundraising. The Children's Fund is financed by voluntary contributions from Governments, the UN and the general public.

---

**United Nations Children's Fund**
3 United Nations Plaza, New York, NY 10017, USA
Web site: www.unicef.org

---

## UNITED NATIONS CONFERENCE ON TRADE AND DEVELOPMENT

The United Nations Conference on Trade and Development (UNCTAD) has 190 member states including the Holy See and Switzerland. UNCTAD was established in 1964 by the General Assembly and is a permanent intergovernmental body. There are 394 staff members who are part of the UN Secretariat. The main goals of UNCTAD are 'to maximize the trade, investment and development opportunities of developing countries, and to help them face challenges arising from globalization and integrate into the world economy on an equitable basis'.

UNCTAD receives an annual budget of US$50 million from the UN budget. It relies on donor and beneficiary countries' contributions to its US$24 million fund for technical activities.

From an organizational point of view, the Conference meets every four years at ministerial level in order to draw up new policies. The 144 member Trade and Development Board meets in Geneva for two weeks each autumn. One-day Executive sessions take place three times a year. The

Board has three commissions, which meet once a year for five days. Each commission may also organize up to ten expert meetings per annum. The three commissions are:

- Commission on Trade in Goods, Services and Commodities
- Commission on Investment, Technology and Related Financial Issues
- Commission on Enterprise, Business Facilitation and Development

UNCTAD and the World Trade Organization (WTO) together run the International Trade Centre, which was originally established in 1964 by the General Agreement on Trade and Tariffs (GATT), the forerunner of the World Trade Organization. UNCTAD became involved in the Trade Centre in 1968. Both organizations contribute equal amounts to the Centre, which promotes trade in developing countries, and in economies in transition. The International Trade Centre is based at the Palais des Nations in Geneva, Switzerland.

Rubens Ricupero has been Secretary General of the Conference since 1995.

Interpreting services are provided by the UN Office in Geneva.

---

**United Nations Conference on Trade and Development**
Palais des Nations, 1211 Geneva, Switzerland
Web site: www.unctad.org

---

## UNITED NATIONS DEVELOPMENT PROGRAMME

Founded in 1965, the aim of the United Nations Development Programme of UNDP is to promote sustainable development. The UNDP is an inter-governmental organization. It is linked to the UN General Assembly through ECOSOC. The UNDP employs 1,000 staff in New York and 4,300 in its 132 offices around the world. As a voluntarily funded programme, the UNDP annual budget in 1999 was US$2 billion, derived from a combination of voluntary contributions and targeted resources.

The Administrator is Mark Malloch Brown.

The UNDP administers the following:

- The UN Capital Development Fund (UNCDF)
- United Nations Development Fund for Women (UNIFEM)
  Established in 1976, this fund aims to promote the empowerment of women and gender equality. Web site: www.unifem.undp.org
- UN Volunteers
- Special Unit for Technical Cooperation among Developing Countries (SU/TCDC)

**United Nations Development Programme**
One United Nations Plaza, New York, NY 10017, USA
Web site: www.undp.org

## UNITED NATIONS ENVIRONMENT PROGRAMME (UNEP)

Founded in 1972, the Environment Programme is a relative latecomer to the UN system. A voluntarily funded programme, it aims to increase public awareness of the environment and to ensure that countries work together so that development will not damage the environment for present and future generations.

UNEP's concerns are various. They include desertification, biotechnology, the conservation of wildlife, the protection of the seas, destruction of forests and clean water in Africa. On a more positive note, UNEP works to develop cleaner industries, ecotourism, green technologies and emergency response to accidents involving chemicals. It has drawn up an International Register of over 8,000 Potentially Toxic Chemicals. UNEP has also got involved in disaster relief in conjunction with the US Department of Humanitarian Affairs.

Along with other organizations, UNEP has been involved in drawing up international treaties to do with the ozone layer and with the movement and disposal of hazardous waste.

UNEP has offices in Bahrain, Bangkok, Geneva, Mexico City, Nairobi and New York. The Executive Director, Klaus Töpfer, heads the Programme. The United Nations General Assembly elects 58 members to four year terms on the Governing Council which is made up of 16 representatives from Africa, 13 from Asia, 6 from Eastern Europe, 13 from Western Europe and 10 from Latin America.

**United Nations Environment Programme**
PO Box 67578, Nairobi , Kenya
Web site: www.unep.org

## UNITED NATIONS HIGH COMMISSIONER FOR HUMAN RIGHTS (UNHCHR)

The Commission on Human Rights met for the first time in 1947 to begin work on the Universal Declaration of Human Rights, which was adopted at the end of the following year. The Commission was also involved in drawing up the International Covenant on Civil and Political Rights and the International Covenant on Economic, Social and Cultural Rights. The Declaration and the two Covenants are collectively known as the International Bill of Human Rights. In 1967 the Economic and Social

Council authorised the Commission to deal with Human Rights violations.

A number of committees have been established to ensure that international treaties are being observed. These include

- Human Rights Committee
- Committee on Economic, Social and Cultural Rights
- Committee against Torture
- Committee on Elimination of All Forms of Racial Discrimination
- Committee on the Rights of the Child

The 53 members of the Human Rights Commission are elected by ECOSOC for a three-year renewable term. The allocation of members is: 15 from Africa, 12 from Asia, 11 from Latin America and the Caribbean, 10 from Western Europe and other European countries and 5 from Eastern Europe.

The office of High Commissioner for Human Rights was created by the General Assembly in 1993. The High Commissioner, Mary Robinson, is accountable to the UN Secretary General. The purpose of the UNHCHR is to promote human rights, to respond to serious violations of human rights and to coordinate the promotion and protection of human rights throughout the UN system. The Commission organizes fact-finding missions to countries in order to ascertain what exactly is happening there. For example, in 1994 a Special Rapporteur on religious intolerance was sent to China and a Rapporteur on contemporary forms of racism was sent to the United States. The Commission also seeks to promote democracy and development as an integral part of human rights.

The UNHCHR budget is US$20 million per annum, or 1.7% of the total UN budget. This is matched by voluntary funds donated by member states.

There are some 200 staff at the Office of the High Commissioner for Human Rights in Geneva. Interpretation is provided by the Conference Services of the Office of the United Nations in Geneva for official meetings such as the Commission on Human Rights and for meetings of the treaty bodies. The Commission also has an office in New York.

---

**United Nations High Commissioner for Human Rights**
Palais des Nations, 8–14 Avenue de la Paix, 1211 Geneva 10, Switzerland
Web site: www.unhchr.ch

---

## UNITED NATIONS HIGH COMMISSIONER FOR REFUGEES (UNHCR)

Founded in 1951 by the General Assembly, the UNHCR acts as a watchdog for refugees, to ensure that they are properly treated. It also helps to look after people who are returning to their native country after a war or people who have been displaced within their own country. In 1998 it worked with 425 different non-governmental organizations to help 22 million people. It employs 5,528 staff of whom 4,670 work in the field. Based in Geneva, the UNHCR is allocated US$19.8 million from the UN budget as a contribution towards administrative costs. The remainder of its budget is funded by governments, the European Commission, non-governmental organizations and individual donations. The 1999 budget was US$918 million. The UNHCR operates general programmes for needs that it can predict and special programmes in emergency cases. UNHCR appeals for funding to finance emergency needs.

The interpreting needs of UNHCR are covered by the UN office in Geneva. However, the UNHCR also has interpreting needs in the field when dealing with crisis situations. At the 1999 Babelea Conference on Community Interpreting, Melita Sunjic of UNHCR in Vienna explained that many UNHCR staff members in the field find themselves interpreting. Local interpreters have to be found, often at very short notice. They are given a short training course. The UNHCR has a booklet called *Interpreting in a Refugee Context.* These interpreters may have to explain that they are interpreters, not decision-makers. Potential refugees have to be interviewed at length in order to ascertain if they have a well-founded fear of persecution under the Geneva Convention. If this is the case, they may be offered places in other countries as programme refugees.

Ruud Lubbers is the High Commissioner.

The fifty UNHCR members are Algeria, Argentina, Australia, Austria, Bangladesh, Belgium, Brazil, Canada, China, Colombia, Democratic Republic of the Congo, Denmark, Ethiopia, Finland, France, Germany, Greece, Holy See, Hungary, India, Iran, Israel, Italy, Japan, Lebanon, Lesotho, Madagascar, Morocco, Namibia, Netherlands, Nicaragua, Nigeria, Norway, Pakistan, Philippines, Russia, Somalia, Spain, Sudan, Sweden, Switzerland, Tanzania, Thailand, Tunisia, Turkey, Uganda, United Kingdom, United States, Venezuela, Yugoslavia.

---

**United Nations High Commissioner for Refugees**
Case Postale 2500, 1211 Geneva 2, Switzerland
Web site: www.unhcr.ch

---

## UNITED NATIONS OFFICE FOR DRUG CONTROL AND CRIME PREVENTION (ODCCP)

Together, the UN International Drug Control Programme and the UN Centre for International Crime Prevention (CICP) make up the UN Office for Drug Control and Crime Prevention based in Vienna. The UNDCP has drawn up model legislation that could be adapted by member states in common law or civil law systems. The UNDCP has regional offices around the world.

The UN Interregional Crime and Justice Research Institute or UNICRI is based in Rome. UNCJIN, the Internet-based UN Crime and Justice Information Network, is a database containing statistics on crime.

The Commission on Crime Prevention and Criminal Justice is made up of 40 representatives of member states. The Commission formulates policies and coordinates activities.

The Executive Director of ODCCP is Pino Arlacchi.

---

**UN Crime and Justice Information Network**
Web site: www.uncjin.org

**United Nations Office for Drug Control and Crime Prevention**
Vienna International Centre, PO Box 500, A-1400 Vienna, Austria
Web site: www.undcp.org

This Web site is amazingly uninformative as regards the workings of the ODCCP.

---

## UNITED NATIONS POPULATION FUND (UNFPA)

The original acronym stands for United Nations Fund for Population Activities, created by UN Secretary General U Thant in 1969. The Population Fund has been controversial because some people felt that it promoted abortion. The UNFPA is a subsidiary organ of the UN General Assembly. It 'assists developing countries to improve reproductive health and family planning services on the basis of individual choice, and to formulate population policies in support of efforts towards sustainable development'. The Population Fund depends on voluntary contributions. Its budget was US$309 million in 1997 and was expected to be in the region of US$290 million in 1998. The United States did not contribute to the fund in 1999. However, it resumed contributions in 2000 with the sum of US$25 million. Fifteen per cent of the Fund is allocated to projects carried out by non-governmental organizations around the world. In 1997 the Fund offered support to 168 countries.

The Executive Director, Thoraya Ahmed Obaid, was appointed in January 2001.

---

**United Nations Population Fund**
220 East 42nd Street, NY 10017, USA
Web site: www.unfpa.org

## WORLD FOOD PROGRAMME

Founded in 1963, the World Food Programme is the world's largest international food aid agency. Its budget is voluntary, and is in fact linked to the amount of food it moves. Expenditure for 1998 amounted to US$1,348 billion and 2.8 million tons of food were delivered to 74 million people. There are 2,116 permanent staff, of whom 1,530 are employed in the field and 586 at headquarters in Rome. Just under 3,000 temporary staff are employed for emergency operations. The WFP targets women, children and the elderly. It provides food to schoolgoing children and in food for work programmes. It helps feed refugees, returnees and internally displaced people. It also helps to feed victims of natural disasters such as hurricanes and floods. Half of the members of WFP are chosen by ECOSOC and half by the Food and Agriculture Organization also based in Rome.

The Executive Director is Ms Catherine Ann Bertini.

**World Food Programme**
Via Cesare Giulio Viola, 68 Parco dei Medici, Rome 00148, Italy
Web site: www.wfp.org

# Courts and Tribunals

## INTERNATIONAL COURT OF JUSTICE

The International Court of Justice is also known as the World Court. It is based in The Hague in the Netherlands. Its brief is limited. It settles legal disputes submitted by states and gives advisory opinions on legal questions referred by UN international organs or specialised agencies. The Court operates in English and French. According to the Rules of the court, any evidence submitted in one of the official languages is interpreted into the other official language. If any other language is used, the evidence is interpreted into English and French and a written translation must be submitted in one of the official languages to become part of the court record. If a party chooses not to use either of the official languages it is their responsibility to organize interpretation. If the Court calls witnesses, then it organizes interpretation. The interpreter is asked to state: 'I solemnly declare upon my honour and conscience that my interpretation will be faithful and complete'.

Fifteen judges are elected to nine-year terms by the General Assembly and the Security Council. There cannot be more than one judge of any nationality. Elections are held every five years for five judges. If a state refuses to submit a case to the Court, then the case cannot go ahead.

**International Court of Justice**
Peace Palace , 2517 KJ The Hague, The Netherlands
Web site: www.icj-cij.org

## INTERNATIONAL CRIMINAL COURT

When it is set up the International Criminal Court (ICC) will be a permanent court based in The Hague in the Netherlands, dealing with war crimes, genocide, crimes of aggression and crimes against humanity. Under Article 24 of the Rome Statute, 'No person shall be criminally responsible under this Statute for conduct prior to the entry into force of this Statute'. The whole process of establishing the court is a lengthy one. Meetings were held in July 1998 in Rome, Italy. China, Iraq, Israel, Libya, Qatar, Sudan and the United States voted against the establishment of the ICC. The Preparatory Commission for the Court held three meetings in 1999. Draft texts were to be finalised by mid 2000. In July 2000 only fourteen countries had ratified the Rome statute. A total of sixty signatories is required.

The International Criminal Court does not have an address yet but the Rome Statute and news are available at www.un.org/icc

In 2000 there were two Criminal Tribunals in operation, one for the former Yugoslavia, the other for Rwanda. UN member states finance these Tribunals, 50% under the regular scale assessment and 50% on the peacekeeping scale.

## INTERNATIONAL CRIMINAL TRIBUNAL FOR THE FORMER YUGOSLAVIA

The ICTY was established in March 1993 by Security Council resolution 827. Based in The Hague in The Netherlands, its mandate is 'to prosecute persons responsible for serious violations of international humanitarian law committed on the territory of the former Yugoslavia since 1991'. In 1999 the Tribunal employed a total of 766 staff from 65 countries and its budget was US$94 million.

**Public Information Services**
Churchillplein 1, PO Box 13888, 2501 EW The Hague, The Netherlands
Web site: www.un.org/icty

## INTERNATIONAL CRIMINAL TRIBUNAL FOR RWANDA

The ICTR was created in November 1994 under Security Council resolution 955. Based in Tanzania, its task is to prosecute those responsible for genocide and serious violations of humanitarian law in Rwanda and neighbouring states. The time frame is limited to the year 1994. There are 511 staff from 71 countries. The 1999 budget was US$57 million. There are two trial chambers with three judges each, appointed for a four-year term.

The Criminal Tribunals for the former Yugoslavia and for Rwanda share the same Chief Prosecutor and five appeals judges. Two deputy prosecutors, one for Rwanda and one for the former Yugoslavia, assist the chief prosecutor.

---

**International Criminal Tribunal for Rwanda**
PO Box 6016, Arusha, Tanzania
Web site: www.ictr.org

---

## INTERNATIONAL TRIBUNAL FOR THE LAW OF THE SEA

The UN Convention on the Law of the Sea is enforced by the International Tribunal based in Hamburg, Germany. There are 21 judges from all over the world but all the work of the Tribunal is carried out in English and French. The judges are elected by the 132 Convention signatories. The Convention covers a huge range of issues including disputes between countries, drug trafficking, hazardous waste, piracy, fishing and minerals. For example, New Zealand and Australia took a case about southern bluefin tuna against Japan to the Tribunal. Panama took a case against France when a Panama registered boat called the 'Camouco' was arrested for illegal fishing off the French owned Crozet Islands. Freelance interpreters are employed. According to George Drummond's article in issue number 6 of AIIC's *Communicate!* on the Internet, the interpreters work into their mother tongue and should 'have a certain amount of experience in legal issues and in working for international institutions'. The Convention also led to the creation of the International Seabed Authority and the Commission on the Limits of the Continental Shelf.

---

**Registry of the International Tribunal for the Law of the Sea**
Wexstrasse 3, 20355 Hamburg, Germany
Web site: www.un.org/Depts/los/ITLOS/ITLOShome.htm

---

## Specialised UN Agencies

The fourteen specialised agencies are part of the UN system. They have their own membership, their own budget and organize their own recruitment. These agencies have been established over the years by means of treaties in response to new developments around the world. They are all intergovernmental organizations that have special agreements with the UN but are not under its authority. The heads of the specialised agencies are appointed by their legislative and governing bodies.

## FOOD AND AGRICULTURE ORGANIZATION

The Food and Agriculture Organization (FAO) was established in 1945. In 1999 it had 175 member nations plus the European Community and employed 4,300 staff, of whom 2,300 were based in Rome and the remainder around the world. Puerto Rico is an associate member. The FAO is the largest autonomous organization within the United Nations. According to the FAO Web site, 800 million people in the world do not have enough to eat. The mission of the FAO is to improve nutrition and living standards, to increase agricultural productivity and to improve the living conditions of rural people. The FAO collects information on all aspects of food and agriculture and provides advice to governments. It is also involved in providing assistance to farmers. The FAO budget for the two years 1998 and 1999 amounted to US$650 million. Agencies and governments contributed a further US$3,000 million for FAO projects.

The Conference, made up of all 175 member states, elects 49 members to the Council. Members are elected for a period of three years. Elections take place each year for a third of the seats. Representation is decided on a regional basis, with twelve seats for Africa, ten for Europe, nine each for Asia and for Latin America (including the Caribbean), six for the Near East, two for North America and one for the South West Pacific. The Council is the decision making body of the FAO. It has the final say on policies and the budget and can make recommendations. Jacques Diouf, the Director General, was re-elected to a second six-year term in November 1999.

The FAO has eight committees:

- Programme Committee
- Committee on Finance
- Committee on Constitutional and legal matters
- Committee on commodity problems
- Fisheries
- Forestry
- Agriculture
- World Food Security

**Food and Agriculture Organization**
Via delle Terme di Caracalla, 00100 Rome, Italy
Web site: www.fao.org

## INTERNATIONAL CIVIL AVIATION ORGANIZATION

The ICAO was established in 1947 and in 1999 had 185 member states. It is a specialised UN agency linked to the Economic and Social Commission. The Organization sets standards and draws up regulations to ensure the safety of air transport. The ICAO has worked to speed up customs and immigration for passengers and has made contributions in the areas of aircraft design, air traffic control and rescue services. More recently, it has begun work on legislation to combat air rage.

The Assembly, composed of representatives from all member states, meets every third year to agree on policies and budget. Thirty-three people elected by the Assembly make up the Council which in turn appoints the Secretary General to the ICAO Secretariat. Council members are drawn firstly from those countries which are considered important in air transport terms, then from those countries which contribute most to the provision of air navigation facilities and finally from the remaining countries.

The ICAO has regional offices in Bangkok, Cairo, Dakar, Lima, Mexico City, Nairobi and Paris. Altogether, it employs 550 in Montreal and 250 in the regional offices. The Secretary General is Renato Cláudio Costa Pereira. The languages of the ICAO are the six official UN languages: Arabic, Chinese, English, French, Russian and Spanish. There are 23 staff interpreters who also work as translators. Freelance interpreters are employed for additional meetings and when a number of bodies are meeting simultaneously at a Conference.

---

**International Civil Aviation Organization**
1000 Sherbrooke Street West, Montreal, Quebec H3A 2R2, Canada
Web site: www.icao.int

---

## INTERNATIONAL FUND FOR AGRICULTURAL DEVELOPMENT

At the 1974 World Food Conference in Rome a decision was made to set up a fund to help the poorest people in developing countries. The IFAD, founded in 1977, is an international financial institution that works with governments, banks and non-governmental organizations. Its loans are repayable over forty years, with a ten-year grace period and a service charge of 0.75% per annum. Its first priorities were farmers who did not own any land and rural women. The IFAD targets communities rather than individuals. The basic tenet is that if more food is produced, more people are employed and the population will be better fed.

Each member country appoints a Governor and an Alternate Governor to the Governing Council, which meets each year and elects the President. The Executive Board is made up of 18 members and the same number of alternate members. The Board oversees the approval of loans and grants. The President is Fawzi Hamad Al-Sultan.

In 1999, IFAD had 160 members made up of 22 industrialised aid contributors, 12 petroleum exporting aid contributors and 126 aid recipients.

The working languages of IFAD are Arabic, English, French and Spanish. IFAD does not employ any staff interpreters but it does employ 170 freelance interpreters who are expected to have knowledge of at least three and preferably all four of the working languages. IFAD has had some difficulty in finding interpreters with knowledge of Arabic. Interpreting is provided at all official meetings and at the six or seven international conferences that IFAD organizes each year.

**International Fund for Agricultural Development**
Via del Serafico, 107, 00142 Rome, Italy
Web site: www.ifad.org

## INTERNATIONAL LABOUR ORGANIZATION

Founded in 1919, the International Labour Organization (ILO) became the first UN specialised agency in 1946. It had 174 members in 1999. The ILO sets minimum standards. It draws up conventions and recommendations. It promotes human rights for all working people and has initiated projects to combat child labour in eleven developing countries.

The International Labour Conference meets each year in June in Geneva to approve the budget, debate issues and adopt new labour standards. One of the unique aspects of the ILO is the way in which it brings together governments, employers and employees. For example, in the case of the International Labour Conference, each country which is a member of the ILO is represented by two government delegates, one employer and one employee and all delegates have equal status.

The Governing Body is elected every three years. It has 56 titular members and 66 deputy members. The titular members consist of 28 Government members, 14 employer members and 14 worker members. Brazil, China, France, Germany, India, Italy, Japan, the Russian Federation, the United Kingdom and the United States permanently hold ten of the 28 government seats. The 66 deputy members are made up of 28 Government members, 19 employers and 19 workers. The Governing Body meets three times a year and functions as the executive body of the ILO. The Governing Body elects the Director General of the Organization. Juan Somavía is the director general.

The Governing Body has ten committees:

- Committee on Freedom of Association
- Programme, Financial and Administrative Committee
- Building Subcommittee
- Committee on Legal Issues and International Labour Standards
- Subcommittee on Multinational Enterprises

- Working Party on Policy regarding the revision of standards
- Committee on Employment and Social Policy
- Committee on Sectoral and Technical Meetings and Related Issues
- Committee on Technical Cooperation
- Working Party on the Social Dimensions of the Liberalization of International Trade

The ILO budget for 1997–1999 was US$481 million made up of contributions from member countries.

ILOTERM is a searchable referral system in English, French, German and Spanish of terms to do with the social and labour spheres. The Terminology and Reference Unit of the Official Documentation Branch manages the system which is available at ilis.ilo.org/ilis/ilisterm/ilin-trte.html

---

**International Labour Organization**
4, Route des Morillons, CH-1211 Geneva 22, Switzerland
Web site: www.ilo.org

---

## INTERNATIONAL MARITIME ORGANIZATION

With a staff of 300, the IMO is the smallest of the UN agencies. It has 156 member states and two associate members (Hong Kong and Macau). The Organization is responsible for improving marine safety and preventing pollution from ships. It works on developing international regulations and maritime legislation.

The IMO governing body is the Assembly, which meets every second year. The Assembly elects a 32 member Council that acts as governing body between Assembly sessions. William A. O'Neil, the Secretary General, has been appointed to three four-year terms since 1990.

The IMO has an interesting system for sharing its costs. The countries with the biggest merchant ship fleets pay the biggest share. Panama pays 15% and Liberia pays 10%.

---

**International Maritime Organization**
4 Albert Embankment, London SE1 7SR, United Kingdom
Web site: www.imo.org

---

## INTERNATIONAL MONETARY FUND

The IMF was established at the Bretton Woods Conference in July 1944 and founded in the following year. It is often referred to as one of the Bretton Woods Institutions. It did not come into operation until 1947. It had 182 member states in 1999 and employed 2,300 people from 122 countries. It has offices in Geneva, Paris, Tokyo, and a United Nations Fund Office in New York.

The IMF oversees the international monetary system. It is in favour of currency convertibility and exchange stability. It provides three to five year term loans to any member country that is experiencing problems with the balance of payments. It uses contributions, known as quota subscriptions, from member states to finance loans. One quarter of the quota subscription is paid in gold or a convertible currency such as the American dollar. This amount is at a country's immediate disposal if it runs into difficulties. The remaining three-quarters of the quota subscription can be paid in local currency, but most borrowing countries prefer to borrow major currencies. If a country borrows in US dollars, the repayments go to the United States. The interest rate will be just under commercial banking rates. The more a country pays in, the more it can borrow and the more votes it has. The United States contributes 18% of quota subscriptions and as a result has 18% of votes.

Members must abide by IMF rules. The IMF carries out annual checks in member countries to assess their economic position. Reports are submitted to the Executive Board. The IMF can and does impose economic conditions before agreeing to make a loan. Many commentators believe that IMF conditions are too stringent and as a result education and health services suffer in order to finance paying off debts. The IMF argues that it does not decide where spending cuts are to take place.

The IMF has given very large loans to help Indonesia and Russia cope with their financial crises. The IMF provides emergency assistance to countries that suffer natural disasters and in post conflict situations. It has also provided technical assistance to the countries of Eastern Europe and Russia and more recently in Africa.

The **Enhanced Structural Adjustment Facility** (ESAF) is targeted at 80 low-income member countries. Under this system, countries can borrow up to a maximum of 140% of their Fund quota. In certain cases the maximum amount can be 185% of the quota. The interest rate is 0.5% per annum.

The Ministers of Finance of the member countries make up the Board of Governors, which is the supreme authority of the IMF. The Executive Board consists of 24 members, 8 of whom are from China, France Germany, Japan, Russia, Saudi Arabia, the UK and the US. The remaining 16 represent groupings of other countries. Horst Köhler of Germany and former President of the European Bank for Reconstruction and Development was appointed Managing Director in March 2000. The Managing Director is usually European. An Interim Committee advises the Board of Governors.

The IMF employs 15 interpreter-translators and hundreds of freelance interpreters around the world. English is the official language of the Fund but interpreting is provided for Arabic, French, Russian and Spanish and to a lesser extent for Chinese, German, Portuguese and Eastern European languages.

**International Monetary Fund**
700 19th Street, NW, Washington, DC 20431, USA
Web site: www.imf.org

## INTERNATIONAL TELECOMMUNICATIONS UNION

The ITU has 187 members. It is concerned with the allocation of frequencies and the positions of geostationary satellites. It aims to ensure
that member states agree on the use and development of television, radio,
telephone and space communications. The ITU organizes international
telecommunications conferences and exhibitions. For example, the World
Radiocommunication Conference is held every two years. The
Telecommunications Standardisation Conference is held every four years.

The Plenipotentiary Conference meets every four years. It is concerned
with radio frequencies, the standardisation of telephone equipment and
assisting developing countries to improve their telecommunications. The
Secretary General is Yoshio Utsumi.

A council carries out the work of the ITU in accordance with the decisions of the Plenipotentiary Conference.

The Union operates a two-year budgetary system. In 1998–1999 the
budget was over 330 million Swiss Francs. Member states can choose the
scale of contribution that they wish to make to the organization. There
are three sectors within the Union. These are telecommunication standardisation, radio communications and development.

The ITU does not employ any staff interpreters but it does employ
between 500 and 600 freelance interpreters annually. The six official UN
languages are used for large meetings such as those of the Council and
at world conferences. The three ITU working languages, English, French
and Spanish, are used for smaller meetings.

The ITU Telecommunication Terminology Database, also known as
TERMITE, and containing all terms from ITU printed glossaries since
1980 is available online in English, French, Russian and Spanish at
www.itu.int/search/wais/Termite/index.html

**International Telecommunications Union**
Place des Nations, 1211 Geneva 20, Switzerland
Web site: www.itu.ch

## UNITED NATIONS EDUCATIONAL SCIENTIFIC AND CULTURAL ORGANIZATION

UNESCO was founded in 1946 to encourage cooperation among its 188
members in the areas of education, science and culture. There are 188

members and five associate members: Aruba, British Virgin Islands, Cayman Islands, Macau and Netherlands Antilles.

The United States withdrew from UNESCO in 1984 and the United Kingdom withdrew in the following year. Singapore also withdrew. Among other things, they were concerned that a large proportion of the UNESCO budget was being spent on administration in Paris rather than on education, science and culture around the world. At the time, the UK and the US contributed almost a third of UNESCO's budget. The United Kingdom rejoined in July 1997.

The regular budget for the two years 2000–2001 amounted to US$544 million. However, in 1997 for example, UNESCO also has extrabudgetary resources of a further US$275 million from other UN agencies (UNDP, UNEP, UNFPA, UNICEF and WFP), from special accounts financed by member states and from funds in trust which are donated by countries for use in other countries.

The General Conference is the supreme governing body and meets every two years. Each country has one vote. The Conference approves the programme and the budget. The Executive Board consists of 58 representatives of member states and meets twice a year. It recommends a candidate for the six-year post of Director General. The recommendation must be approved by the General Conference. The Executive Board prepares the work of the General Conference. There are over 2,000 staff at the Secretariat in Paris and a further 500 people work in field offices around the world. The majority of member states have permanent delegations to UNESCO. The Organization has regular contact with a large number of non-governmental and intergovernmental organizations.

The Director General, Koichiro Matsuura, was appointed to a six-year term in November 1999.

The Interpretation Division at UNESCO is made up of a small group of staff interpreters plus a large number of freelance interpreters. Most interpreters begin employment as freelancers. UNESCO interpreters must have three of the UN official languages including English and French. As UNESCO does not provide any training, interpreters should have attended a recognised interpreting school. Most bilingual meetings are either in English and French or in English and Spanish. Other combinations may also occur, sometimes in non-official UN languages. Meetings are held either in Paris or in member states. In both cases local interpreters are recruited. According to its Web site, UNESCO 'welcomes inquiries' from interpreters.

---

**UNESCO**
7, Place de Fontenoy, 75352 Paris, 07 SP, France
Web site: www.unesco.org

This Web site includes articles by David Fox, Ingrid Kurz and Ruth A. Roland on the history of interpreting at www.unesco.org/int/cldinfen.html

## UNITED NATIONS INDUSTRIAL DEVELOPMENT ORGANIZATION

The Committee for Industrial Development was established in 1961 to help developing countries to build up industry and thereby strengthen their economies. In 1966 the United Nations Industrial Development Organization or UNIDO was established by the United Nations General Assembly to replace the Committee. In 1985 UNIDO became a UN specialised agency. The development of new industry was a very worthy aim in the 1960s but as time went by other issues such as the environment gained importance. As a result, UNIDO went through a period of uncertainty as to what exactly its role should be. The United States and Australia withdrew from UNIDO in 1996. The following year the organization developed its 'Business Plan for the Future Role and Functions of UNIDO'. This highlighted the importance of three core features: sound environment, competitive economy and productive employment.

By 1999 UNIDO had 168 members and employed 750 staff. UNIDO decided to concentrate on the world's poorest countries, particularly in Africa. It also helps Eastern European countries to reduce industrial pollution levels.

The biennial budget for the years 1998 and 1999 was US$129.5 million made up of assessed contributions from member states. Japan contributed 21.8%, Germany 12.6%, France 8.9%, Italy and the United Kingdom 7.3% each. UNIDO earns a further US$27.4 million from the projects which it implements. Member states also make voluntary contributions to help fund technical cooperation.

The General Conference, governing body of the organization, meets every second year and appoints the Director General. Carlos Alfredo Magariños is the present Director General. The 53 member Industrial Development Board ensures that the organization adheres to the budget and work programme prepared by the 27 member Programme and Budget Committee. UNIDO is based in Vienna and has offices in New York and Geneva as well as a number of field offices around the world.

The United Nations Office in Vienna covers UNIDO's interpreting needs.

---

**UNIDO**

PO Box 300, Vienna International Centre, A-1400 Vienna, Austria
Web site: www.unido.org

---

## UNIVERSAL POSTAL UNION

The Universal Postal Union (UPU) was founded in 1874 and became a specialised UN agency in 1948. There are 189 member countries. The UPU fixes international postal rates. According to the UPU Web site, over 6 million people work in the postal services in 700,000 post offices around the world. They handle 430 billion letters and parcels in their own countries plus a further 10 billion in the international service.

The Universal Postal Congress meets every five years and is the supreme authority. Thomas Leavey is the director general. The Council of Administration meets each year in Bern and consists of a Chairman and forty member countries. A further forty member countries are elected to the Postal Operations Council which meets each year. There is an International Bureau that is basically the Secretariat and uses English as a second working language along with French. The total number of staff employed by the UPU is 175. The UPU budget in 2000 was 35.7 million Swiss francs. Member states contribute under a contribution class system.

French is the official language of the UPU. The other working languages are English, Russian and Spanish. Interpretation is provided at annual and five yearly meetings. Interpretation is also provided at selected meetings for Arabic, Chinese, German, Japanese and Portuguese. Interpreters are employed on a freelance basis at meetings of the Congress and Councils. They are recruited by the head interpreter or via member countries in the case of Chinese, Japanese and Russian.

---

**Universal Postal Union**
Head Interpreter, 16 Chemin des Erables, CH-1213 Petit-Lancy, Switzerland
Web site: www.upu.int

---

## WORLD BANK

The World Bank is made up of the following entities:

- International Bank for Reconstruction and Development (IBRD)
- International Development Association (IDA)
- International Finance Corporation (IFC)
- Multilateral Investment Guarantee Agency (MIGA)
- International Centre for the Settlement of Investment Disputes (ICSID)

The World Bank is often referred to as one of the Bretton Woods Institutions because the IBRD and the International Monetary Fund were established at the Monetary and Financial Conference held in Bretton Woods, New Hampshire, in 1944. The original purpose of the IBRD was to help reconstruct Europe after the Second World War.

Once the task of reconstructing Europe was accomplished the World Bank began to concentrate its energies on the developing countries throughout the world. At first it concentrated on electricity and transport. In more recent times it has promoted agriculture, small businesses and urban development. The World Bank has drawn up Comprehensive

Development Frameworks with developing countries. These are long term plans that are backed by governments, the private sector and the citizens of a country.

The World Bank borrows money on the international bond market to finance loans for projects in developing countries. Each year the World Bank lends almost US$30 billion, making it the largest source of development assistance in the world.

The Board of Executive Directors meets twice a week in Washington to decide on policies and to approve loans. There are 24 executive directors, five of whom represent France, Germany, Japan, the United Kingdom and the United States because these are the largest shareholders in the bank. The remaining 19 executive directors represent either their own country or a group of countries.

James D. Wolfensohn is the President. As the United States is the largest shareholder in the World Bank, the President is always an American. The President serves a five-year term.

The **International Bank for Reconstruction and Development** sells AAA rated bonds on the international capital markets and uses the money thus raised to provide loans to middle income countries and to poor but creditworthy countries. The term of the loans is between 15 and 20 years. When countries join the IBRD they pay in some money to purchase shares in the Bank. The more capital a country can subscribe to the Bank, the greater its voting power. About three-quarters of World Bank lending is through the IBRD.

The **International Development Association** (IDA), established in 1960, makes long term interest free loans to the governments of the poorest developing nations. Otherwise, these countries would not be able to borrow money anywhere. Repayment is spread over 35 to 40 years. Borrowers pay a 1% fee to cover administrative costs. The funds for these loans are provided by about 40 richer member states. One quarter of World Bank lending is through the IDA. The IBRD and the IDA target different categories of countries in financial terms.

The **International Finance Corporation** (IFC), an affiliate of the World Bank, encourages private enterprises in developing countries.

If a foreign investor is interested in investing in a developing country, the **Multilateral Investment Guarantee Agency** (MIGA) may guarantee the investor against loss but not against business risks. MIGA also provides information to potential foreign investors. MIGA has its own Council of Governors.

The **International Centre for Settlement of Investment Disputes** (ICSID) intervenes in the case of disputes between countries and foreign investors. ICSID was established in 1966 in accordance with the Convention on the Settlement of Investment Disputes between States and Nationals of Other States. The members are those states that have ratified the Convention. The Centre has an Administrative Council and a Secretariat. The World Bank provides funding for the Secretariat. The President of the World Bank is the Chairman of the Administrative Council.

The Boards of Governors of the World Bank and the International Monetary Fund meet up once a year. Joint annual meetings are also held. Total attendance at these meetings is close on 10,000. In September 2000 the meeting was held in Prague in the Czech Republic amid protests similar to those which seriously disrupted the World Trade Organization Millennium Round meeting in Seattle in December 1999. The Prague protests focused on poverty, debt and inequality in the Third World.

The World Bank has 182 member countries, employs 7,000 people and has 40 offices around the world. The majority of the staff are based in Washington. Because the World Bank is concerned with development its staff is not just composed of economists but also of engineers, lawyers, statisticians, experts in telecommunications, rural development and health care.

**World Bank**
1818 H Street, NW, Washington, DC 20433, USA
Web site: www.worldbank.org

## WORLD HEALTH ORGANIZATION

Founded in 1948, the World Health Organization (WHO) has 191 member states. It collaborates with 160 non-governmental organizations. WHO was very involved in the successful campaign to eradicate small-pox – this was achieved in 1977. Nowadays its mission is concerned with basic issues such as infant and maternal mortality, health care and childhood diseases, polio, tuberculosis, as well as AIDS and illnesses caused by smoking.

WHO's regular budget for the two years 1998 and 1999 reached US$842 million. This was made up of assessed contributions from member states and associate members. However, voluntary funding for the two years at an estimated US$956 million exceeded the regular budget considerably.

The Pan American Health Organization (PAHO) is a section of the World Health Organization based in the Americas.

The World Health Assembly, which meets every May in Geneva, approves the annual budget and decides on policies. The Executive Board, made up of 32 health professionals, meets in January and May. The Board ensures that the programme decided on by the Assembly is carried out. The Secretariat in Geneva and in six regional offices employs 3,800 staff. The Director General, Dr Gro Harlem Brundtland, is over the Secretariat. She took up her five year appointment in July 1998.

**World Health Organization**
20, Avenue Appia, 1211 Geneva 27, Switzerland
Web site: www.who.int

This Web site includes a section titled 'Health-related terminology in Cyberspace'. The terminology is in the form of medical dictionaries and glossaries on topics from AIDS to biotechnology to pharmaceuticals to tropical diseases at: www.who.int/terminology/ter/dicfair/htm

## WORLD INTELLECTUAL PROPERTY ORGANIZATION

The roots of the World Intellectual Property Organization (WIPO) date back to the International Union for the Protection of Industrial Property, founded in 1883. WIPO itself was founded in 1967.

In the year 2000 WIPO had 175 member states. Intellectual property includes inventions, trademarks, industrial designs as well as copyright on literature, music, art, photography and film. WIPO's brief covers the promotion and protection of intellectual property around the world and the administration of 21 treaties, 15 on industrial property and 6 on copyright. The counterfeiting of goods has become a widespread problem with imitations becoming very difficult to distinguish from *bona fide* goods. Examples include sports clothes, videocassettes and perfumes. WIPO has also been involved in researching the problem of Internet domain names and cybersquatting where individuals use established company trademarks on the Internet. It is often cheaper for a company to buy back its rights to the trademark than to go to court.

The Secretariat comprises 760 staff from 83 countries. There is a Conference and a Coordination Committee. WIPO's earnings from its registration systems make the organization 85% self-financing. The budget for the biennium 2000–2001 was 410 million Swiss francs.

The Director General is Dr. Kamil Idris.

WIPO also operates an Arbitration and Mediation Centre for settling disputes to do with intellectual property. Arbitration and mediation can be carried out in any country, any language, and under any law chosen by the parties to the dispute.

WIPO does not employ any staff interpreters. Freelance interpreters are employed for conferences.

**World Intellectual Property Organization**
34 Chemin des Colombettes, 1211 Geneva 20, Switzerland
Web site: www.wipo.int

## WORLD METEOROLOGICAL ORGANIZATION

The World Meteorological Organization (WMO) had 185 members in June 1996 including Hong Kong, New Caledonia, the Netherlands Antilles, French Polynesia and the British Caribbean Territories. Originally formed in 1950, the WMO became a specialised UN agency in 1951. It coordinates the work of scientists in collecting data in order to provide information on climate. The Organization is also concerned with water resource assessment and environmental problems such as air and water pollution.

The World Meteorological Congress is the governing body of the WMO. It meets every four years to decide on policies and set the programme and budget. The Executive Council is made up of 36 members, including the President and three Vice Presidents, and meets each year. The Secretary General is Prof. G.O.P. Obasi. There are six regional associations, which meet every four years to coordinate work on a regional basis.

The WMO has eight technical commissions that meet every four years and concentrate on different aspects of meteorology. These are aeronautical meteorology, agricultural meteorology, atmospheric sciences, basic systems, climatology, hydrology, instruments and methods of observation and marine meteorology.

**World Meteorological Organization**
Case Postale No. 2300, Geneva, Switzerland
Web site: www.wmo.ch

## Autonomous Organizations

### INTERNATIONAL ATOMIC ENERGY AGENCY

The IAEA was founded in 1957. At the end of 1999 it employed over 2,200 staff and there were 130 member states. In 2000, Tajikistan and Azerbaijan applied for membership. The Agency promotes the safe application of nuclear technology. It is involved in inspecting nuclear programmes to ensure that they are destined for peaceful use only. It has drawn up standards for the transport of radioactive material and for its management. In April 2000 a total of 16 states had ratified the Joint Convention for the safety of radioactive waste management and spent fuel management.

The Agency is also involved in an amazing variety of projects around the world. Examples include the eradication of the tsetse fly in Zanzibar, irradiation, breeding more productive plants and managing freshwater resources. In the case of the tsetse fly, gamma radiation was used to sterilise the males. Ionising energy is used to irradiate food. Seeds are treated with bacteria so that they become self-fertilising. Isotope hydrology can provide information on water reserves and on groundwater. The IAEA works closely with other UN organizations such as the World Health Organization and the International Fund for Agricultural Development.

All member states are represented at the General Conference, which meets once a year. The Board of Governors meets five times a year. The

Board of Governors appoints thirteen of its 35 members and the General Conference elects 22. The Board of Governors organizes the programme and budget of the IAEA. It also appoints the Director General to a four-year term subject to the approval of the General Conference, which also approves the programme and budget formulated by the Board of Governors. The Director General is Mohamed ElBaradei. There are also six deputy Director Generals who head the departments of Nuclear Science and Applications, Administration, Nuclear Energy, Technical Cooperation, Nuclear Safety and Safeguards. In 1999 the regular budget totalled US$224 million and extrabudgetary contributions amounted to US$17.5 million.

Interpreting is provided by the United Nations Office in Vienna at the Board of Governors, General Conference and at technical meetings.

---

**International Atomic Energy Agency**
PO Box 100, Vienna International Centre, A-1400 Vienna, Austria
Web site: www.iaea.org/worldatom/

---

## WORLD TOURISM ORGANIZATION

The World Tourism Organization (WTO) is an intergovernmental body entrusted by the United Nations with the task of developing tourism around the world. The membership is made up of 138 countries and territories. The staff in Madrid is quite small consisting of 80 people. There are also 350 affiliates including airlines, hotel groups and tour operators. Tourism is the fastest growing industry in the world. According to the WToO, there were 594 million arrivals in 1996. This number is expected to rise to 700 million in the year 2000 and one billion in 2010.

The Executive Council consists of a Chairman, two Vice Chairmen and representatives from 27 member countries, a representative from the Affiliate Members and a representative from the Associate Members (Aruba, Macau, Madeira, Netherlands Antilles and the Flemish community in Belgium).

---

**World Tourism Organization**
Capitán Haya, 42, 28020 Madrid, Spain
Web site: www.world-tourism.org

---

# Other

## UNAIDS

UNAIDS or the Joint UN Programme on HIV/AIDS was founded because it was felt that the task of tackling AIDS was too big for the World Health Organization alone. The programme includes the heads of the Children's Fund, UN Development Programme, UNESCO, UN Population Fund, the World Health Organization, UNDCP and the World Bank. UNAIDS has an annual budget of US$60 million which is made up of voluntary contributions from the United States government (US$15 million) and the governments of the Netherlands, United Kingdom, Sweden, Norway, Denmark, China, South Africa and Thailand. ECOSOC organizes the distribution of 22 seats on the Programme Coordinating Board among member states. The seven UN organizations mentioned above are also represented on the Board. Unusually, the Board includes five representatives of non-governmental organizations. UNAIDS draws up the UN policy on HIV/AIDS and provides technical support in developing countries. The Secretariat is in Geneva and the staff comprises 129 professionals. Dr. Peter Piot was appointed executive director in December 1994.

**UNAIDS**
20 avenue Appia, CH-1211 Geneva 27, Switzerland
Web site: www.unaids.org

# 9 Other International Organizations

This chapter concentrates on those international and regional organizations (apart from the European Union and the United Nations) where interpreting is provided.

A number of organizations have elected to use English for all meetings. For example, OPEC, the Organization of Petroleum Exporting Countries, made up of eleven member countries drawn from the Middle East, Africa, Asia and South America, uses English for all meetings. The International Air Transport Association (IATA) and the Association of South East Asian Nations (ASEAN) use English exclusively.

For readers interested in finding out about international organizations not covered in this volume, the *CIA World Factbook* is a very useful source. It gives a one-line summary of the activities of each organization, its address and a full list of member states. It also provides a country listing with basic facts and figures about geography, people, economy, communications, transport, military and transnational issues and a full list of all international organizations that each country belongs to.

*CIA World Factbook (2000)*
Web site: www.odci.gov/cia/publications/factbook/

## ACP

The ACP group is made up of 71 countries in Africa, the Caribbean and the Pacific, all of which are former European colonies. About 80 staff work in the Secretariat in Brussels. There is a joint ACP-EU Assembly that consists of one member from each ACP country and 71 members of the European Parliament. The Joint Assembly meets twice a year in plenary session for one week. The Assembly elects two co-presidents who along with 24 elected Vice Presidents make up the Bureau of the Joint Assembly. The Bureau meets several times a year.

The principal focus of ACP and the Joint Assembly is the Lomé Convention. The EU signed the Lomé Convention with the 71 African, Caribbean and Pacific States (ACP) in 1975, 1979, 1984, 1989, 1995 and 2000. The Convention covers financial aid to these countries and trade agreements. In January 2000 a development aid package was agreed whereby the ninth European Development Fund was established. The European Union provided a development aid package of 13.5 billion euros over five years. A European Investment Bank loan of 1.7 billion euros was included in the package. Under the terms of the agreement the EU gives tariff free access to 95% of ACP exports in exchange for more limited access to ACP markets. In the long term, the aim is to establish free trade zones between the EU and regions within the ACP zone.

Jean-Robert Goulongana, the Secretary General, was selected by the ACP Council of Ministers and took up his appointment on the 1st March 2000.

The official languages of the ACP countries are English, French and Portuguese. Eight staff interpreters work at ACP. There are no freelance interpreters. Both the EU and ACP provide interpreters at the joint ACP-EU Assembly.

*Members:* Angola, Antigua and Barbuda, Bahamas, Barbados, Belize, Benin, Botswana, Burkina Faso, Burundi, Cameroon, Cape Verde, Central African Republic, Chad, Comores, Congo, Democratic Republic of the Congo, Djibouti, Dominica, Dominican Republic, Eritrea, Ethiopia, Equatorial Guinea, Fiji, Gabon, The Gambia, Ghana, Grenada, Guinea, Guinea-Bissau, Guyana, Haiti, Jamaica, Kenya, Kiribati, Lesotho, Liberia, Madagascar, Malawi, Mali, Mauritania, Mauritius, Mozambique, Namibia, Niger, Nigeria, Papua New Guinea, Rwanda, Sao Tome and Principe, Senegal, Seychelles, Sierra Leone, Solomon Islands, Somalia, South Africa, St Kitts and Nevis, St Lucia, St Vincent and the Grenadines, Sudan, Suriname, Swaziland, Tanzania, Togo, Tonga, Trinidad and Tobago, Tuvalu, Uganda, Vanuatu, Western Samoa, Zambia and Zimbabwe.

---

**ACP**
451 avenue Georges Henri, 1200 Brussels, Belgium
Web site: www.acpsec.org

---

## AFRICAN DEVELOPMENT BANK

The African Development Bank (ADB) was established in 1964 by the Organization of African Unity. It now includes the original Development Bank plus the African Development Fund and the Nigeria Trust Fund. The original start-up capital was 250 million dollars. The capital at the end of the nineties was 33 billion dollars. There are 53 African and 24 other shareholders.

The Bank provides low cost loans to member countries for development purposes. It also offers technical assistance to projects. For example, the Bank gave Burkina Faso a fifty-year loan with a ten-year grace period in order to build twenty-five primary schools, two high schools and one hundred women's literacy centres. Loans have been made to improve water supplies, to build roads and to diversify agriculture.

The Board of Governors includes ministerial representatives from each member country. The Executive Council is made up of nine members. The Board of Directors, which is responsible for the day to day running of the bank, includes eighteen executive directors, twelve of whom represent regional members and six non-regional member states. The President, Omar Kabbaj, was elected in 1995 and is the Chief Executive of the Bank. There are three vice-presidencies: planning and finance, corporate management and operations.

The working languages of the Bank are English and French. Arabic is also used at the annual meeting of the Board of Governors. The total number of personnel employed by the bank is just over one thousand. Of these 10 are permanently employed interpreters. A small number of freelance interpreters are also employed for conferences. Interpreting vacancies are advertised in *Time, The Economist, Jeune Afrique* and local newspapers.

*Members:* Algeria, Angola, Benin, Botswana, Burkina-Faso, Burundi, Cameroon, Cape Verde, Central African Republic, Chad, Comoros, Congo, Democratic Republic of the Congo, Côte d'Ivoire, Djibouti, Egypt, Equatorial Guinea, Eritrea, Ethiopia, Gabon, The Gambia, Ghana, Republic of Guinea, Guinea-Bissau, Kenya, Lesotho, Liberia, Libyan Arab Jamahiriya, Madagascar, Malawi, Mali, Mauritania, Mauritius, Morocco, Peoples' Republic of Mozambique, Namibia, Niger, Nigeria, Rwanda, Sao Tome and Principe, Senegal, Seychelles, Sierra Leone, Somalia, South Africa, Sudan, Swaziland, Tanzania, Togo, Tunisia, Uganda, Zambia, Zimbabwe.

*Non-Regional Member Countries:* Argentina, Austria, Belgium, Brazil, Canada, China, Denmark, Finland, France, Germany, India, Italy, Japan, Korea, Kuwait, Netherlands, Norway, Portugal, Saudi Arabia, Spain, Sweden, Switzerland, United Kingdom, United States of America.

---

**African Development Bank**
Human Resources Management Department, 01 BP 1387, Abidjan, Côte d'Ivoire
Web site: www.afdb.org

---

## ASIAN DEVELOPMENT BANK

The Asian Development Bank was founded by 31 member governments in 1966 and in early 2000 had expanded considerably to 58 members – 42 in Asia and 16 outside Asia. In 1999 the Bank lent US$5 billion, of which 40% targeted poverty reduction. Japan and the United States are the two largest shareholders. The Bank draws on its reserves and borrows money in order to offer loans to promote higher levels of economic development. It also uses members' contributions and repayments from former loans to provide loans at very favourable rates to developing member countries. The Bank provides technical assistance to projects in member countries.

The aims of the Bank are as follows:

- promote economic growth
- reduce poverty
- support human development
- improve the status of women
- protect the environment

English is the official language of the Bank. Freelance interpreters cover interpreting needs. The total number of staff was just under 2,000 in 1998.

*Members:* Afghanistan, Australia, Azerbaijan, Bangladesh, Bhutan, Cambodia, People's Republic of China, Cook Islands, Fiji Islands, Hong Kong (China), India, Indonesia, Japan, Kazakhstan, Kiribati, Republic of Korea, Kyrgyzstan, Lao People's Democratic Republic, Malaysia, Maldives, Marshall Islands, Micronesia, Mongolia, Myanmar, Nauru, Nepal, New Zealand, Pakistan, Papua New Guinea, Philippines, Samoa, Singapore, Solomon Islands, Sri Lanka, Tajikistan, Taipei, Thailand, Tonga, Tuvalu, Uzbekistan, Vanuatu, Vietnam.

*Non regional members:* Austria, Belgium, Canada, Denmark, Finland, France, Germany, Italy, the Netherlands, Norway, Spain, Sweden, Switzerland, Turkey, United Kingdom, United States of America.

---

**Asian Development Bank**
PO Box 789, 0980 Manila, Philippines
Web site: www.adb.org

---

## CERN aka EUROPEAN ORGANIZATION FOR NUCLEAR RESEARCH aka EUROPEAN LABORATORY FOR PARTICLE PHYSICS

This organization is known by its French acronym, which stands for Centre européen de recherche nucléaire. Particle physics is about what matter is made of and what forces hold it together. CERN was founded in 1954. It is a very large organization with just under 3,000 staff. Over 6,000 scientists go to Geneva each year to use the state of the art laboratories at CERN. These scientists come from many countries, not just CERN member states. Scientists at CERN were involved in developing medical imaging and the World Wide Web, which they originally used to share information with other physicists around the world.

The Council is made up of two members from each member state, one from the world of science, the other a civil servant. There are two committees, a Finance Committee and a Scientific Policy Committee. The Director General is appointed for five years. In 2000 the director general was Luciano Maiani.

*Members:* Austria, Belgium, Czech Republic, Denmark, Finland, France, Germany, Greece, Hungary, Italy, Netherlands, Norway, Poland, Portugal, Slovak Republic, Spain, Sweden, Switzerland, United Kingdom.

*Observer states and organizations:* Israel, Japan, the Russian Federation, Turkey, United States of America, European Commission, UNESCO.

*Non member states (whose scientists may use CERN research facilities):* Algeria, Argentina, Armenia, Australia, Azerbaijan, Belarus, Brazil, Bulgaria, Canada, China, Croatia, Cyprus, Estonia, Georgia, Iceland, India, Iran, Ireland, Israel, Japan, Kazakhstan, Mexico, Morocco, Pakistan, Peru, Romania, Russia, Slovenia, South Africa, South Korea, Taiwan, Turkey, Ukraine, United States, Uzbekistan.

---

**CERN**
Geneva 23, CH-1211, Switzerland
Web site: public.web.cern.ch/Public

---

## EUROCONTROL

Eurocontrol, or the European Organization for the Safety of Air Navigation, was founded in 1960. There are 2,000 staff across Belgium, France, Germany, Luxembourg and the Netherlands. The Maastricht Upper Area Control Centre in Belgium handles over a million flights a year. Eurocontrol is involved in training Air Traffic Management personnel, operating a charges system and in improving and expanding air traffic control in Europe.

Eurocontrol has a General Assembly, which is made up of the relevant government Ministers from each member state. The Council, which supervises activities, is made up of Director Generals of Civil Aviation.

There are 27 member states and 19 languages within Eurocontrol. Interpreting can be provided for twelve languages. In 1997 interpreting was provided at 54 meetings. Of these, 32 were multilingual, covering twelve languages and 22 were bilingual (mainly English and French). This worked out as 1,739 interpreter days over the year. However, most of this work is done by freelance interpreters.

*Member states:* Austria, Belgium, Bulgaria, Croatia, Cyprus, Czech Republic, Denmark, France, Germany, Greece, Hungary, Ireland, Italy, Luxembourg, Malta, Monaco, the Netherlands, Norway, Portugal, Romania, Slovak Republic, Slovenia, Spain, Sweden, Switzerland, Turkey, United Kingdom.

---

**Eurocontrol**
rue de la Fusée, 96, B-1130 Brussels, Belgium
Web site: www.eurocontrol.be

---

## EUROPEAN FREE TRADE ASSOCIATION

The European Free Trade Association (EFTA) was founded in 1960. Originally quite a big organization, it now consists of Iceland, Liechtenstein, Norway and Switzerland. The former members of EFTA are Austria, Denmark, Portugal, Sweden and the United Kingdom. All five countries left the EFTA to join the European Union.

The Council is the governing body of EFTA and meets once a month. It is made up of the heads of permanent delegations to EFTA. Each country has one vote but decisions are usually reached by consensus.

In 1994 the European Economic Area came into effect. It consists of Iceland, Liechtenstein and Norway plus the 15 EU countries. Switzerland is not a member. The EEA council is made up of members of the EU and Iceland, Liechtenstein and Norway. The EFTA court exerts judicial control over the implementation of EEA rules and regulations. The EFTA Surveillance Court ensures that rules are observed.

The EEA Joint Committee meets once a month. Its members are representatives of the three EFTA countries that are members of the EEA, the European Commission and the 15 EU member states.

The EFTA has free trade agreements with Bulgaria, Czech Republic, Estonia, Hungary, Israel, Latvia, Lithuania, Morocco, PLO on behalf of the Palestinian Authority, Poland, Romania, Slovakia, Slovenia and Turkey.

EFTA is in the process of negotiating free trade agreements with Canada, Cyprus, Egypt, Jordan, Macedonia and Tunisia.

English is the working language of EFTA. There are no staff interpreters. Freelance interpreters are employed when the need arises. About 80 staff are employed at the three offices in Geneva, Brussels and Luxembourg.

---

**European Free Trade Association (EFTA)**
9–11 rue de Varembé, CH-1211 Geneva 20, Switzerland
Web site: www.efta.int

## EUROPEAN PATENT OFFICE

The European Patent Organization (EPO) was founded in 1973 with the objective of setting up a uniform patent system in Europe. The Organization consists of the Administrative Council, which is a legislative body, the European Patent Office (established in 1977) which is the executive body, and the contracting states.

The total number of staff at the different EPO centres in Munich, The Hague, Berlin and Vienna is about 5,000. Surprisingly for such a large organization, the European Patent Office is self-financing. Procedural fees cover its costs.

The working languages of the European Patent Office are English, French and German. Other languages such as Danish, Dutch, Italian, Japanese, Norwegian, Portuguese, Spanish, Swedish and Russian are used on occasion. About 130 interpreters are employed on a freelance basis. They are recruited by word of mouth. They all work into their mother tongue, which should be English, French or German. Ninety nine per cent of interpreting is simultaneous. Interpreting is provided at Oral Proceedings (oppositions and appeals), conferences, exhibitions and informal meetings with delegates from other national offices or organizations.

*Member Countries:* Austria, Belgium, Cyprus, Denmark, Finland, France, Germany, Greece, Ireland, Italy, Liechtenstein, Luxembourg, Monaco, Netherlands, Portugal, Spain, Sweden, Switzerland, United Kingdom.

*Extension countries (these are expected to become members):* Albania, Latvia, Lithuania, Macedonia, Romania and Slovenia.

---

**European Patent Office**
Language Service, Erhardstrasse 27, D-80298 Munich, Germany
Web site: www.european-patent-office.org

---

## EUROPEAN SPACE AGENCY

The European Space Agency (ESA) is the result of the 1973 amalgamation of the European Launcher Development Organization and the European Space Research Organization, both founded in 1962. Some programmes are mandatory while others are optional. All member states contribute to mandatory programmes. The amount contributed is based on national income. Member states can decide on their level of involvement in optional programmes. Along with the North American, Japanese and Russian Space Agencies, the European Space Agency is a partner in the International Space Station which is due to be completed in 2004.

Just under 300 staff are employed at ESA headquarters in Paris. A much larger number, 1,850, is involved in cooperative ventures with other space stations and in work on satellites, space technology and Ariane 5.

The working languages at the ESA are English, French and German. Freelance interpreters are recruited from a pool of interpreters. There is an occasional need for interpreters with Italian, Japanese and Russian.

*Members:* Austria, Belgium, Denmark, Finland, France, Germany, Ireland, Italy, Netherlands, Norway, Spain, Sweden, Switzerland and the United Kingdom. Canada is involved in some programmes.

**European Space Agency**
8–10 rue Mario Niki, 85738 Paris Cedex 15, France
Web site: www.esrin.esa.it

## INTELSAT

The International Telecommunications Satellite Organization or INTEL-SAT, a non-profit making cooperative, was founded in 1964. It had 141 member nations in 1999. Its nineteen satellites serve people in over 200 countries. INTELSAT customers include television and radio stations, airlines, banks and multinational manufacturers. There are over three hundred customers throughout the world. INTELSAT provided television coverage on such occasions as the Apollo moon landing in 1969 and the 1992 Barcelona Olympic Games.

**Intelsat**
3400 International Dr. NW, Washington DC 20008–3098, USA
Web site: www.intelsat.int

## INTER AMERICAN DEVELOPMENT BANK

The Inter-American Development Bank (IADB) was established in 1959 by the Organization of American States. Its purpose is to speed up economic and social development in Central and South America and in the Caribbean. In 1999 the bank was comprised of 46 nations including Canada and a number of European countries such as France and the United Kingdom. The Bank uses money contributed by member countries and borrows funds on the world's financial markets to lend money to the poorer countries of Latin America. In the early years of the bank's existence it concentrated on infrastructure, agriculture, industry and public health. More recently it has become involved in poverty reduction, modernisation and protection of the environment. The Bank's funds have increased from 294 million dollars in 1961 to 6.7 billion dollars in 1996.

The Board of Governors is made up of a representative, usually the Minister for Finance or the President of the Central Bank, from each member country. The Board of Executive Directors is responsible for the day to day operations of the Bank. The Inter-American Investment Corporation (IIC) is a separate 34-member affiliate of the Bank which finances small and medium sized private companies.

The total number of staff employed at the IADB is 1,800. There are three staff interpreters. Between 20 and 30 freelance interpreters are employed on a daily basis. The last open competition for interpreting posts was held in 1989. The official languages of the bank are English, French, Portuguese and Spanish. Some difficulty has been experienced in finding qualified interpreters with Portuguese. Interpreting into the four official languages is provided at annual or twice yearly meetings of the Board of Governors. Interpreting from the four official languages is provided into English and Spanish at daily meetings of the Board of Executive Directors and senior management.

The President of the IADB is Enrique V. Iglesias.

*Members:* Argentina, Austria, Bahamas, Barbados, Belgium, Belize, Bolivia, Brazil, Canada, Chile, Colombia, Costa Rica, Croatia, Denmark, Dominican Republic, Ecuador, El Salvador, Finland, France, Germany, Guatemala, Guyana, Haiti, Honduras, Israel, Italy, Jamaica, Japan, Mexico, Netherlands, Nicaragua, Norway, Panama, Paraguay, Peru, Portugal, Slovenia, Spain, Suriname, Sweden, Switzerland, Trinidad and Tobago, United Kingdom, United States of America, Uruguay, Venezuela.

---

**Inter American Development Bank**
1300 New York Avenue, NW, Washington, DC 20577, USA
Web site: www.iadb.org

---

## INTERNATIONAL AMATEUR ATHLETICS FEDERATION

Founded in 1912 the IAAF promotes athletics around the world and organizes competitions. Corporate sponsorship and the sale of television broadcasting rights have bolstered its budget. In 1999, the Federation had 210 affiliated federations. Each country has one vote. The Council is made up of 27 members: the President, four Vice Presidents, one Honorary Treasurer, one representative from each of six regions and fifteen individual members. Each member is elected by Congress to a four-year term. The Council is an administrative body that appoints the General Secretary and all delegates to IAAF competitions. It also submits a report and budget to Congress every two years. The Council has six committees and eight commissions.

The Congress consists of the Council, Honorary Members and a maximum of three delegates from each National Federation. Congress meets every two years during the World Championships. The Congress is the decision making body of the IAAF.

Over 40 full time professional staff are employed at the IAAF Headquarters in Monaco and its office in Rome.

---

**International Amateur Athletics Federation**
17 rue Princesse Florestine, BP 359, MC 98007 Monaco Cedex
Web site: www.iaaf.org

---

## INTERNATIONAL ELECTROTECHNICAL COMMISSION

The International Electrotechnical Commission (IEC) was founded in 1906 to draw up and publish standards for electrical, electronic and other such technologies. The work is carried out by some two hundred technical committees and subcommittees and by seven hundred working groups.

The IEC Council, which is made up of a general assembly of all the national committees that are IEC members, is the highest authority in the Commission. The Council Board is a decision-making body. There is also an Executive Committee. The IEC works closely with other organizations such as ISO and ITU. M.R. Fünfschilling was appointed to a three-year term as President in 1999.

English, French and Russian are the official languages of the IEC. Apart from the Council where English is the working language, discussions may be held in English and/or in French. The IEC annual general meeting is held at a different location each year. Four freelance interpreters are employed for one day each year at the Council meeting where simultaneous interpreting is provided for the French/English combination and for Russian/French/English.

*Members:* Australia, Austria, Belarus, Belgium, Brazil (suspended 1st October 1999), Bulgaria, Canada, China, Croatia, Czech Republic, Denmark, Egypt, Finland, France, Germany, Greece, Hungary, India, Indonesia, Ireland, Israel, Italy, Japan, Republic of Korea, Luxembourg, Malaysia, Mexico, Netherlands, New Zealand, Norway, Pakistan, Philippines, Poland, Portugal, Romania, Russian Federation, Saudi Arabia, Singapore, Slovakia, Slovenia, South Africa, Spain, Sweden, Switzerland, Thailand, Turkey, Ukraine, United Kingdom, United States of America, Yugoslavia.

*Associate members:* Bosnia and Herzegovina, Cyprus, Estonia, Iceland, Latvia, Lithuania, Malta, Tunisia.

*Pre-Associates:* Colombia, Costa Rica, Cuba, Eritrea, Kenya, Uruguay.
*Note:* pre-associate membership lasts for a five-year period after which these countries will become associate members.

**International Electrotechnical Commission**
3, rue de Varembé, CH-1211 Geneva 20, Switzerland
Web site: www.iec.ch

## THE RED CROSS MOVEMENT

The Red Cross Movement is made up of:

- The International Committee of the Red Cross
- The International Federation of the Red Cross and Red Crescent Societies
- The Red Cross and Red Crescent societies throughout the world

The Committee and the Federation have divided humanitarian work between them. The Committee deals with war situations while the Federation deals with natural disasters.

The International Committee of the Red Cross (ICRC) was founded in 1863 by Henry Dunant, a Swiss citizen. He was shocked when he saw soldiers dying on the battlefield in Solferino, Italy, with no one to treat them. The Committee is made up of 25 Swiss citizens and meets ten times a year. The ICRC deals with situations of armed conflict. The Central Tracing Agency helps reunite families separated by war. The ICRC is funded by voluntary contributions from states that have signed the Geneva Convention, the European Union, the Swiss public and the 175 national societies of the Red Cross and the Red Crescent. The Red Crescent Societies are based in the Muslim countries.

The International Federation of Red Cross and Red Crescent Societies was founded in 1919. The General Assembly of all national Red Cross and Red Crescent societies meets every two years. Each member society has one vote. The General Assembly elects the president and the Secretary General of the Federation. The members of the Executive Council are also elected by the General Assembly. The Secretariat employs 250 people from 50 different countries. The Federation coordinates international relief assistance in the case of natural and technological disasters.

The Council of Delegates is an assembly made up of representatives of the ICRC, the International Federation and the national societies. The Council meets every second year.

The International Conference of the Red Cross and Red Crescent i.e. the ICRC, the Federation, the 188 states that have signed the Geneva Convention and the national societies, meets every four years.

The Standing Commission of the Red Cross and Red Crescent Societies meets twice a year. There are nine members: five elected by the International Conference, the ICRC president and another ICRC representative and the Federation president and another Federation representative. The ICRC does not employ interpreters.

**International Committee of the Red Cross**
19 avenue de la Paix, CH 1202 Geneva, Switzerland
Web site: www.icrc.org

**International Federation of the Red Cross and Red Crescent Societies**
PO Box 372, CH-1211 Geneva 19, Switzerland
Web site: www.ifrc.org

## INTERNATIONAL OLYMPIC COMMITTEE

Founded in 1894, the Olympic movement is an international non-governmental, non-profit organization made up of the IOC, the International Sports Federations, the National Olympic Committees and the Organizing Committees of the Olympic Games along with national associations, clubs and athletes.

The IOC has 110 members and 24 honorary members. Retirement age is 80 years. The President is first elected by the members to eight years in office. After that he may be elected to four-year terms. The Session is the annual general assembly and is the supreme organ of the IOC. The Executive Board, which meets four or five times each year and proposes decisions, is made up of the IOC president, four Vice Presidents and six members elected by the Session. The Vice Presidents and six members serve a four-year term. There are 23 commissions on areas ranging from marketing to philately to radio and television. They meet in plenary session at least once a year.

The 1999 IOC budget was just under 40 million Swiss Francs. It is privately financed and does not receive public funding. Most of its budget comes from television rights to the Olympic Games. However, countries wishing to host the Olympic Games pay for the privilege.

The official languages of the IOC are English and French. There are no staff interpreters but freelance interpreters work at meetings all over the world. Examples of meetings include the Session, which is held every six months, once in Lausanne, and once in another country, the Executive Board and the Commissions mentioned above. The Session uses Arabic, English, French, German, Russian and Spanish.

The organization of interpreting for the Olympic Games is quite complex. About fifty consecutive interpreters from Sydney or nearby were hired for the 2000 Olympic Games. A further forty to fifty simultaneous interpreters were also required to work at the Main Press Centre, with some International Sports Federation Congresses, at IOC meetings and at press conferences. Simultaneous interpreters covered eleven languages: Arabic, English, French, German, Italian, Japanese, Korean, Mandarin, Portuguese, Russian and Spanish. These eleven languages were mainly for the more popular Olympic events such as athletics, aquatics and gymnastics. Interpreters were also to be provided for daily meetings of the IOC Medical Commission and the Coordinating

Committee. Most interpreters were accredited by the Australian National Accreditation Authority for Translators and Interpreters (NAATI).

---

**International Olympic Committee**
Château de Vidy, 1007 Lausanne, Switzerland
Web site: www.olympic.org

---

## INTERNATIONAL ORGANIZATION FOR MIGRATION

The International Organization for Migration (IOM) is an intergovernmental body originally established in 1951 as the Provisional Intergovernmental Committee for Movement of Migrants from Europe. During the fifties and sixties it concentrated on migration within Europe. For example, it was active in the resettlement of Hungarian refugees in 1956. In 1968 it helped resettle Czechoslovakian refugees from Austria. In the 1970s it spread its wings and was involved in helping over 30,000 Chileans move to fifty receiving countries and in helping Asians move out of Uganda. The IOM is also involved in moving people back into their own countries after some displacement. There are 71 member states and 47 observer states plus the Order of Malta. A number of international governmental and non-governmental organizations also have observer status at IOM meetings. There is a Council and an Executive Committee. Brunson Mc Kinley was elected Director General and took office in 1998.

The official languages are English, French and Spanish. There are no staff interpreters. Freelance interpreters are employed as the need arises.

*Members:* Albania, Angola, Argentina, Armenia, Australia, Austria, Bangladesh, Belgium, Bolivia, Bulgaria, Canada, Chile, Colombia, Costa Rica, Croatia, Cyprus, Czech Republic, Denmark, Dominican Republic, Ecuador, Egypt, El Salvador, Finland, France, Germany, Greece, Guatemala, Guinea-Bissau, Haiti, Honduras, Hungary, Israel, Italy, Japan, Jordan, Kenya, Latvia, Liberia, Lithuania, Luxembourg, Mali, Morocco, Netherlands, Nicaragua, Norway, Pakistan, Panama, Paraguay, Peru, Philippines, Poland, Portugal, Republic of Korea, Romania, Senegal, Slovakia, South Africa, Sri Lanka, Sudan, Sweden, Switzerland, Tajikistan, Tanzania, Thailand, Tunisia, Uganda, United States of America, Uruguay, Venezuela, Yemen, Zambia.

*Observers:* Afghanistan, Algeria, Belarus, Belize, Bosnia and Herzegovina, Brazil, Cambodia, Cape Verde, Congo, Democratic Republic of the Congo, Cuba, Estonia, Ethiopia, Georgia, Ghana, Guinea, Holy See, India, Indonesia, Iran, Ireland, Jamaica, Kazakhstan, Kyrgyzstan, Madagascar,

Malta, Mexico, Moldova, Mozambique, Namibia, New Zealand, Papua New Guinea, Russian Federation, Rwanda, San Marino, Sao Tome and Principe, Slovenia, Somalia, Spain, Turkey, Turkmenistan, Ukraine, United Kingdom, Vietnam, Yugoslavia, Zimbabwe.

**International Organization for Migration**
BP 71, CH-1211 Geneva 19, Switzerland
Web site: www.iom.int

## INTERNATIONAL ORGANIZATION FOR STANDARDISATION (ISO)

ISO is not an acronym; it is derived from the Greek word 'isos' meaning equal. The International Organization for Standardisation is known as ISO all around the world. The ISO 9000 quality assurance will be familiar to most readers. Established in 1947, ISO brings together 90 national standards bodies, 36 correspondent members and 9 subscriber members. There are also regional standards organizations in Africa, the Arab countries, the Commonwealth of Independent States, Europe, Latin America, Pacific Asia and South East Asia.

ISO has worked on establishing standards for all kinds of products. For example, it has established the ISO film speed code, it ensured that banking cards would work in ATM machines in all countries, it standardised paper sizes and it developed international symbols for car controls. To date ISO has established 12,000 international standards and these are reviewed every five years. In 1999, 1,493 technical meetings were held in 32 countries. There are 160 full time staff from 18 countries at the Central Secretariat in Geneva. ISONET is the ISO information network on the Internet. ISO has links with the International Telecommunications Unit, the International Electrotechnical Commission and the World Trade Organization. Member bodies contribute to the cost of running the Secretariat. The technical committees are organized separately. Their costs are covered by 35 member bodies, which provide them with administrative and technical resources. Decisions are reached by consensus. Standards are applied across the world and this in turn facilitates trade.

**International Organization for Standardisation**
1, rue de Varembé, CH-1211 Geneva 20, Switzerland
Web site: www.iso.ch

## INTERPOL

Founded in 1914, Interpol had 178 member countries in the year 2000. It is also known as the International Criminal Police Organization or ICPO. Interpol facilitates cooperation between police forces in different countries around the world. Each national police force has a National Central Bureau to coordinate the sharing of information with other national police forces and with Interpol. Interpol has its own independent email system, which uses encryption to ensure that messages are not intercepted. Interpol also has an Automated Search Facility whereby the police at any National Central Bureau can gain access to automated records. Each member country sends delegates to the General Assembly which in turn elects 13 members from different countries and regions to the Executive Committee – a President who is elected to a four year term, three Vice Presidents and nine ordinary members who are all elected to three year terms. The Executive Committee meets three times a year. The General Secretariat is based in Lyon, France. The Secretary General is appointed by the General Assembly to a five year tenure. Each member government makes a financial contribution to Interpol. The size of the contribution varies but each country has one vote at the General Assembly. There are four divisions within the organization:

- General Administration
- Liaison and General Intelligence
- Legal Matters
- Information Technology

In 1997 there were 318 staff, of whom 203 were French. The four official languages of Interpol are Arabic, English, French and Spanish. All interpreters are freelance.

---

**Interpol**
Quai Charles de Gaulle, 69006 Lyon, France
Web site: www.interpol.int

---

## ORGANIZATION OF AFRICAN UNITY

The Organization of African Unity (OAU) was founded in 1963 by thirty heads of state. In 1999 almost every country in Africa was a member and the organization employed 570 staff from 44 African countries. The OAU has been active in the decolonisation of Africa, the struggle against apartheid, placement of refugees and resolving boundary conflicts. A treaty establishing an African Economic Community was signed in 1991.

The General Secretariat is based in Addis Ababa in Ethiopia. The Secretary General is elected by the Assembly of Heads of State and

Government to a four year term. In 2000 the Secretary General was Dr Salim Ahmed Salim. There are also five Assistant Secretaries General. The OAU has offices in Brussels, Cairo, Dar es Salaam (Tanzania), Geneva, Lagos (Nigeria), Niamey (Niger) and New York. There are five specialised commissions:

- Economic and Social Commission
- Educational, Scientific, Cultural and Health Commission
- Commission of fifteen on refugees
- Defence Commission
- Mediation, Conciliation and Arbitration Commission

Member states make a contribution to the annual budget based on their national income.

The official OAU languages are Arabic, English, French and Portuguese.

*Member states:* Algeria, Angola, Benin, Botswana, Burkina Faso, Burundi, Cameroon, Cape Verde, Central African Republic, Chad, Comoros, Côte d'Ivoire, Democratic Republic of the Congo, Republic of the Congo, Djibouti, Egypt, Equatorial Guinea, Eritrea, Ethiopia, Gabon, Gambia, Ghana, Guinea, Guinea-Bissau, Kenya, Lesotho, Liberia, Libya, Madagascar, Malawi, Mali, Mauritania, Mauritius, Mozambique, Namibia, Niger, Nigeria, Rwanda, Saharawi Arab Democratic Republic, Sao Tome and Principe, Senegal, Seychelles, Sierra Leone, Somalia, South Africa, Sudan, Swaziland, Tanzania, Togo, Tunisia, Uganda, Zambia, Zimbabwe.

---

**Organization of African Unity**
PO Box 3243, Addis Ababa, Ethiopia
Web site: www.oau-oua.org

---

## ORGANIZATION OF AMERICAN STATES

The Organization of American States or OAS is the world's oldest regional organization. It dates back to the establishment of the First International Conference of American States in 1890. In 1910 the Conference changed its name to the Pan American Union. In 1948 it was renamed the Organization of American States.

The OAS is made up of 35 member states; in other words every sovereign state in North, Central and South America. The European Union and 44 other countries have permanent observer status.

Permanent observers are permitted to attend the public meetings of the General Assembly and the Permanent Council. They may also be invited to attend private meetings. In return, permanent observers help with the provision of expertise, training and financial contributions to various programmes.

The purposes of the OAS are very wide-ranging. They include the promotion of democracy, strengthening of peace and security, peaceful settlement of disputes, common action against aggression, economic and social development. In recent years trade and the environment have become more important. The OAS plans to establish a free trade area, the Free Trade Area of the Americas, by 2005.

The Inter-American Development Bank was established by the OAS in 1959.

The OAS has sent election observation missions to various countries. The American Commission on Human Rights consists of seven members elected by the General Assembly from lists submitted by the governments of member states. The Commission is based in Washington and meets several times a year. It visits different countries in order to assess their record on human rights. If it sees infringements of human rights it can submit a case to the Inter-American Court of Human Rights in San José, Costa Rica, which deals with infringements of the American Convention on Human Rights. Individuals and non-governmental organizations can also take cases to the Court if they have exhausted all legal avenues in their own country.

CIDI is the Inter-American Council for Integral Development. Established in 1996, it is directly answerable to the General Assembly. Member state governments appoint one representative at ministerial level. CEPCIDI is the permanent executive committee of CIDI and SEDI is the Executive Secretariat for Integral Development.

The OAS is responsible for over a hundred conventions on international law.

The total number of staff employed by the OAS in 1999 was over six hundred, of whom only two were permanently employed interpreters. However, the OAS also employed about 64 freelance interpreters on a *per diem* basis. The OAS organizes at least one meeting each month outside Washington. The official languages of the OAS are English, French, Portuguese and Spanish. Interpreters should be able to work into at least two of these official languages and out of the other two official languages.

*Member states:* Antigua and Barbuda, Argentina, Bahamas, Barbados, Belize, Bolivia, Brazil, Canada, Chile, Colombia, Costa Rica, Dominica, Dominican Republic, Ecuador, El Salvador, Grenada, Guatemala, Guyana, Haiti, Honduras, Jamaica, Mexico, Nicaragua, Panama, Paraguay, Peru, Saint Lucia, Saint Vincent and the Grenadines, Suriname, St.Kitts and Nevis, Trinidad and Tobago, USA, Uruguay, Venezuela.

*Permanent Observers:* Algeria, Angola, Austria, Belgium, Bosnia and Herzegovina, Bulgaria, Croatia, Cyprus, Czech Republic, Egypt, Equatorial Guinea, European Union, Finland, France, Germany, Ghana, Greece, Holy See, Hungary, India, Israel, Italy, Japan, Kazakhstan,

Republic of Korea, Latvia, Lebanon, Morocco, Netherlands, Pakistan, Poland, Portugal, Romania, Russian Federation, Saudi Arabia, Spain, Sweden, Sri Lanka, Switzerland, Thailand, Tunisia, Turkey, Ukraine, United Kingdom, Yemen.

---

**Organization of American States**
Department of Human Resources, 1889 F Street NW, Washington, DC 20006, USA
Web site: www.oas.org

---

## ORGANIZATION FOR ECONOMIC COOPERATION AND DEVELOPMENT

The OECD was founded in 1961 and has grown from a European based organization to a twenty-nine member international organization that includes Australia, Japan, Korea, Mexico and the United States. Slovakia is to become the thirtieth member state. Based in Paris, the OECD employs 1,850 staff of whom 700 are economists, lawyers and scientists. Donald J. Johnston has been Secretary General since 1996. The Secretary General chairs the Council, which is made up of one representative from each member country and a representative from the European Commission. The Council meets regularly at Ambassador level. It also meets annually at ministerial level. Some 40,000 senior officials attend meetings of the two hundred OECD committees each year. There are a number of directorates within the Organization which collect statistics, do research, analyse data and develop economic and social policy. Over the coming years the OECD plans to concentrate on such issues as ageing populations, education, electronic commerce, sustainable development, trade and taxation.

The official languages of the Organization are English and French.

*Members:* Australia, Austria, Belgium, Canada, Czech Republic, Denmark, Finland, France Germany, Greece, Hungary, Iceland, Ireland, Italy, Japan, Korea, Luxembourg, Mexico, the Netherlands, New Zealand, Norway, Poland, Portugal, Spain, Sweden, Switzerland, Turkey, United Kingdom, United States of America.

---

**OECD**
2 rue André-Pascal, 75775 Paris Cedex 16, France
Web site: www.oecd.org

---

## PAN AMERICAN HEALTH ORGANIZATION

The Pan American Health Organization or PAHO was established by the Second International Conference of American States (now the Organization of American States) in 1902. PAHO aims to combat disease, increase life expectancy and improve people's physical and mental health.

The Pan American Sanitary Conference, which meets every four years, is PAHO's supreme governing body. Each member government is represented at the Conference, which decides on the Organization's policies.

The Directing Council meets annually to review the programme and budget. All member governments are represented on the Council.

The Executive Committee meets twice yearly. This is a group of representatives of nine member governments who are elected by the Conference of the Council for staggered three-year terms. This committee looks after administration and the budget.

The Subcommittee on Planning and Programming of the Executive Committee also meets twice a year. Its composition is however different as it is made up of delegates from seven member states.

The Pan American Sanitary Bureau is the Secretariat of the Organization. The Director General is George Alleyne. PAHO has 27 offices in various member countries. PAHO is the World Health Organization Regional Office of the Americas and as a result is part of the United Nations System.

PAHO employs only freelance interpreters. Bilingual interpreters are employed for technical workshops and seminars, which are held in English and Spanish. In the case of governing body meetings, interpreting is provided in the four official PAHO languages – English, French, Portuguese and Spanish.

*Member states:* Antigua and Barbuda, Argentina, Bahamas, Barbados, Belize, Bolivia, Brazil, Canada, Chile, Colombia, Costa Rica, Cuba, Dominica, Dominican Republic, Ecuador, El Salvador, Grenada, Guatemala, Guyana, Haiti, Honduras, Jamaica, Mexico, Nicaragua, Panama, Paraguay, Peru, St. Kitts and Nevis, Saint Lucia, Saint Vincent and the Grenadines, Suriname, Trinidad and Tobago, United States of America, Uruguay and Venezuela.

*Participating states:* France, Netherlands, United Kingdom.

*Associate Member:* Puerto Rico.

*Observer states:* Spain and Portugal.

**Pan American Health Organization**
525 23rd St., NW, Washington, DC 20037, USA
Web site: www.paho.org

## SECRETARIAT OF THE PACIFIC COMMUNITY

Founded in 1947, and known as the South Pacific Commission until 1998, the Secretariat of the Pacific Community (SPC) is a regional intergovernmental organization which includes 26 members: Australia, France, New Zealand, the United States and 22 Pacific island countries and territories. The Netherlands and the United Kingdom were founding members of the Commission but the Netherlands withdrew after transferring administration of Netherlands New Guinea to Indonesia in 1962 and the United Kingdom withdrew in 1996. France, New Zealand and the United States have close connections with many of these islands. New Caledonia, French Polynesia and Wallis and Futuna are French territories. The Mariana Islands, Marshall Islands, Federated States of Micronesia, Guam and Palau are closely linked to the United States or indeed are US territories. Many of the islands are members of the British Commonwealth. The Secretariat provides technical assistance in social and economic areas to these islands. Each member has one vote at the annual South Pacific Conference where decisions are reached by consensus. The Committee of Representatives of Governments and Administrations decides on the Secretariat's programme and budget. The Executive Committee is made up of a Director General, a director of programmes and a director of services.

English and French are the official languages of the SPC. Over seven hundred languages are spoken in Papua New Guinea alone. The Commission employs a total of 253 people, 142 in New Caledonia and 111 in Fiji and the Solomon Islands. The staff includes a Chief Interpreter and two interpreters who also double as translators.

*Members:* American Samoa, Australia, Cook Islands, Federated States of Micronesia, Fiji, France, French Polynesia, Guam, Kiribati, Marshall Islands, Nauru, New Caledonia, New Zealand, Niue, Commonwealth of the Northern Mariana Islands, Palau, Papua New Guinea, Pitcairn Islands, Solomon Islands, Tokelau, Tonga, Tuvalu, United Kingdom, United States of America, Vanuatu, Wallis and Futuna, Western Samoa.

**Secretariat of the Pacific Community**
BP D5, 98848 Noumea Cedex, New Caledonia
Web site: www.spc.org.nc

## WORLD CUSTOMS ORGANIZATION

The World Customs Organization (WCO) is an independent intergovernmental body that was founded in 1952 as the Customs Cooperation Council. It had 146 member countries in 1999. Each member has one representative at the WCO and each country has one vote. The WCO aims to harmonise and simplify customs systems across its member countries. In some cases it is fighting against inefficiency and corruption. It works closely with other international organizations such as the World Trade Organization and the United Nations Conference on Trade and Development (UNCTAD).

The 146 member Council, 24 member Policy Commission and the 18 member Finance Committee direct the WCO. The Council approves a Strategic Plan each year. Five committees work on different aspects of customs coordination. Michel Danet is the Secretary General.

The working languages of the World Customs Organization are English and French, with some Spanish. The WCO employs a total of 142 staff, three of whom are interpreters. Freelance Arabic and Russian interpreters are employed for about thirty days a year. Simultaneous interpreting is provided at meetings throughout the year.

---

**World Customs Organization**
30 rue du Marché, B-1210 Brussels, Belgium
Web site: www.wcoomd.org

---

## WORLD TRADE ORGANIZATION

The World Trade Organization (WTO) was established in 1995 when it replaced the General Agreement on Tariffs and Trade (GATT) which had been founded in 1948. A number of problems had arisen with GATT – one country could block the settlement of a dispute and the Agreement applied only to goods. The World Trade Organization has a broader brief; as well as trade it deals with service sectors such as banking, insurance, tourism, transport and telecommunications. It also deals with copyrights, patents and trademarks. Member countries are not allowed to discriminate against other countries as regards trade. They are encouraged to use customs tariffs rather than attempting to restrict trade on the basis of quantity for example.

In 1999 the World Trade Organization was made up of 134 member countries and over thirty other countries were in the process of negotiating membership. Among these were China and the Russian Federation. All WTO decisions are reached by consensus. The Secretarial staff amounts to five hundred. The WTO makes and administers trade agreements, handles trade disputes such as the banana war between Europe and the United States, is a forum for negotiation and provides assistance to developing countries. WTO rules are legally binding on its members. It also cooperates with other international organizations.

The Ministerial Conference meets every two years. The Conference has decision making power in relation to the trade agreements. The Organization is controlled by the General Council, which is made up of ambassadors from the member states. Each country has one vote but the aim is to reach agreement by consensus. The General Council also meets as the Dispute Settlement Body and the Trade Policy Review Body. The WTO budget in 1998 was 116 million Swiss francs. Member states' contributions are based on their share of world trade. Part of the WTO budget goes to help finance the International Trade Centre which works to help developing countries promote their exports. The Director General Mike Moore of New Zealand was appointed to a four-year term in 1999.

In December 1999 the Seattle or Millennium Round of talks began in Seattle but had to be abandoned due to street protests against the domination of the WTO by Canada, the European Union, Japan and the United States.

The working languages of the WTO are English, French and Spanish. There are four staff interpreters for each of these three languages.

---

**World Trade Organization**
Centre William Rappard, rue de Lausanne 154, CH-1211 Geneva 21, Switzerland
Web site: www.wto.org

---

# 10 Interpreters' Associations

Most of the associations covered in this section are interesting for the contribution they have made to furthering the role of the interpreter or as sources of up to date information. The Internet has made this information accessible to everyone. A list of national associations affiliated to FIT, the International Federation of Interpreters, appears in the Appendix to this volume.

## AIIC

AIIC (Association Internationale des Interprètes de Conférence) was founded in Paris in 1953. The Secretariat is based in Geneva. There are two membership categories, active and associate. An active interpreter is a practising interpreter whereas an associate member works at interpreting for twenty days or less per year. In 1998 there were over 2,300 members in 78 countries. Of these 2,000 are freelance and only 300 are permanently employed in international organizations. The majority of members are based in Europe and the United States with a smaller number in Asia and Africa. Three quarters of AIIC members are women. This Association is for Conference Interpreters only.

AIIC makes a distinction first of all between active languages and passive languages. Active languages may be either A or B. All interpreters will have at least one A language, usually the mother tongue. The conference interpreter will work into the A language when interpreting consecutively or simultaneously.

A B language is another language into which the interpreter can work simultaneously or consecutively or both.

A passive language or a C language is a language from which the interpreter works.

AIIC has done some important work in laying down standards for interpreting. For example, it stipulates that interpreters should not work for more than two three-hour sessions per day. Depending on the number of languages required at a conference, AIIC provides guidelines on the number of interpreters required. Interpreters should not have to work alone in the booth, and should have a clear view of the speaker. Some of these points are covered in the AIIC Code of Professional Ethics, (included in section 5 in the present volume), others in the document on Professional Standards. AIIC has been actively involved in negotiating agreements on working conditions between interpreters and the European Commission, with the Consultative Committee on Administrative Questions (CCAQ) which is a subsidiary of the UN Administrative Committee on Coordination, and with International Trade Secretariats associated with the International Confederation of Free Trade Unions (ICFTU).

AIIC publishes an annual directory of members' names, addresses, contact numbers and active and passive languages. The directory contains two lists, one alphabetical and the other geographical. It is a useful resource for international organizations and conference organizers.

Becoming an AIIC member is not an easy task. The first requirement is two hundred working days as an interpreter. The next requirement is at least five sponsors. A sponsor is someone who has been an active AIIC member for five years or more. The idea is that the sponsor should be familiar with the candidate's work at conferences and prepared to vouch for the candidate. A sponsor has to state for which languages they intend to sponsor the candidate. Two of the sponsors must be based in the same region as the applicant. All of this means that an interpreter who is based in Geneva (where many international organizations are based and many conferences are held) has firstly a better chance of getting an opportunity to interpret as a freelance and in addition potentially has access to some 250 AIIC members. In comparison, there are three AIIC interpreters in the Czech Republic, one in Bulgaria, two in Bolivia and one in Zimbabwe.

---

**AIIC**

10 avenue de Sécheron, CH-1202 Geneva, Switzerland
Web site: www.aiic.net

---

This Web site contains quite a lot of information about AIIC. Occasionally, it includes interpreter vacancies in various international organizations. The contents of the Web site include a 'webzine' called *'Communicate!'* made up of articles by AIIC members. The site also has advice for speakers at conferences, conference organizers and even hotel managers! Unfortunately, what would appear to be the most interesting section of the Web site, the AIIC Extranet, is for paid up members, candidates and applicants only.

## AMERICAN TRANSLATORS ASSOCIATION (ATA)

Founded in 1959, the ATA is made up of almost 7,000 interpreters and translators. ATA holds a conference each year and is a member of FIT. There are a number of different levels of membership from active to corresponding to associate to associate-student to institutional to corporate. The Association has 16 committees, one of which is concerned with interpretation. There are also 12 divisions, one of which is an interpreters' division. Each division publishes a newsletter, is involved in the annual conference and is useful for networking. The *ATA Chronicle* is not available in full online.

---

**American Translators Association**
225 Reinekers Lane, Suite 590, Alexandria, VA 22314, USA
Web site: www.atanet.org

---

## AUSTRALIAN INSTITUTE OF INTERPRETERS AND TRANSLATORS INC. (AUSIT)

Founded in 1987, AUSIT is an association of professional interpreters and translators. Its quarterly publication, *AUSIT Newsletter,* is available online. AUSIT is a member of FIT and has drawn up its own code of ethics.

---

**Australian Institute of Interpreters and Translators Inc. (AUSIT)**
National Office, PO Box A202, Sydney South, NSW 1235, Australia

There are also regional offices in each state.
Web site: www.ausit.org

---

## BABELEA

Founded in 1996, the European Babelea Association for Community Interpreting represents community interpreting organizations in France, the Netherlands and the United Kingdom. The principal members are Language Line from the UK, ISM Interprétariat in France and a network of six interpreter centres *(Tolkencentra)* in the Netherlands. Cospe of Italy is also involved. Babelea publishes *Babel Info.*

Annual membership of Babelea is available to organizations and costs 575 euros. Babelea organized a three-day conference on Community Interpreting in November 1999 in Vienna, Austria. The conference was aimed at a wide spectrum of organizations involved in providing interpreting services. For example, government agencies, local authorities, refugee groups and interpreting agencies.

---

**Secrétariat Babelea**
12, rue Guy de la Brosse, 75005 Paris, France
Web site: www.babelea.org

## CALIFORNIA HEALTHCARE INTERPRETERS ASSOCIATION

The California Healthcare Interpreters Association (CHIA) 'is committed to setting standards of excellence that ensure equal access to quality medical care for all people by supporting and promoting the healthcare interpreting profession'. In order to achieve this aim, CHIA members would like to establish Standards of Practice and a Code of Ethics. They believe that a Certification programme is a necessity. The *CHIA Newsletter* is a quarterly and is available online.

**California Healthcare Interpreters Association**
343 Lunada Court, Los Altos, California 94022, USA
Web site: www.interpreterschia.org

## COUNCIL FOR THE ADVANCEMENT OF COMMUNICATION WITH DEAF PEOPLE (CACDP)

Set up in 1982, the Council is a registered charity which organizes examinations in British Sign Language, Lipspeaking (a communication service for those who lip-read), communication with Deafblind people and Speech to Text Reporting. Deaf and deafblind people are actively involved as tutors and examiners. There are 8.7 million deaf or hearing impaired people in the United Kingdom alone. The Council also maintains registers of people qualified in sign language interpreting and publishes an annual national Directory of Sign Language Interpreters, Lipspeakers, Interpreters for Deafblind People and Speech to Text Reporters.

In Scotland provision has been made in the courts to ensure the presence of professional sign language interpreters and lipspeakers since 1984. The Lord Chancellor has agreed that only fully qualified interpreters and lipspeakers who are registered with CACDP will be employed in England and Wales from the year 2001.

**Council for the Advancement of Communication with Deaf People (CACDP)**
Head Office, Pelaw House, School of Education, University of Durham, Durham
DH1 1TA, United Kingdom

(CACDP also has offices in London, Belfast and Glasgow).
No Web site at the time of writing.

## FIT INTERNATIONAL FEDERATION OF TRANSLATORS

FIT is an international federation of sixty translators' and interpreters' organizations. For example, the Institute of Translation and Interpreting and the Institute of Linguists are members. As a non-governmental organization FIT has consultative status with UNESCO. It also has four committees that deal with interpreting issues:

- Committee for Community based Interpreting. Community Interpreting was only recognised as an important issue by FIT in 1996. This committee is an Australian venture and specifically an AUSIT venture in deference to the fact that Australia has been providing community based interpreting services to immigrant communities since the 1970s. In 1998 the Committee made out a questionnaire which was distributed to community interpreters around the world. An interim report was delivered at the XV FIT Congress in Mons, Belgium in 1999 and is available online in the January 2000 edition of The Critical Link Newsletter. (Web site: www.criticallink.org).
- Committee for Interpreters
- Committee on Media Translators and Interpreters
- At the time of writing the Committee on Legal and Court Interpreters was in the process of collecting data about court interpreters and translators from FIT member organizations.

FIT organizes conferences every three years and publishes the proceedings. The 1996 Conference was held in Melbourne and the 1999 one in Mons, Belgium. The 2002 conference will be held in Montreal, Canada. Adolfo Gentile was elected president of the Federation at the Mons Conference.

**FIT General Secretariat**
PO Box 21, Dr. H. Maierstrasse 9, A-1184 Vienna, Austria
Web site: fit-ift.org

## INSTITUTE OF LINGUISTS

Founded in 1901, the Institute of Linguists is both an examining body and an association for professional translators, interpreters and educationalists. Success in the IoL examinations leads to membership. It is probably best known for its Diploma in Translation.

With the help of the charitable trust the Nuffield Foundation, the Institute of Linguists has developed a Diploma in Public Service Interpreting to provide a qualification for interpreters interested in working in Community Interpreting. From 2001 the Diploma will be a prerequisite for all government-employed interpreters in the United Kingdom. The examination is available in Arabic, Bengali, Cantonese Chinese, Czech, Farsi, French, German, Greek, Gujarati, Hindi, Italian, Polish, Portuguese, Punjabi, Russian, Serbo-Croat/Croatian, Somali,

Spanish, Turkish, Urdu and Vietnamese. It is a practical exam covering the following three areas:

- Consecutive and Simultaneous Interpreting
- Sight translation from and into English
- Written translation from and into English

A ten-minute explanatory video of the examination is available from the Institute of Linguists. The options are health, English law, Scottish law and local government services. DPSI training courses are offered on a part time basis at the following centres in the United Kingdom:

Bradford and Ilkley Community College
Burnley College
Cambridgeshire Interpreting and Translation Agency (CINTRA)
Cardonald College, Glasgow
College of NE London
College of NW London
De Montfort University
East Birmingham College
Foleshill Women's Training Centre
Goldsmiths College, London SE14
Greenhill College
Greenheys Adult Education Centre
Hackney Community College
Huddersfield Technical College
Lewisham College
Newcastle College
South Tyneside College, South Shields (distance learning course)
South Birmingham College
Stevenson College, Edinburgh
Tile Hill College of Further Education
Westminster Adult Education Service
Wood Green AEC

The Institute of Linguists Web site includes a list of colleges with the languages and options available in each at www.iol.org.uk/dpsi.htm

There is also a more recent version with less information at www.iol.org.uk/DPSI%20HANDBOOK.doc

Successful candidates can be included on the National Register of Public Service Interpreters (administered by the Institute of Linguists), can use the letters 'DPSI' after their name and may become members of the Institute. The National Register of Public Service Interpreters has drawn up a Code of Conduct for Public Service Interpreters. This code is included in Chapter 5 on ethics in the present volume.

**Institute of Linguists Educational Trust**
Saxon House, 48 Southwark Street, London SE1 1UN, United Kingdom
Web site: www.iol.org.uk

The Links List for Languages on this site provides links to a number of areas of interest to linguists. The sites are divided into categories: sites for translators and interpreters, sites for teachers and students, dictionaries and reference works, language bodies, language-specific sites and commercial sites.

## INSTITUTE OF TRANSLATION AND INTERPRETING (ITI)

The ITI was founded in 1986. It holds an annual conference on translation and interpreting. It has a directory of members and has carried out surveys on rates and salaries for translators and interpreters.

The ITI has a number of different categories for membership. These include subscriber for anyone with an interest in translation and interpreting and student membership for any student aged over 18 who is studying to be a translator or an interpreter. The categories of associated and qualified member are the most important for interpreters.

To become an associate member of ITI the following conditions apply:

*Over 21 years of age*
Degree in a relevant subject.
Recommendations from 3 interpreters.
100 days professional experience.

To become a qualified member (MITI) the conditions are:

*Over 25 years of age*
A degree in a relevant subject.
Recommendations from 3 interpreters for *ad hoc* interpreters or recommendations from 5 interpreters for conference interpreters.
A pass in the ITI interpreters' exam. In order to be permitted to sit the exam, candidates must first present documentary proof that they have 120 days of interpreting experience over the previous three years. The examination lasts one hour and consists of five sections:

- 250 word sight translation from English (10%)
- 250 word sight translation into English. (10%)
- the examiner reads a 300 word text which the candidate summarises in his or her A language (15%)
- the candidate interprets a ten minute general discussion between the two examiners (20%)
- The candidate chooses between Court and community interpreting,

business interpreting and conference interpreting (simultaneous with equipment or consecutive) (45%)

According to the ITI examination syllabus, 'a single serious error may be enough to fail'.

Corporate membership is available to educational institutions, translation agencies and other companies involved in translation or interpreting.

---

**Institute of Translation and Interpreting (ITI)**
377 City Road, London EC1V 1NA, United Kingdom
Web site: www.iti.org.uk

---

This site contains an excellent links page to a wide range of topics, including accountancy, advertising, aeronautics, dictionaries, music, philosophy and the Social Sciences. Another useful section is Events, a list of upcoming conferences around the world in the areas of translation and interpreting.

## IRISH TRANSLATORS' ASSOCIATION (ITA)

The Irish Translators' Association accepts applications from both ordinary members and professional translators and interpreters. At the time of writing the Association did not organize any examination for translators or interpreters.

Bilateral interpreters who wish to join the Association should have three years of professional experience or a minimum of 40 days interpretation per annum during the five years previous to their application.

Conference interpreters should also have three years of professional experience or a minimum of 75 hours of conference interpretation during the five years preceding their application. Both bilateral and conference interpreters are required to supply documentary evidence of commercial experience to support their applications.

The Association keeps a register of translators and interpreters and publishes a quarterly newsletter called *Translation Ireland*. The Irish Translators' Association is a member of FIT

---

**Irish Writers' Centre**
19 Parnell Square, Dublin 1, Ireland
Web site: homepage.eircom.net/~translation/

---

## NATIONAL ASSOCIATION OF JUDICIARY INTERPRETERS AND TRANSLATORS (NAJIT)

An American Association founded in 1978, NAJIT operates an online directory containing the names of 800 interpreters and translators. It also publishes a newsletter called *Proteus,* which is available online and usually contains interesting articles on Court interpreting in America and elsewhere. NAJIT holds a conference each year. Through the Society for the Study of Translation and Interpretation, a non-profit making association, NAJIT is planning to set up certification examinations in Spanish first of all, and then possibly in other languages.

The NAJIT site includes two mailing lists. COURTINTERP-L is for court and interpreting and legal translation problems or issues and court-interp-Spanish is for specific issues to do with Spanish and English.

**National Association of Judiciary Interpreters and Translators**
551 Fifth Avenue, Suite 3025, New York, NY 10176, USA
Web site: www.najit.org

## REGISTRY OF INTERPRETERS FOR THE DEAF INC.

The Registry of Interpreters for the Deaf was founded in the United States in 1964 and now comprises over 20,000 members in eight different categories. The RID provides training for sign language interpreters and runs a national Testing System.

**Registry of Interpreters for the Deaf Inc.**
National Office, 8630 Fenton Street, Suite 324, Silver Spring, Maryland 20910, USA
Web site: www.rid.org

## SOCIETY OF FEDERAL LINGUISTS, INC.

The Society was founded in 1930 and comprises United States government employees who use foreign languages in the course of their work. The United States Department of State employs a large number of linguists including about twenty staff interpreters. According to the Society of Federal Linguists Web site, the Department of State has a roster of 1,000 freelance escort interpreters who are contracted for thirty days at a time to interpret for foreign delegations visiting the United States.

The Society of Federal Linguists aims to promote linguistic professionalism, to further the knowledge of languages and to provide a discussion forum for its members. The Society holds meetings and publishes a Newsletter that is distributed to members.

**Society of Federal Linguists, Inc.**
PO Box 7765, Washington DC 20044–7765, USA
Web site: www.federal-linguists.org

## THE AMERICAN ASSOCIATION OF LANGUAGE SPECIALISTS (TAALS)

Founded in 1957 and American based, TAALS is an organization of some 150 interpreters and translators. The majority of members are based in America but the Association includes interpreters and translators in Europe, South America, Africa and Japan. The conditions for membership are similar to those of AIIC. Interpreters who wish to join should have 200 days of conference interpreting experience. They must also be sponsored by a minimum of five active existing members of the Association. Three A sponsors are required for an interpreter's A language, two A sponsorships for a B language and two B or A sponsorships for a C language.

**TAALS**
PO Box 39339, Washington DC 20016, USA
Web site: www.taals.net

# Bibliography

AIIC, (1997) *Conseils aux étudiants souhaitant devenir interprètes de conférence.* Geneva: AIIC.

*Babelea First Conference on Community Interpreting* (1999). London: Language Line Ltd.

Baistow, Dr Karen (1999) *Interpreter Trauma Research Project.* London: Language Line Ltd.

Borchardt, Dr Klaus-Dieter (1995) *European Integration – The Origins and Growth of the European Union.* Luxembourg: Office for Official Publications of the European Communities.

Bowen, Margareta, Bowen, David, Kaufmann, Francine and Kurz, Ingrid (1995) Interpreters and the making of history. In *Translators through History,* edited and directed by Jean Delisle and Judith Woodsworth. Amsterdam and Philadelphia: John Benjamins Publishing Company.

Carr, Silvana, Roberts, Roda, Dufour, Aideen and Steyn, Dini (eds) (1999) *The Critical Link 2: Interpreters in the Community.* Amsterdam and Philadelphia: John Benjamins Publishing Company.

Drummond, George (2000) *Interpreting at the International Tribunal for the Law of the Sea.* Issue 6, *Communicate!* at www.aiic.net

*Encarta 98 Encyclopedia* (1998). Microsoft Corporation CD-ROM.

Fadiman, Anne (1997) *The Spirit Catches You and You Fall Down.* New York: The Noonday Press.

Fontaine, Pascal (1998) *Europe in Ten Points.* Luxembourg: Office for Official Publications of the European Communities.

Gile, Daniel (1995) *Regards sur la recherche en interprétation de conférence.* Lille: Presses Universitaires de Lille.

Herbert, Jean (1978) How conference interpretation grew. In *Language Interpretation and Communication,* edited by David Gerver and H.Wallace Sinaiko. London and New York: Plenum Press.

Kurz, Ingrid (1997) Getting the message across: Simultaneous interpreting for the media. In *Translation as Intercultural Communication*, edited by Mary Snell-Hornby, Klaus Kaindl and Zuzana Jettmarova. Amsterdam and Philadelphia: John Benjamins Publishing Company.

Matyssek, Heinz (1989) *Handbuch der Notizentechnik für Dolmetscher Teil I and II*. Heidelberg: Julius Groos Verlag.

Mintz, David (1998) Hold the phone: Telephone interpreting scrutinized. In *Proteus* Volume VII, No.1. Available online at: www.najit.org/proteus/back_issues/phoneinterp.html

Rozan, Jean-François (1979) *La prise de notes en consécutive*. Geneva: Librairie de l'Université.

Seleskovitch, Danica (1968) *L'interprète dans les conférences internationales: problèmes de langage et de communication*. Paris: Minard Lettres Modernes.

Thomson, David (1973) *Europe Since Napoleon*. Middlesex: Pelican.

UNHCR (1993) *Interpreting in a Refugee Context*. Geneva: United Nations High Commission for Refugees.

Viaggi, Sergio (1996) Keynote presentation at XIV FIT World Congress. *Proceedings* Volumes I and II. Sydney, NSW: Australian Institute of Interpreters and Translators (AUSIT Inc.).

Weber, Wilhelm K. (1990) *Interpretation in the United States (Annals of the American Academy of Political Social Sciences*, reprinted by Sage Publications, Inc.)

Western European Union (1998) *WEU Today*. Brussels: Western European Union.

Wong, Edward (2000) Filtering the doctor–patient relationship through a translator. *The New York Times*, 6th April.

# Internet Sites

This is a list of Internet sites visited in connection with the present volume. All sites were functioning in September 2000. Please note that Web site addresses may change.

| Name | Web site |
| --- | --- |
| ACEBO | www.acebo.com |
| ACP | www.acpsec.org |
| African Development Bank | www.afdb.org |
| Agnese Haury Institute for Court Interpretation (Arizona) | nci.arizona.edu/ahi.htm |
| AIIC | www.aiic.net |
| Alphatrad (France) | www.alphatrad.com |
| American Translators Association | www.atanet.org |
| Arte TV station | www.arte.fr/ |
| Asian Development Bank | www.adb.org |
| AT&T Video Center (US) Tips and Techniques – the basics of Video Conferencing | www.att.com/conferencing/vid_bas.html |
| AUSIT (Australian Insititute of Interpreters and Translators) | www.ausit.org |
| Babelea | www.babelea.org |
| California Courts | www.courtinfo.ca.gov |
| California Healthcare Interpreters Association | www.interpreterschia.org |
| Canadian Parliament | www.parl.gc.ca |
| CEDEFOP European Centre for the Development of Vocational Training | www.cedefop.gr |
| CERN | cern.web.cern.ch/CERN/ and public.web.cern.ch/Public/ |
| Challenge Europe | www.theepc.be/Challenge_Europe/top.asp |
| CIA World Factbook 2000 | www.odci.gov/cia/publications/factbook/ |
| Committee of the Regions (EU) | www.cor.eu.int |
| Community Plant Variety Rights Office (EU) | www.cpvo.fr |
| Conference Interpreters' Web site (Brian Huebner) | web.wanadoo.be/brian.huebner/interp.htm |

| Name | Web site |
|------|----------|
| Cospe | www.Cospe.it |
|  | (in Italian) |
| Council of Europe | www.coe.fr |
| Council of the European Union | ue.eu.int/en/summ.htm |
| Court of Justice of the European Communities | europa.eu.int/cj |
| Critical Link (The) | www.criticallink.org |
| Critical Link 3 Conference (The) | www.rrsss06.gouv.qc.ca/english/colloque/index2.html |
| Cross Cultural Health Care Program (Seattle) | www.xculture.org |
| Department of Immigration and Multicultural Affairs (Australia) | www.immi.gov.au |
| Department of Social and Health Services (Washington) | www.wa.gov/dshs/index.html |
| Department of State (US) | www.state.gov/www/issues/fs-unsc_expan_000105.html |
| Economic and Social Commission for Asia and the Pacific | unescap.org |
| Economic and Social Commission for Western Asia | www.escwa.org.lb |
| Economic and Social Committee (EU) | www.esc.eu.int |
| Economic Commission for Africa | www.un.org/depts/eca |
| Economic Commission for Europe | www.unece.org |
| Economic Commission for Latin America and the Caribbean | www.eclac.cl |
| Eionet | www.eionet.eu.int |
| Emergency Room Interpreter Bill (Massachusetts) | www.healthlaw.org/pubs/Alert000426.html |
| Eurocontrol | www.eurocontrol.be |
| Eurodicautom | eurodic.ip.lu |
| European Agency for Health and Safety at Work | agency.osha.eu.int |
| European Agency for the Evaluation of Medicinal Products | www.eudra.org/emea.html |
| European Anti Fraud Office (OLAF) | europa.eu.int/comm/anti_fraud/index_en.htm |
| European Bank for Reconstruction and Development | www.ebrd.org |
| European Central Bank | www.ecb.int |
| European Commission | europa.eu.int/comm/index_en.htm |
| European Community Humanitarian Office (ECHO) | europa.eu.int/comm/echo/en/index_en.html |
| European Court of Auditors | www.eca.eu.int |
| European Court of Human Rights | www.dhcour.coe.fr |

| Name | Web site |
|------|----------|
| European Environment Agency | www.eea.eu.int |
| European Foundation for the Improvement of Living and Working Conditions | www.eurofound.ie |
| European Free Trade Association | www.efta.int |
| European Investment Bank | eib.eu.int |
| European Monitoring Centre for Drugs and Drug Addiction (EMCDDA) | www.emcdda.org |
| European Monitoring Centre on Racism and Xenophobia | www.eumc.at |
| European Ombudsman | www.euro-ombudsman.eu.int |
| European Parliament | www.europarl.eu.int |
| European Parliament Interpretation Directorate | www.europarl.eu.int/interp/public/en/default.htm |
| European Patent Office | www.european-patent-office.org |
| European Policy Centre | www.theepc.be |
| European Space Agency | www.esrin.esa.it |
| European Training Foundation | www.etf.eu.int |
| European Union | europa.eu.int |
| European Voice | www.european-voice.com |
| Europol | www.europol.eu.int/home.htm |
| Eurostat | europa.eu.int/comm/eurostat |
| FIT | fit-ift.org |
| Food and Agriculture Organization | www.fao.org |
| Gallaudet Research Institute | gri.gallaudet.edu |
| Gallaudet University | www2.gallaudet.edu |
| Guide to Best Practice for Lawyers, Interpreters and Translators (Law Society of New South Wales) | www.lawsocnsw.asn.au/about/papers/translators_interpreters/translators_interpreters.html |
| Habitat | www.unchs.org |
| Health-related terminology in Cyberspace (WHO) | www.who.int/terminology/ter/dicfair.html |
| Hospital for Sick Children, Toronto | www.sickkids.on.ca |
| ILIS Referral System (ILO databases) | ilis.ilo.org |
| ILOTERM | ilis.ilo.org/ilis/ilisterm/ilintrte.html |
| Institute of Linguists (UK) | www.iol.org.uk |
| Institute for Interpretation & Translation Studies (Stockholm University) | lisa.tolk.su.se |
| Institute of Translation and Interpreting (UK) | www.iti.org.uk |
| Intelsat | www.intelsat.int |
| Inter-American Development Bank | www.iadb.org |
| International Amateur Athletics Federation | www.iaaf.org |
| International Atomic Energy Agency | www.iaea.org/worldatom/ |
| International Civil Aviation Organization | www.icao.int |
| International Committee of the Red Cross | www.icrc.org |

| Name | Web site |
|------|----------|
| International Court of Justice | www.icj-cij.org |
| International Criminal Court | www.un.org/icc |
| International Criminal Tribunal for Rwanda | www.ictr.org |
| International Criminal Tribunal for the former Yugoslavia | www.un.org/icty |
| International Federation of the Red Cross and Red Crescent Societies | www.ifrc.org |
| International Fund for Agricultural Development | www.ifad.org |
| International Labour Organization | www.ilo.org |
| International Maritime Organization | www.imo.org |
| International Monetary Fund | www.imf.org |
| International Olympic Committee | www.olympic.org |
| International Organization for Migration | www.iom.int |
| International Organization for Standardisation | www.iso.ch |
| International Telecommunications Union | www.itu.ch |
| International Tribunal for the Law of the Sea | www.un.org/Depts/los/ITLOS/ITLOShome.htm |
| Interpol | www.interpol.int |
| Irish Translators' Association | homepage.tinet.ie/~translation/ **or** homepage.eircom.net/~translation/ |
| Language Line Ltd. (UK) | www.languageline.co.uk |
| Language Line Services (US) | www.languageline.com |
| Monterey Institute of International Studies (International Interpretation Resource Centre) | www.miis.edu/iirc/iirc2.html |
| Multicultural Health Communication Service (New South Wales, Australia) | www.mhcs.health.nsw.gov.au |
| National Accreditation Authority for Translators and Interpreters (NAATI), Australia | www.naati.com.au |
| National Assembly for Wales | www.wales.gov.uk |
| National Association of Judiciary Translators and Interpreters (US) | www.najit.org |
| National Center for Interpretation Testing, Research and Policy (US) | nci.arizona.edu |
| National Geographic | www.nationalgeographic.com/xpeditions |
| NATO | www.nato.int |
| NetworkOmni® | www.networkomni.com |
| Office for Harmonization in the Internal Market (EU) | www.oami.eu.int |
| Oregon OHSU Medical Interpreter Program | www.ohsu.edu/interpreters/interpreter.html |
| Organization for Economic Cooperation and Development | www.oecd.org |

| Name | Web site |
| --- | --- |
| Organization for Security and Cooperation in Europe | www.osce.org |
| Organization of African Unity | www.oau-oua.org |
| Organization of American States | www.oas.org |
| Pan American Health Organization | www.paho.org |
| Proteus | www.najit.org/proteus/proteus.html |
| Registry of Interpreters for the Deaf (US) | www.rid.org |
| Resources for Cross Cultural Health Care (US) | www.diversityrx.org |
| SCIC – Joint Interpreting and Conference Service at EU Commission | europa.eu.int/comm/scic/index_en.htm |
| Site for Conference Interpreters | web.wanadoo.be/brian.huebner/interp.htm |
| Secretariat of the Pacific Community | www.spc.org.nc |
| Society of Federal Linguists Inc. | www.federal-linguists.org |
| Southern California School of Interpretation | www.interpreting.com |
| Staffordshire Social Services Department | www.staffordshire.gov.uk/locgov/county/ socserv/ssasoff.htm |
| TAALS (The American Association of Language Specialists) | www.taals.net |
| TERMITE (ITU terminology database) | www.itu.int/search/wais/Termite/index.html |
| Texas Department of Human Services | www.dhs.state.tx.us/regions/03 |
| The Interpreters' Network | www.terpsnet.com |
| Tolkencentrum | www.tolkencentrum-non.nl/ (in Dutch) |
| Transcultural and Multicultural Health Links | www.lib.iun.indiana.edu/trannurs.htm |
| Translation Centre for Bodies in the European Union | www.cdt.eu.int |
| Translator's Home Companion (The) | www.rahul.net/lai/companion.html |
| UNAIDS | www.unaids.org |
| UNESCO articles on interpreting | www.unesco.org/int/cldinfen.html |
| United Nations | www.un.org |
| United Nations Association of the United States of America (UNA-USA) | www.unausa.org |
| United Nations Centre for Human Settlements | www.unchs.org |
| United Nations Children's Fund | www.unicef.org |
| United Nations Conference on Trade and Development | www.unctad.org |
| United Nations Crime and Justice Information Network | www.uncjin.org |
| United Nations Development Programme | www.undp.org |
| United Nations Drug Control Programme | www.undcp.org |
| United Nations Educational Scientific and Cultural Organization | www.unesco.org |
| United Nations Environment Programme | www.unep.org |

| Name | Web site |
|---|---|
| United Nations High Commissioner for Human Rights | www.unhchr.ch |
| United Nations High Commissioner for Refugees | www.unhcr.ch |
| United Nations Industrial Development Organization | www.unido.org |
| United Nations Office Geneva | www.unog.ch |
| United Nations Office Nairobi | www.unon.org |
| United Nations Office Vienna | www.un.or.at |
| United Nations Population Fund | www.unfpa.org |
| United Nations System of Organizations | www.unsystem.org |
| United Nations Vacancies | www.un.org/Depts/icsc/vab/index.htm |
| Universal Postal Union | www.upu.int |
| University of Charleston, South Carolina | univchas.cofc.edu/programs/legal-int.html |
| University of Minnesota (Program in Translation and Interpreting) | cla.umn.edu/pti |
| Western European Union | www.weu.int |
| World Bank | www.worldbank.org |
| World Customs Organization | www.wcoomd.org |
| World Food Programme | www.wfp.org |
| World Health Organization | www.who.int |
| World Intellectual Property Organization | www.wipo.int |
| World Meteorological Organization | www.wmo.ch |
| World Tourism Organization | www.world-tourism.org |
| World Trade Organization | www.wto.org |

**Table 11** *Internet sites visited*

# Appendix

---

## European Master's in Conference Interpreting

This is a list of Universities participating in the European Master's in Conference Interpretation in 2000. The number of universities will probably increase in the future as the Joint Interpreting and Conference Service of the European Commission develops more contacts with different universities.

**Austria**
Karl-Franzens Universität Graz
Prof. Dr. E. Prunc
IÜD Institut für Übersetzer – und Dolmetscherausbildung
Merangaße, 70
A-8010 Graz

**Belgium**
Hoger Instituut voor Vertaalers en Tolken
Hogeschool Antwerpen (HIVT)
Dr. H. Antonissen
Schildersstraat, 41
B-2000 Antwerp

**Czech Republic**
Charles University
Institute of Translation
Ms Zuzana Jettmarova
Hybernska 3
110 00 Praha 1

**Denmark**
Copenhagen Business School
Prof. O. Helmersen
Faculty of Modern Languages
Dalgas Have, 15
DK-2000 Frederiksberg C

**Finland**
Turku University
Turun Yliopisto
Mr Yves Gambier
Centre de Traduction et d'Interprétation
Kääntämisen ja Tulkkauksen Keskus
Tykistökatu, 4
FIN-20520 Turku

**France**
Université de la Sorbonne Nouvelle – Paris III
Prof. M. Lederer
Ecole Supérieure d'Interprètes et de Traducteurs (ESIT)
Centre Universitaire Dauphine
F-75775 Paris Cédex 16

**Germany**
Universität Mainz Johannes Gutenberg
Institut für Französiche und Italienische Sprache und Kultur (FB 23)
Prof. Dr. M. Forstner
An der Hochschule, 2
D-76711 Germersheim

**Hungary**
Eotvos Lorand University
Interpreter and Translator Training Centre
Amerikai Út 96
H-1145 Budapest

**Italy**
Universita di Trieste
Prof. Dr. J. Dodds
Scuola Superiore di Lingue Moderne per Interpreti e Traduttori
Via Filzi, 14
I-34132 Trieste

**Portugal**
Universidade do Minho
Prof. D.A. da silva Estanqueiro Rocha
Instituto de Letras e Ciencias Humanas
Largo Do Paço
P-4710 Braga Codex

**Spain**
Universidad de La Laguna
Master en Interpretación de Conferencia
Campus de Guajara
E-38071 Tenerife

**Sweden**
Universitet Stockholms
Mr D. Jones
S-10691 Stockholm

**Switzerland**
Université de Genève
Prof. B. Moser-Mercer
Ecole de Traduction et d'Interprétation
102, Boulevard Carl-Vogt
CH-1211 Genève

**United Kingdom**
University of Westminster
Ms I. Smallwood
School of Languages
Faculty of Law, Languages and Communication
9-18, Euston Centre
London NW1 3ET

## Other Universities Which Have Links with JICS/SCIC at the European Commission

**Austria**
Leopold-Franzens-Universität Innsbruck
Prof. Dr. A. Schmid
Institut für Übersetzer – und Dolmetscherausbildung der Leopold-Franzens
Fischnalerstraße, 4
Innrain, 52
A-6020 Innsbruck

Universität Wien
Docteur B. Strolz
Institut für Übersetzer – und Dolmetscherausbildung der Universitaët Wien
Gymnasiumstraße, 50
A-1190 Wien

**Belgium**
Erasmus Hogeschool
Departement Tolken
Trierstraat 84
B-1040 Brussels

Haute Ecole de Bruxelles
Institut Supérieur de Traducteurs et Interprètes
Mr J.M. Van Der Meerschen
rue J. Hazard, 34
B-1180 Bruxelles

Haute Ecole Leonardo de Vinci
Institut Libre Marie Haps
11 rue d'Arlon
B-1050 Bruxelles

Katholieke Vlaamse Hogeschool (K.V.H.)
Departement Tolken
Sint-Andriesstraat 2
B-2000 Antwerpen

Mercator Hogeschool
Mr A. Brisau
Meerstraat, 158 D
B-9000 Gent

Université de Mons-Hainaut
Prof. J. Klein
Ecole d'Interprètes Internationaux
Avenue du Champ de Mars, 17
B-7000 Mons

**France**
Institut Supérieur d'Interprétation et de Traduction (ISIT)
Prof. F. de Dax
rue d'Assas, 21
F-75270 Paris Cédex 06

Université Catholique de l'Ouest
Institut de Langues Vivantes
3, Place André-Leroy
BP 808
F-49008 Angers Cedex 01

Université des Sciences Humaines
Institut de traducteurs, d'interprètes et de relations internationales
22, rue Descartes
F-67084 Strasbourg

**Germany**
Fachbereich 8 Der Universität des Saarlandes
Prof. Dr. Heidrun Gerzymisch-Arbogast
Angewandte Sprachwissenschaft Sowie Übersetzen und Dolmetschen
Postfach 151150
D-66041 Saarbrucken

Ruprecht-Karls-Universität Heidelberg
Prof. Dr. J. Albrecht
Prüfungsausschuss für die Studiengänge
Übersetzen und Dolmetschen
Der Gerschäftsfuhrer
Plöck 57 A
D-69117 Heidelberg

Universität Mainz Johannes Gutenberg
Institut für Französiche und Italienische Sprache und Kultur (FB 23)
Prof. Dr. M. Forstner
An der Hochschule, 2
D-76711 Germersheim

**Greece**
EKEM
Mr P. Grigoriou
1, rue G. Prassa & Didotou
GR-10680 Athens

Université Ionienne-Corfu
Prof. Dr. I. Mazis
Département des Langues Étrangères, Traduction et Interprétation
Megaro Kapodistria
GR-49100 CORFU

**Italy**
Università di Trieste
Prof. Dr. J. Dodds
Scuola Superiore di Lingue Moderne per Interpreti e Traduttori
Via Filzi, 14
I-34132 Trieste

Università di Bologna
Prof. M. Soffritti
Scuola Superiore di Lingue Moderne per Interpreti e Traduttori
Corso Repubblica, 136
I-47100 Forlì

**Portugal**
Universidade Autonoma de Lisboa
Prof. Emmanuel Sabino
Departamento de Línguas, Literatura e Tradução
Palácio dos Condes do Redondo
Rua de Sta Marta
P-1150 Lisboa

**Spain**
Universidad europea de Madrid
Sr. D. Antonio Argüeso González
Decano de la Facultad de Traducción e Interpretación
Campus Universitario
Villaviciosa de Odón
E-28670 Madrid

Universidad de Las Palmas de Gran Canaria
Sr. D. Manuel Wood
Decano de la Facultad de Traducción e Interpretación
C/ Pérez del Toro n° 1
E-35003 Las Palmas de Gran Canaria

Universidad Pontificia Comillas
Facultad de Filosofía y Letras
Traducción e Interpretación
Quintana 21
E-28008 Madrid

Universidad de Salamanca
Sr. Don Carlos Figuerola
Decano de la Facultad de Filosofía y Letras
Paseo de San Vicente s/n
E-37007 Salamanca

**Switzerland**
Université de Genève
Prof B. Moser-Mercer
Ecole de Traduction et d'Interprétation
102, Bld. Carl-Vogt
CH-1211 Genève

**United Kingdom**
Herriot Watt University
Mrs B. Böser
Department of Languages
Riccarton
Edinburgh EH14 4AS

University of Bath
Prof. Dr. M. Croft
School of Modern Languages and International Studies
Bath BA2 7AY

University of Bradford
Mr B. Griffiths
Department of Modern Languages
Bradford, West Yorkshire BD7 1DP

University of Salford
Dr M. Carr/Mr A. Riddell
Department of Modern Languages
Salford M5 4WT

## University Courses Recognised by AIIC

This is a list of worldwide University Interpreting Courses recognised by the International Association of Conference Interpreters (AIIC) which has a star system to classify these courses. The AIIC Training Committee has a set of ten requirements for interpreting courses. These are, in brief:

1. Courses should be at postgraduate level.
2. Oral testing is essential, preferably before the start of the course.
3. Languages should match market demands.
4. The course should cover both Consecutive and Simultaneous interpreting.
5. The course should include a module on ethics.
6. The teaching staff should be made up of trained, practising interpreters, preferably AIIC members.
7. The target language should be the teacher's A language.
8. A fail in any Consecutive or Simultaneous interpreting examination should mean that the student has failed the course and all exams should be repeated.
9. The exam board should include professional interpreters from outside the University. They should be AIIC members and they should have a say.
10. The Diploma should clearly state the language combination covered in the course and the student's active and passive languages.

One star means that the course satisfies some of AIIC's requirements. Two stars mean that the course satisfies most of AIIC's requirements and three stars mean that the course satisfies all or almost all of the Association's requirements.

**Australia**
Department of Asian Languages and Studies **
University of Queensland
Brisbane, Queensland 4072
(English and Japanese)

**Austria**
Institut für Übersetzer- und Dolmetscherausbildung der Universität
Wien*
Gymnasiumstrasse 50
A-1190 Wien
(German mother tongue with English and French)

Institut für Übersetzer- und Dolmetscherausbildung der Universität
Graz*
Merangasse 70
A-8010 Graz
(German mother tongue)

**Belgium**
Hoger Instituut voor Vertalers en Tolken *
Schildersstraat 41
B-2000 Antwerp

Institut Supérieur de Traducteurs et d'Interprètes *
rue Joseph Hazard 34
B-1180 Brussels

Ecole d'interprètes internationaux *
Université de Mons
Avenue du Champ de Mars
B-7000 Mons

**Cameroon**
Advanced School of Translators and Intepreters **
PO Box 63
Buea, South West Province
Republic of Cameroon

**Denmark**
Center for Konferencetolkgning ***
1 København
Dalgas Have 15
DK-2000 Frederiksberg

## Finland
Center for Translation and Interpreting **
University of Turku
Tykistökatu 4
FIN-20520 Turku

## France
ESIT ***
Université Paris III
Centre Universitaire Dauphine
F-75116 Paris

ISIT **
21, rue d'Assas
F-75006 Paris

## Germany
Fachbereich angewandte Sprachenwissenschaft *
An der Hochschule 2
D-76711 Germersheim

Institut für Übersetzen und Dolmetschen der Universität Heidelberg *
Plöck 57 A
D-69117 Heidelberg

Sprachen und Dolmetscher Institut München *
Amalienstrasses 73
D-80799 Munich

## Israel
Bar Ilan University Department of Translation and Interpretation **
52900 Ramat Gan

## Italy
Scuola Superiore per Interpreti e Traduttori dell Comune di Milano *
Piazzale G. Cantore 10
I-20213 Milan

Scuola Superiore di Lingue Moderne per Interpreti e Traduttori *
Università di Trieste
Via D'Alviano 15/1
I-34144 Trieste

**Korea**
Hankuk University of Foreign Studies *
Graduate School of Interpretation and Translation
270 Imun-dong
Dongdaemun-gu
Seoul 130-791

**Lebanon**
Ecole de traducteurs et interprètes ***
Université Saint Joseph de Beyrouth
BP 175-208 Beirut
(Arabic with English and French)

**Portugal**
Instituto de Letras e Ciencias Humanas ***
Universidade do Minho
Largo do Paço
P-4719 Braga

**Spain**
Universidad de La Laguna **
Calle Molinos de Agua s/n
E-38207 La Laguna
Tenerife

**Sweden**
Tolk-Och Översättarinstitutet ***
Konferenstolkutbildningen
Stockholms Universtitet
S-10691 Stockholm

**Switzerland**
Dolmetscherschule Zurich *
Thurgauerstrasse 56
CH-8050 Zurich

Ecole de Traduction et d'interprétation de l'Université de Genève ***
102, boulevard Carl-Vogt
CH-1211 Genève 4

**Taiwan**
Graduate Institute of Translation and Interpretation Studies **
Conference Interpreting Section
Fu Jen University
Hsinchuang 242
Taipei
(Mandarin and English or Mandarin and Japanese)

**United Kingdom**
Postgraduate Diploma in Conference Interpreting Techniques **
University of Westminster
9-18 Euston Centre
London NW1 3ET

**United States**
Division of Translation and Interpretation **
Georgetown University
Box 571053
Washington, DC 20057-1053

Monterey Institute of International Studies**
425 Van Buren Street
Monterey, CA 93940

# FIT Member Associations

This is the FIT list, available at www.ift-ift.org/english/members.html
Readers are advised that this information may change: other associations may join FIT, some may change address. Web site addresses in
particular can change or cease to exist. Also, this list includes some
associations that are clearly more for translators than for interpreters.
The problem is that often Translators' Associations include interpreters.

**Argentina**
Asociación Argentina de Traductores e Intérpretes
Carlos Pellegrini 1515
1011 Buenos Aires
Mail: 863 Maipú St., 3° C
1006 Buenos Aires

Colegio de Traductores Públicos de la Ciudad de Buenos Aires
Callao 289 – 4 Piso
1022 Buenos Aires
Web site: www.traductores.org.ar

**Australia**
Australian Institute of Interpreters and Translators (AUSIT)
PO Box A202
Sydney South, NSW 1235
Web site: www.ausit.org

**Austria**
Österreichischer Übersetzer-und Dolmetscherverband "Universitas"
Gymnasiumstrasse 50
A-1190 Vienna
Web site: www.universitas.org

Österreichischer Verband der Gerichtsdolmetscher
Museumstraße 12
A-1016 Vienna
Web site: www.gerichtsdolmetscher.at

Übersetzergemeinschaft im Literaturhaus, Interessengemeinschaft von
Übersetzern literarischer und wissenschaftlicher Werke
Seidengasse 13
A-1070 Vienna
Web site: www.translators.at

**Belgium**
Chambre belge des traducteurs, interprètes et philologues
rue des Sapins, 19
B-4100 Seraing
Web site: www.cbtip-bkvtf.org

**Brazil**
Sindicato Nacional dos Tradutores (SINTRA)
Rua da Quitanda 194-10°
Sala 1206-1207
Rio de Janeiro RJ-CEP 20.091-000
Web site: www.sintra.ong.org

**Bulgaria**
Bulgarian Translators' Union
ul. Graf Ignatiev 16
BG-1000 Sofia

**Canada**
Canadian Translators and Interpreters Council (CTIC)
1, Nicholas Street
Suite 1402
Ottawa (Ontario) K1N 7B7
Web site: www.synapse.net/~ctic

Literary Translators' Association of Canada (LTAC)
Maison des écrivains
3492, avenue Laval
Montreal (Quebec) H2X 3C8

**Chile**
Asociación Gremial de Traductores de Santiago
Luis Thayer Ojeda 95, Of. 207
Providencia, Santiago 9

**China**
Science and Technology Translators' Association of the Chinese
Academy of Sciences (STTACAS)
Bureau of International Cooperation
52 Sanlihe Road
CN-Beijing 100864

Translators' Association of China
Wai Wen Building
24 Baiwanzhuang Road
CN-Beijing 10037

**Croatia**
Croatian Association of Scientific and Technical Translators
Hrvatsko Drua.tvo Znanstvenih i Tehni kih Prevoditelja (HDZTP)
Amru eva 19
10000 Zagreb

**Cyprus**
Cyprus Association of Translators and Interpreters
51A Riga Fereou Street
CY-3091 Limassol

**Czech Republic**
Translators Guild – Obec prekladatelú
Pod nuselsk_mi schody 3
CZ-120 00 Praha 2

Union des Interprètes et Traducteurs/ Jednota tlumocníku a prekla-
datelu
Senovázné nám. 23
CZ-112 82 Praha 1

**Denmark**
The Danish Association of Business Language Graduates/
Erhvervssprogligt Forbund
Skindergade 45-47
Postboks 2246
DK-1019 Copenhagen V
Web site: www.esf.dk

Dansk Translatørforbund
Nørre Farimagsgade 35
DK-1364 Copenhagen K
Web site: www.translators-association.dk

Dansk Forfatter Forening
Strandgade 6, st.
DK-1401 Copenhagen K

## Finland
Suomen Kääntäjien ja tulkkien liitto
Finlands översättar – och tolkförbund r.y.
Museokatu 9 B 23
FIN-00100 Helsinki

## France
Société française des traducteurs (SFT)
22, rue des Martyrs
F-75009 Paris
Web site: www.sft.fr

Union Nationale des Experts Traducteurs-Interprètes près les Cours
d'Appel (UNETICA)
Att. Charles Roé
7, rue André Chénier
F-66000 Perpignan

## Germany
Bundesverband der Dolmetscher und Übersetzer e. V. (BDÜ)
Geschäftsstelle: Rüdigerstrasse 79a
D-53179 Bonn-Bad Godesberg
www.bdue.de

Verband der Übersetzer und Dolmetscher Berlin e. V. (VÜD)
Chausseestr. 111 (Raum 230)
D-10115 Berlin

Assoziierte Dolmetscher und Übersetzer in Norddeutschland e V.
(ADÜ Nord)
Wendenstrasse 435
D-20537 Hamburg
Web site: www.adue-nord.de

## Greece
Hellenic Association of Translators – Interpreters in the Public Sector
Kazanova 80
GR-18539 Piraeus

Panhellenic Association of Professional Translators
Trisevgeni Papaioannou
28 M. Drakou str.
GR-114 76 Athens
Web site: www.psem.gr

Panhellenic Association of Translators
8 Komninon Street
GR-54624 Thessaloniki

Hellenic Society of Translators of Literature (EEML)
7, E. Tsakona Street
Paleo Psychiko
GR-15452 Athens

**Guatemala**
Asociación Guatamalteca de Intérpretes y Traductores (AGIT)
20 Calle, 5-65 Zona 10 (3° nivel)
Guatemala City
www.agit-gua.org

**Hong Kong**
Hong Kong Translation Society Ltd.
PO Box 20186
Hennessy Road Post Office

**Hungary**
A Magyar Írók Szövetségének Müforditói Szakosztálya
Bajza utca 18
H-10061 Budapest VI

**Indonesia**
Himpunan Penterjemah Indonesia
Jalan Semarang No. 12
Djakarta 10310

**Iraq**
Iraqi Translators Association
Ali Building, 3rd Floor
Sinak-Al-Khulafa Avenue
Baghdad

**Ireland**
Irish Translators' Association
Irish Writers' Centre
19 Parnell Square
Dublin 1
Web site: homepage.eircom.net/~translation

**Israel**
Israel Translators' Association
c/o Mrs Ophira Rahat
PO Box 9082
Jerusalem 91090

**Italy**
Associazione Italiana Traduttori ed Interpreti (AITI)
Mme. Vittoria Lo Faro
Via dei Prati Fiscali 158
I-00141 Rome
Web site: www.mix.it/AITI/

**Japan**
Japan Society of Translators (JST)
a/s: Orion Press
1-13 Kanda Jimbocho
Chiyoda-ku
Tokyo 101

**Jordan**
Jordanian Translators' Association (JTA)
c/o Dr Abdulla Shunnaq
PO Box 4990
Yarmouk University
211-63 Irbid

**Macedonia**
Union of Literary Translators of the Republic of Macedonia
P.P. 3
91001 Skopje

**Mexico**
Asociación de Traductores Profesionales (ATP)
Bajio 335-104
Col. Roma Sur
06760 México, D.F.

Organización Mexicana de Traductores, A.C.
Matias Romero 99
Desp. 2, Col. del Valle
03100 México, D.F.

**Netherlands**
Nederlands Genootschap van Vertalers (NGV)
Postbus 8138
NL-3503 RC Utrecht
Web site: www.metacom.org/ngv/

**New Zealand**
New Zealand Society of Translators and Interpreters Inc.
c/o Dr Sabine Fenton, Director
Center for Translation and Interpreting Studies
Auckland Institute of Technology
Private Bag 92006
Auckland 1020

**Nigeria**
Nigerian Association of Translators and Interpreting (NATI)
24 Eric Manuel Street
Surulere, Lagos
Mail: PO Box 1861
Marina, Lagos

**Norway**
Norsk Oversetterforening
Postboks 579, Sentrum
N-0105 Oslo 1
Web site: www.boknett.no/no/

Norwegian Non-Fiction Writers and Translators Association
Bygdøy allé 21
N-0262 Oslo
Web site: www.boknett.no/nff/

Statsautoriserte Translatørers Forening (STF)
Kongensgate 15
N-0153 Oslo
Web site: www.statsaut-translator.no

**Panama**
Panamanian Association of Translators and Interpreters
Apartado 1745
Panama 9A

**Poland**
Stowarzyszenie Tlumaczy Polishk (STP)
ul. Hoza 29/31 m.92
PL-00-521 Warsaw

TEPIS – Polish Society of Economic, Legal and Court Translators
PO Box 23
PL-00-967 Warsaw 86
Web site: www.aim.com.pl

**Portugal**
Associação Portuguesa de Tradutores
Rua de Ceuta 4/B – Gar 5
P-2795 Linda-a-Velha
Web site: www.apt.pt

**Russia**
Union of Translators of Russia
PO Box 136
Moscow 125047

**Slovakia**
Association of Slovak Translators and Interpreters Organizations
Laurinská 2
81508 Bratislava

**Slovenia**
Association of Scientific and Technical Translators of Slovenia (DZTPS)
Petkova.kovo nabre je 57
61000 Ljubljana
Web site: www.drustvo-ztps.si

**South Africa**
South African Translators' Institute (SATI/SAVI)
PO Box 27711
Sunnyside 0132

**South Korea**
Korean Society of Translators (KST)
2F. Shinmunro Bldg. 238 Shinmunro 1-ga
Jongro-gu
Seoul 110-061

**Spain**
Agrupación de Interpétes de Conferencia de España (AICE)
Apartado de Correos 50680
E-28080 Madrid

Asociación Profesional Española de Traductores e Intérpretes (APETI)
Calle Recoletos 5, 3 izqda.
E-28001 Madrid

Asociación Profesional de Traductores, Correctores e Interprétes de
Lengua Vasca
Zurriola pasealekua, 14-1 ezk.
E-20003 Donostia-San Sebastian
Web site: www.eizie.org

Asociación dos Traductores Galegos
c/o Sr Gómez Clemente
Facultade de Humanidades, Aptdo. 874
E-36200 Vigo

Traductors i Interprets Associats Pro-Col.legi (TRIAC)
Casal de Transformadors
C/ Ausiàs March 60
E-08010 Barcelona

**Sri Lanka**
Translators' Committee of the People's Writers' Front of Sri Lanka
57/10 Sirinivasa
Ratnavali Road
Kalubovila West, Dehiwala

**Sweden**
Federation of Authorized Translators in Sweden (FAT)
Rimbogatan 19
S-753 24 Uppsala

Swedish Association of Professional Translators (SFÖ)
Kansliet
Drottinggatan 29
S-411 14 Göteborg
Web site: www.sfoe.se

**Switerland**
Association Suisse des Traducteurs, Terminologues et Interprètes
(ASTTI)
Postgasse 17
CH-3011 Bern
Web site: www.astti.ch

**Syria**
Association des Traducteurs dans l'Union des Écrivains Arabes
Mazzé–Auto-Strad
BP 3230 Damas

**United Kingdom**
Insitute of Translation and Interpreting
377 City Road
London EC1V 1NA
Web site: www.iti.org.uk

The Translators' Association
84 Drayton Gardens
London SW10 9SB
Web site: www.writers.org.uk/society/trans.htm

**United States**
American Translators' Association (ATA)
225 Reineckers Lane, Suite 590
Alexandria, VA 22314
Web site: www.atanet.org

American Literary Translators Association (ALTA)
The University of Texas at Dallas
Box 830 688
Richardson, Texas 75083-0688
Web site: www.utdallas.edu/research/cts/alta.html

**Uruguay**
Colegio de Traductores Públicos del Uruguay
Colonia 892
Piso 6 esc. 604
11.100 Montevideo

**Venezuela**
Colegio Nacional de Traductores e Intérpretes
Apartado Postal 52108
Sabana Grande 1050, Colinas de Bello Monte
VE-Caracas
Web site: www.conalti.org

**Yugoslavia**
Savez drua.tava udruzenja knijizevnih prevodilaca Jugoslavije
Francuska 7
YU-11000 Belgrade

# Trilingual Glossary of International Organizations in English, French and Spanish

| English | French | Spanish |
| --- | --- | --- |
| Africa Caribbean and Pacific Group (ACP) | Afrique-Caraïbes-Pacifique (ACP) | los países ACP |
| African Development Bank (ADB) | Banque africaine de développement | Banco Africano de Fomento |
| Atlantic Treaty Association | Association du Traité Atlantique | Asociación Atlántica |
| Committee of the Regions | Comité des régions | Comité de las Regiones |
| Community Plant Variety Rights Office (CPVO) | Office communautaire des variétés végétales (OCVV) | Oficina Comunitaria de Variedades Vegetales (OCVV) |
| Council of Europe | Conseil de l'Europe | Consejo de Europa |
| Council of the European Union | Conseil de l'Union européenne | Consejo de la Unión Europea |
| Court of First Instance | Tribunal de première instance | Tribunal de Primera Instancia |
| Court of Justice of the European Communities | Cour de Justice | Tribunal de Justicia de las Comunidades Europeas |
| Economic and Social Commission for Asia and the Pacific (ESCAP) | Commission économique et sociale pour l'Asie et le Pacifique (CESAP) | Comisión Económica y social para Asia y el Pacífico (CESPAP) |
| Economic and Social Commission for Western Asia (ESCWA) | Commission économique et sociale pour l'Asie occidentale (CESAO) | Comisión Económica y Social para Asia occidental (CEPAO) |
| Economic and Social Committee (ESC) | Comité économique et social | Comité Económico y Social |
| Economic and Social Council (ECOSOC) | Conseil économique et social (ECOSOC) | Consejo Económico y Social (ECOSOC) |
| Economic Commission for Africa (ECA) | Commission économique pour l'Afrique (CEA) | Comisión Económica para África (CEPA) |
| Economic Commission for Europe (ECE) | Commission économique pour l'Europe (CEE) | Comisión Económica para Europa (CEPE) |
| Economic Commission for Latin America and the Caribbean (ECLAC) | Commission économique pour l'Amérique latine et les Caraïbes (CEPALC) | Comisión Económica para América Latina y el Caribe (CEPAL) |

| English | French | Spanish |
|---|---|---|
| European Agency for Health and Safety at Work (ESHA) | Agence européenne pour la sécurité et la santé au travail | Sistema de Seguridad y Salud en el Trabajo de la UE |
| European Agency for the Evaluation of Medicinal Products | Agence européenne du médicament | Agencia de Evaluación de Medicamentos |
| European Anti Fraud Office (OLAF) | Office européen de lutte antifraude (OLAF) | Oficina europea de lucha antifraude (OLAF) |
| European Bank for Reconstruction and Development (EBRD) | Banque européenne pour la reconstruction et le développement (BERD) | Banco Europeo para la Reconstrucción y el Desarrollo (BERD) |
| European Central Bank (ECB) | Banque centrale européenne | Banco Central Europeo |
| European Centre for Development of Vocational Training (CEDEFOP) | Centre Européen pour le développement de la Formation Professionnelle (CEDEFOP) | Centro Europeo para el Desarrollo de la Formación Profesional (CEDEFOP) |
| European Commission | Commission européenne | Comisión Europea |
| European Court of Auditors | Cour des comptes | Tribunal de Cuentas Europeo |
| European Court of Human Rights | Cour européenne des Droits de l'Homme | Tribunal Europeo de Derechos Humanos |
| European Economic Area (EEA) | Espace économique européen (EEE) | Espacio Económico Europeo (EEE) |
| European Environment Agency (EEA) | Agence européenne de l'environnement | Agencia Europea de Medio Ambiente |
| European Foundation for the Improvement of Living and Working Conditions | Fondation européenne pour l'amélioration des conditions de vie et de travail | Fundación Europea para la mejora de las condiciones de vida y de trabajo |
| European Free Trade Association (EFTA) | Association européenne de libre-échange | Asociación Europea de Libre Comercio |
| European Investment Bank (EIB) | Banque européenne d'investissement | Banco Europeo de Inversiones |
| European Monitoring Centre for Drugs and Drug Addiction (EMCDDA) | Observatoire européen des drogues et des toxicomanies (OEDT) | Observatorio europeo de la droga y las toxicomanías (OEDT) |

| English | French | Spanish |
|---|---|---|
| European Ombudsman | le médiateur européen | el Defensor del Pueblo Europeo |
| European Organization for Nuclear Research (CERN) | Organisation européenne pour la recherche nucléaire (CERN) | Organización Europea para la Investigación Nuclear (El CERN) |
| European Parliament | Parlement européen | Parlamento Europeo |
| European Patent Office (EPO) | Office européen des brevets (OEB) | Oficina Europea de Patentes (OEP) |
| European Space Agency (ESA) | Agence spatiale européenne | Agencia Espacial Europea |
| European Training Foundation | Fondation européenne pour la formation | Fundación Europea de Formación |
| Food and Agriculture Organization (FAO) | Organisation des Nations Unies pour l'alimentation et l'agriculture (FAO) | Organización de las Naciones Unidas para la Agricultura y la Alimentación (FAO) |
| Intelsat – International Telecommunications Satellite Organization | Organisation internationale des télécommunications par satellite (Intelsat) | Organización Internacional de Telecomunicaciones por Satélite (INTELSAT) |
| Inter-American Development Bank (IADB) | Banque Interaméricaine pour le développement (BID) | Banco Interamericano de Desarrollo (BID) |
| International Amateur Athletics Federation (IAAF) | Fédération Internationale d'Athlétisme | Federación Internacional de Atletismo Amateur (IAAF) |
| International Atomic Energy Agency (IAEA) | Agence internationale de l'énergie atomique (AIEA) | Organismo Internacional de Energía Atómica |
| International Bank for Reconstruction and Development (IBRD) | Banque internationale pour la reconstruction et le développement (BIRD) | Banco Internacional de Reconstrucción y Fomento (BIRF) |
| International Centre for Settlement of Investment Disputes | Centre international pour le règlement des différends relatifs aux investissements | Centro Internacional de Arreglo de Diferencias Relativas a Inversiones |
| International Civil Aviation Organization (ICAO) | Organisation de l'aviation civile internationale (OACI) | Organización de Aviación Civil Internacional (OACI) |
| International Committee of the Red Cross (ICRC) | Comité international de la Croix-Rouge (CICR) | Comité Internacional de la Cruz Roja (CICR) |

| English | French | Spanish |
|---------|--------|---------|
| International Court of Justice | Cour internationale de justice | Corte Internacional de Justicia |
| International Criminal Court | Cour Criminelle Internationale | Corte Penal Internacional |
| International Criminal Police Organization (ICPO/Interpol) | Organisation internationale de la police criminelle (OIPC/Interpol) | Organización Internacional de Policía Criminal |
| International Criminal Tribunal for Rwanda (ICTR) | Tribunal international pénal pour le Rwanda | Tribunal Penal Internacional para Rwanda |
| International Criminal Tribunal for the former Yugoslavia (ICTY) | Tribunal international pénal pour l'ex-Yougoslavie | Tribunal Penal Internacional para la antigua Yugoslavia |
| International Development Association (IDA) | Association internationale de développement | Asociación Internacional de Fomento |
| International Federation of the Red Cross and Red Crescent Societies (IFRC) | Fédération Internationale des Sociétés de la Croix-Rouge et du Croissant Rouge (FICR) | Federación Internacional de Sociedades de la Cruz Roja y de la Media Luna Roja |
| International Finance Corporation (IFC) | Société financière internationale | Corporación Financiera Internacional |
| International Fund for Agricultural Development (IFAD) | Fonds international de développement agricole (FIDA) | Fondo Internacional de Desarrollo agrícola (FIDA) |
| International Labour Organization (ILO) | Organisation internationale du travail (OIT) | Organización Internacional del Trabajo (OIT) |
| International Maritime Organization (IMO) | Organisation maritime internationale (OMI) | Organización Marítima Internacional (OMI) |
| International Monetary Fund (IMF) | Fonds monétaire international (FMI) | Fondo Monetario Internacional (FMI) |
| International Olympic Committee (IOC) | Comité international Olympique | Comité Internacional Olímpico |
| International Organization for Migration (IOM) | Organisation internationale pour les migrations (OIM) | Organización Internacional para las Migraciones (OIM) |
| International Organization for Standardisation (ISO) | Organisation internationale de normalisation (ISO) | Organización Internacional de Normalización (ISO) |

| English | French | Spanish |
|---------|--------|---------|
| International Telecommunications Union (ITU) | Union internationale des télécommunications (UIT) | Unión Internacional de Telecomunicaciones |
| Joint UN Programme on HIV/AIDS (UNAIDS) | Programme commun des Nations Unies sur le VIH/SIDA (ONUSIDA) | Programa Conjunto de las Naciones Unidas sobre el VIH/SIDA (ONUSIDA) |
| Multilateral Investment Guarantee Agency (MIGA) | Agence multilatérale de garantie des investissements (MIGA) | Organismo Multilateral de Garantía de Inversiones |
| North Atlantic Treaty Organization (NATO) | Organisation du Traité de l'Atlantique Nord (OTAN) | Organización del Tratado del Atlántico Norte |
| Office for Harmonization in the Internal Market | Office de l'harmonisation dans le marché intérieur | Oficina de Armonización del Mercado Interior |
| Organization for Security and Cooperation in Europe (OSCE) | Organisation pour la sécurité et la coopération en Europe (OSCE) | Organización para la Seguridad y Cooperación en Europa |
| Organization for Economic Cooperation and Development (OECD) | Organisation de coopération et de développement économiques (OCDE) | Organización de Cooperación y Desarrollo Económicos (OCDE) |
| Organization of African Unity OAU) | Organisation de l'Unité Africaine (OUA) | Organización para la Unidad Africana (OUA) |
| Organization of American States (OAS) | Organisation des États Américaines (OEA) | Organización de los Estados Americanos (OEA) |
| Pan American Health Organization (PAHO) | Organisation panaméricaine pour la santé (OPS) | Organización Panamericana de la Salud (OPS) |
| Partnership for Peace (PfP) | Partenariat pour la paix (PPP) | Asociación para la Paz (APP) |
| Security Council | Conseil de sécurité | Consejo de seguridad |
| UN Centre for Human Settlements (UNCHS/Habitat) | Centre des Nations Unies pour les établissements humains (CNUEH/Habitat) | Centro de las Naciones Unidas para los Asentamientos Humanos (CNUAH/Habitat) |
| UN Children's Fund (UNICEF) | Fonds des Nations Unies pour l'enfance (UNICEF) | Fondo de las Naciones Unidas para la Infancia (UNICEF) |

| English | French | Spanish |
|---|---|---|
| UN Conference on Trade and Development (UNCTAD) | Conférence des Nations Unies sur le commerce et le développement (CNUCED) | Conferencia de las Naciones Unidas sobre Comercio y Desarrollo (UNCTAD) |
| UN Development Programme (UNDP) | Programme des Nations Unies pour le développement (PNUD) | Programa de las Naciones Unidas para el Desarrollo (PNUD) |
| UN Environment Programme (UNEP) | Programme des Nations Unies pour l'environnement (PNUE) | Programa de las Naciones Unidas para el Medio Ambiente (PNUMA) |
| UN High Commissioner for Human Rights (UNHCHR) | Haut Commissaire aux droits de l'homme (HCDH) | Alto Comisionado de las Naciones Unidas para los Derechos Humanos (ACNUDH) |
| UN High Commissioner for Refugees (UNHCR) | Haut Commissariat des Nations Unies pour les réfugiés (HCR) | Alto Comisionado de las Naciones Unidas para los Refugiados (ACNUR) |
| UN International Drug Control Programme (UNDCP) | Programme des Nations Unies pour le contrôle international des drogues | Programa de las Naciones Unidas para la Fiscalización Internacional de Drogas (PNUFID) |
| UN Population Fund (UNFPA) | Fonds des Nations Unies pour la population (FNUAP) | Fondo de Población de las Naciones Unidas (FNUAP) |
| United Nations (UN) | Organisation des Nations Unies (ONU) | Organización de las Naciones Unidas (ONU) |
| United Nations Development Fund for Women (UNIFEM) | Fonds de développement des Nations Unies pour la femme (UNIFEM) | Fondo para el Desarrollo de la Mujer (UNIFEM) |
| United Nations Educational Scientific and Cultural Organization (UNESCO) | Organisation des Nations Unies pour l'éducation, la science et la culture (UNESCO) | Organización de las Naciones Unidas para la Educación, la Ciencia y la Cultura (UNESCO) |
| United Nations Industrial Development Organization (UNIDO) | Organisation des Nations Unies pour le développement industriel (ONUDI) | Organización de las Naciones Unidas para el Desarrollo Industrial (ONUDI) |
| Universal Postal Union (UPU) | Union postale universelle (UPU) | Unión Postal Universal (UPU) |

| English | French | Spanish |
|---|---|---|
| Western European Union (WEU) | Union de l'Europe occidentale (UEO) | Unión Europea Occidental (UEO) |
| World Bank | Banque mondiale | Banco Mundial |
| World Customs Organization (WCO) | Organisation Mondiale des Douanes (OMD) | Organización Mundial de Aduanas (OMA) |
| World Food Programme (WFP) | Programme alimentaire mondial (PAM) | Programa Mundial de Alimentos (PMA) |
| World Health Organization (WHO) | Organisation mondiale de la santé (OMS) | Organización Mundial de la Salud (OMS) |
| World Intellectual Property Organization (WIPO) | Organisation mondiale de la propriété intellectuelle (OMPI) | Organización Mundial de la Propiedad Intelectual (OMPI) |
| World Meteorological Organization (WMO) | Organisation météorologique mondiale (OMM) | Organización Meteorológica Mundial (OMM) |
| World Tourism Organization (WtoO) | Organisation mondiale du tourisme (OMT) | Organización Mundial del Turismo (OMT) |
| World Trade Organization (WTO) | Organisation mondiale du commerce (OMC) | Organización Mundial del Comercio (OMC) |

**Table 12** *Trilingual Glossary of International Organizations in English, French and Spanish*

## List of Members of United Nations

The following 189 countries were UN members in September 2000:

Afghanistan, Albania, Algeria, Andorra, Angola, Antigua and Barbuda, Argentina, Armenia, Australia, Austria, Azerbaijan, Bahamas, Bahrain, Bangladesh, Barbados, Belarus, Belgium, Belize, Benin, Bhutan, Bolivia, Bosnia and Herzegovina, Botswana, Brazil, Brunei Darussalalam, Bulgaria, Burkina Faso, Burundi, Cambodia, Cameroon, Canada, Cape Verde, Central African Republic, Chad, Chile, China, Colombia, Comoros, Democratic Republic of the Congo, Republic of the Congo, Costa Rica, Côte d'Ivoire, Croatia, Cuba, Cyprus, Czech Republic, Denmark, Djibouti, Dominica, Dominican Republic, Ecuador, Egypt, El Salvador, Equatorial Guinea, Eritrea, Estonia, Ethiopia, Fiji, Finland, France, Gabon, Gambia, Georgia, Germany, Ghana, Greece, Grenada, Guatemala, Guinea, Guinea-Bissau, Guyana, Haiti, Honduras, Hungary, Iceland, India, Indonesia, Iran, Iraq, Ireland, Israel, Italy, Jamaica, Japan, Jordan, Kazakhstan, Kenya, Kiribati, North Korea, South Korea, Kuwait, Kyrgyzstan, Laos,

Latvia, Lebanon, Lesotho, Liberia, Libyan Arab Jamahiriya, Liechtenstein, Lithuania, Luxembourg, Macedonia, Madagascar, Malawi, Malaysia, Maldives, Mali, Malta, Marshall Islands, Mauritania, Mauritius, Mexico, Federated States of Micronesia, Moldova, Monaco, Mongolia, Morocco, Mozambique, Myanmar, Namibia, Nauru, Nepal, Netherlands, New Zealand, Nicaragua, Niger, Nigeria, Norway, Oman, Pakistan, Palau, Panama, Papua New Guinea, Paraguay, Peru, Philippines, Poland, Portugal, Qatar, Romania, Russia, Rwanda, St Kitts and Nevis, Saint Lucia, St Vincent and the Grenadines, Samoa, San Marino, Sao Tome and Principe, Saudi Arabia, Senegal, Seychelles, Sierra Leone, Singapore, Slovakia, Slovenia, Solomon Islands, Somalia, South Africa, Spain, Sri Lanka, Sudan, Suriname, Swaziland, Sweden, Syria, Tajikistan, Tanzania, Thailand, Togo, Tonga, Trinidad and Tobago, Tunisia, Turkey, Turkmenistan, Tuvalu, Uganda, Ukraine, United Arab Emirates, United Kingdom, United States of America, Uruguay, Uzbekistan, Vanautu, Venezuela, Vietnam, Yemen, Yugoslavia, Zambia, Zimbabwe.

*Observers:* the Holy See, Palestine Liberation Organization (PLO) and Switzerland.

*Non Members:* East Timor and Taiwan.

*Note:* North Korea is also known as the Democratic People's Republic of Korea and South Korea as the Republic of Korea.

## United Nations English Acronyms

| Acronym | Full title |
| --- | --- |
| ACC | Administrative Committee on Coordination |
| CCAQ | Consultative Committee on Administrative Questions |
| ECA | Economic Commission for Africa |
| ECE | Economic Commission for Europe |
| ECLAC | Economic Commission for Latin America and the Caribbean |
| ECOSOC | Economic and Social Council |
| ESCAP | Economic and Social Commission for Asia and the Pacific |
| ESCWA | Economic and Social Commission for Western Asia |
| FAO | Food and Agriculture Organization |
| IACSD | Inter Agency Committee on Sustainable Development |
| IAEA | International Atomic Energy Association |
| IBRD | International Bank for Reconstruction and Development |
| ICAO | International Civil Aviation Organization |
| ICSC | International Civil Service Commission |
| IDA | International Development Association |
| IFAD | International Fund for Agricultural Development |
| IFC | International Finance Corporation |
| ILO | International Labour Organization |
| IMF | International Monetary Fund |

| Acronym | Full title |
|---------|------------|
| IMO | International Maritime Organization |
| INSTRAW | International Research and Training Institute for the Advancement of Women |
| ITC | International Trade Center |
| ITU | International Telecommunications Union |
| MIGA | Multilateral Investment Guarantee Agency |
| PAHO | Pan American Health Organization |
| UNAIDS | Joint UN Programme on HIV/AIDS |
| UNCHS | United Nations Centre for Human Settlement (HABITAT) |
| UNCJIN | United Nations Criminal and Justice Information Network |
| UNCTAD | United Nations Conference on Trade and Development |
| UNDCP | United Nations Drug Control Programme |
| UNDP | United Nations Development Programme |
| UNEP | United Nations Environment Programme |
| UNESCO | United Nations Educational Scientific and Cultural Organization |
| UNFPA | United Nations Population Fund |
| UNHCHR | United Nations High Commissioner for Human Rights |
| UNHCR | United Nations High Commissioner for Refugees |
| UNICEF | United Nations Children's Fund |
| UNIDIR | United Nations Institute for Disarmament Research |
| UNIDO | United Nations Industrial Development Organization |
| UNIFEM | United Nations Development Fund for Women |
| UNITAR | United Nations Institute for Training and Research |
| UNNY | United Nations Office New York |
| UNOG | United Nations Office Geneva |
| UNOV | United Nations Office Vienna |
| UNRISD | United Nations Research Institute for Social Development |
| UNU | United Nations University |
| UPU | Universal Postal Union |
| WFP | World Food Programme |
| WHO | World Health Organization |
| WIPO | World Intellectual Property Organization |
| WMO | World Meteorological Organization |
| WToO | World Tourism Organization |

**Table 13** *UN acronyms in English*

# United Nations Peacekeeping Missions in Operation in 2000

| Mission Title | Full name of mission | commencement date |
|---|---|---|
| MINURCA | UN Mission in Central African Republic | April 1998 |
| MINURSO | UN Mission for the Referendum in Western Sahara | April 1991 |
| MIPONUH | UN Civilian Police Mission in Haiti | December 1997 |
| MONUC | UN Organization Mission to the Democratic Republic of the Congo | November 1999 |
| UNAMSIL | UN Mission in Sierra Leone | October 1999 |
| UNDOF | UN Disengagement Observer Force (Golan Heights) | June 1974 |
| UNFICYP | UN Peacekeeping Force in Cyprus | March 1964 |
| UNIFIL | UN Interim Force in Lebanon | March 1978 |
| UNIKOM | UN Iraq-Kuwait Observation Mission | April 1991 |
| UNMIBH | UN Mission in Bosnia and Herzegovina | December 1995 |
| UNMIK | UN Interim Administrative Mission in Kosovo | June 1999 |
| UNMOGIP | UN Military Observer Group in India and Pakistan | January 1949 |
| UNMOP | UN Mission of Observers in Prevlaka (Croatia) | January 1996 |
| UNMOT | UN Mission of Observers in Tajikistan | December 1994 |
| UNOMIG | UN Observer Mission in Georgia | August 1993 |
| UNTAET | UN Transitional Administration in East Timor | October 1999 |
| UNTSO | UN Truce Supervision Force (Middle East) | June 1948 |

**Table 14** *UN Peacekeeping Missions*

## English Acronyms of International Organizations

This list is in alphabetical order and does not include EU and UN organizations.

| Acronym | Full title |
|---|---|
| ACI | Airports Council International |
| ACP | Africa, Caribbean, Pacific |
| ACS | Association of Caribbean States |
| ADB | African Development Bank |
| ADB | Asian Development Bank |
| APEC | Asia-Pacific Economic Cooperation |
| APPF | Asia Pacific Parliamentary Forum |
| ASEAN | Association of South East Asian Nations |
| ATAG | Air Transport Action Group |
| Caricom | Caribbean Community |

| Acronym | Full title |
| --- | --- |
| CBSS | Council of Baltic Sea States |
| CERN | European Organization for Nuclear Research |
| COMESA | Common Market for Eastern and Southern Africa |
| ECOWAS | Economic Community of West African States |
| EFTA | European Free Trade Association |
| EPO | European Patent Office |
| ESA | European Space Agency |
| Eurocontrol | European Organization for Safety of Air Navigation |
| IAAF | International Amateur Athletics Federation |
| IADB | Inter American Development Bank |
| IATA | International Air Transport Association |
| ICFTU | International Confederation of Free Trade Unions |
| ICPO | International Criminal Police Organization (INTERPOL) |
| ICRC | International Committee of the Red Cross |
| ICVA | International Council of Voluntary Agencies |
| IFRC | International Federation of the Red Cross and Red Crescent Societies |
| IICA | Inter-American Institute for Cooperation in Agriculture |
| Intelsat | International Telecommunications Satellite Organization |
| IOC | International Olympic Committee |
| IOM | International Organization for Migration |
| IPU | Inter Parliamentary Union |
| ISO | International Organization for Standardisation |
| ITC | International Trade Center |
| ITS | International Trade Secretariat |
| NAM | Non Aligned Movement |
| NATO | North Atlantic Treaty Organization |
| OAS | Organization of American States |
| OAU | Organization of African Unity |
| OECD | Organization for Economic Cooperation and Development |
| OPEC | Organization of Petroleum Exporting Countries |
| OSCE | Organization for Security and Cooperation in Europe |
| PAHO | Pan American Health Organization |
| USAID | US Agency for International Development |
| WCO | World Customs Organization |
| WEU | Western European Union |
| WTO | World Trade Organization |

**Table 15** *English acronyms of international organizations*

# Regional Maps of the World

## Africa

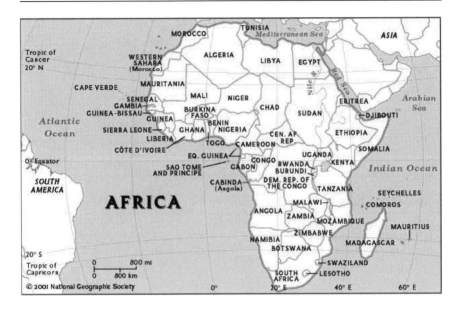

## Asia

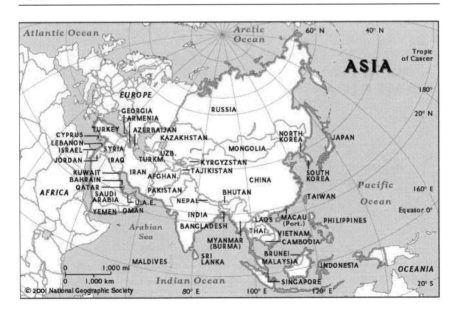

# Europe

# North America

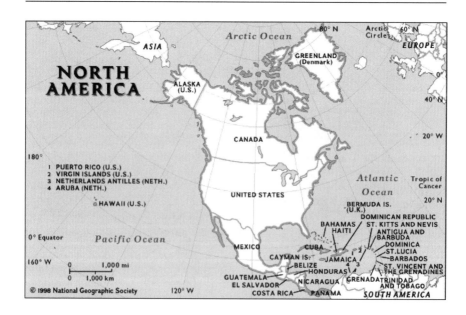

## Oceania

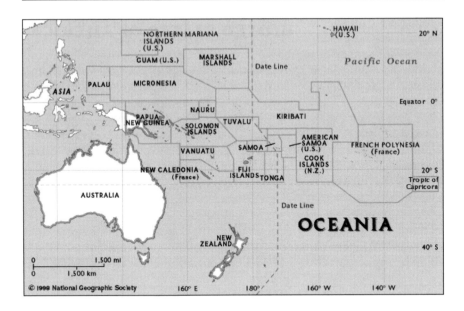

## South America

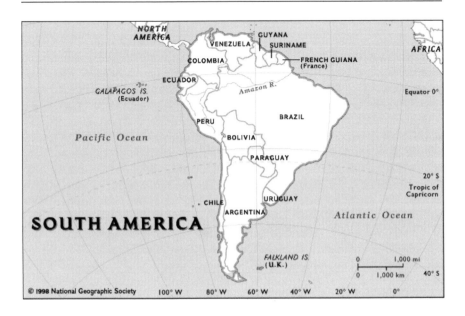

# United States of America

# Index